HOW to EAT a SMALL COUNTRY

HOW to EAT a SMALL COUNTRY

A FAMILY'S PURSUIT of HAPPINESS, ONE MEAL at a TIME

AMY FINLEY

CLARKSON POTTER/PUBLISHERS
NEW YORK

All rights reserved.

Published in the United States by Clarkson Potter/Publishers, an imprint of the Crown Publishing Group, a division of Random House, Inc., New York.

www.crownpublishing.com

www.clarksonpotter.com

CLARKSON POTTER is a trademark and POTTER with colophon is a registered trademark of Random House, Inc.

Library of Congress Cataloging-in-Publication Data

Finley, Amy.

How to eat a small country / Amy Finley.—1st ed.

p.   cm.

1. Food habits—France.   2. Finley, Amy—Travel—France.   3. France—Description and travel.   4. Agriculture—France—Anecdotes.   5. Finley, Amy—Family.   6. Television personalities—United States.   I. Title.

GT2853.F7F56 2011

394.1´20944—dc22

2010034504

ISBN 978-0-307-59138-8

eISBN 978-0-307-95243-1

Printed in the United States of America

Book design and jacket photographs by Amy Sly

Front jacket lettering by Jessica Hische

10 9 8 7 6 5 4 3 2 1

First Edition

For Mama, who's taught me to hold tight

HOW to EAT a SMALL COUNTRY

≈ PROLOGUE ≈

DESPERATE TIMES CALL FOR DESPERATE MEASURES.
While Greg and Marc are in the house, fetching knives and
Marc's paddle, I am outside, gnawing my fingernails and pacing back and
forth between the deck and the small stone shed where a black-and-white
bunny perches in the window, oblivious. I'm a Catholic (though not a
very good one since I believe a little bit in everything) and the symbolism
of the weather isn't lost on me: it is blustery and cold, with dark clouds
racing across the sky, threatening rain. I have learned now firsthand that
this kind of weather is typical of Burgundy in *any* season, and entirely
reasonable for an early spring day just after Easter, but in my schoolgirl's
heart, fraught with catechisms and morality tales, I've always associated
it with Good Friday and the murder of innocence. And so I squirm rest-
lessly and try not to make eye contact with the rabbit.

On the one hand, I want dearly to eat the bunny: it was I who suggested that we have a bunny feast in the first place. And on the other, I
want desperately not to have to kill the bunny. Every time the little creature in the window wiggles his nose at me my anguish rises afresh. It's a
terrible circular argument. A bunny has to die for me to eat it, but I know
I can't kill it myself—and I don't want anyone else to kill it; yet I really
do want to eat a bunny. Damn! Around and around, it's a carnivorous
quandary.

I am fantasizing about freeing all the rabbits from the shed, experi-
ment in old-fashioned sustainable eating be damned—am envisioning
myself striding purposefully (and rather heroically) toward the door to
throw it open and chase the furry creatures toward the relative safety of

the green, grassy fields—when Greg and Marc come out of the house. I slink behind them, nervously nibbling my fingers, as they approach the shed discussing which rabbit to dispatch for dinner.

I have set death into motion, and, apparently, there will be no zero-hour reprieve.

I haven't done so lightly. Greg and I and our two kids, Indiana and Scarlett, are in France specifically to eat. The rabbit, which was always intended to be eaten, is to be cooked in the classic Burgundy fashion—*à la moutarde,* coated in spicy mustard and then sautéed with onions and garlic, crisp white wine, and crème fraîche—and enjoyed with our neighbor Marc and his wife, Sophie, as a celebration of our eightieth day in France. For eighty days Greg and the kids and I have been driving into the nooks and crannies of a country the size of Texas, consuming ridiculous amounts of food—and certainly enough pig fat, goose fat, butter, and cheese to send certain cardiologists into shock. We've eaten bouillabaisse in Marseilles and choucroute in Strasbourg; fat, crimson sausages in Lyon and thick chops of lamb speckled with rosemary and lavender in Provence. We've eaten the head of a baby cow, the innards of a pig, the hearts and leathery combs of several unfortunate roosters, and now count among our friends a butcher, a baker, and a husband-and-wife team of fromagers who keep us in aged Brie and Morbier. The rabbit is just part of a growing record of consumables, but it is the first animal we have confronted in its living state. And that makes all the difference.

I am now, though, officially the only member of the butchering party with any lingering qualms as to the moral implications of our dinner. Even Indiana and Scarlett are unconcerned about the fate of the poor rabbit. Our days in Brianny—a small hamlet of less than a hundred souls where we live in a drafty farmhouse on Marc Verlez's sprawling property—have a calm, pastoral rhythm. In the morning, Greg drives the kids to their respective schools. Indiana goes to kindergarten with Marc's youngest child, Lulu, in Semur-en-Auxois, the medieval village five miles to our north; and Scarlett, who is two, is the newest member of the crèche—a state-sponsored preschool for which we pay all of sixty cents an hour—in Précy-sous-Thil, three miles to the south. While Greg drives the loop on the narrow country lanes, winding through fields and pasture land for the hundreds of lazily grazing white Charolais cattle, I clean up from breakfast, stoke the fire, do a little research on the computer, fetch wood from the wood pile, and start preparations for lunch. The bulk of my day is devoted to food in one form or another: buying it, making it, eating it, planning a trip to eat it, cooking it, or cleaning up from cooking it. Mid-morning passes in companionable silence, me in the kitchen, Greg slouched over the computer in the office, working. He takes a break at noon, and lunch is a slow affair after he fetches the kids from school. Today, over a salad of endives, beets, and walnuts, with slices of toasted bread topped with Morvan ham and melted comté, we began in all earnestness to broach the subject of the bunny.

"How would you like to eat a rabbit?" I asked Indiana.

"I wouldn't."

"But why not?"

"Because I don't want to make anything die." I'll admit to a little glow of pride at my logical, sensitive son.

"But everything that we eat used to be alive, dude. This ham used to be alive when it was a pig," Greg informed him. Indy eyeballed his ham thoughtfully. "Was pasta alive?" he asked me, avoiding looking at Greg. I am considered the authority on all things food in the family, and besides, Greg has a reputation for straight-faced lying just to get a rise out of the kids, especially Indiana. "No," I assured him. "Pasta was never alive. The wheat to make the flour was alive, but it was a plant. And nobody knows if plants suffer or feel pain or anything like that."

"Then I think I'll just eat pasta," Indy replied pragmatically.

"I'll eat the bunny!" Scarlett announced. And this doesn't surprise me at all. Scarlett is the gourmande of the family. Even though I serve her the exact same meals as the rest of us, she distrusts her tiny morsels of carefully cubed meat, preferring instead to crawl onto Greg's lap and direct him with admonitions of "More sauce, Daddy," as he cuts and feeds her little bites off his plate.

Without going into great detail, Greg described the way we intended to kill the rabbit by whacking it very hard in the head, which got Scarlett to giggling her great, burbly laugh. The dining table sits in a corner of the one warm downstairs room of the house, near the massive fireplace. Scarlett rolled around on the rug, pretending to be a bunny that had been whacked hard in the head, sticking out her tongue and saying, "Bleah . . . and now I'm dead." Soon Indy was joining in, pantomiming getting whacked in the head and sprawling on the floor dead, all concerns over killing abandoned.

During lunch, when the idea of the dead bunny had been mere comedic fodder, I was fine with it. Only the ringing phone, summoning us to the big house—Indy and Scarlett stayed behind to play—had awakened me to the reality that we really were going to kill the rabbit. Now my mounting distress magnifies my admiration for Greg as he emerges from the shed clutching a wiggling chocolate-brown rabbit. (I am so glad it isn't the black-and-white bunny, with which I've developed a sense of kinship.) He cradles it gently and tries to soothe it—*Shh, shh*—as if it were a frightened child. We all begin to speak in solemn, subdued whispers as we move toward Marc's patio, where he has assembled a wooden table, a bowl, and several layers of newspaper.

"Hold it by the back legs and it will stop struggling," Marc tells Greg, and sure enough, the rabbit goes completely still as soon as Greg hoists it by its hindquarters. Somehow, this deepens my despair. I am terrified of death. Before I had children I could calmly contemplate the certainty of my eventual demise, but now the very idea sends me into white-hot panic. There are few happy instances in which the rabbit would ever naturally find itself in its current position—dangling precariously in midair—and it seems to sense, and even to accept, its doom. I once heard Olivia Harrison on the radio describing the time her husband George (my favorite Beatle) was attacked and stabbed nearly to death. In the aftermath, when there was finally time to ask such questions, she'd asked him what had he been thinking during those terrifying, calamitous moments? And the sage, mustachioed Beatle, who'd assumed he was about to die, had replied, "I was thinking I'd better start thinking about God." I wonder if the rabbit, like George, is thinking about God, and the possibility constricts my chest, quickens my pulse, and makes me want to weep.

"Come closer, Amy. You're the cook. You have to come closer if you want to see this," Marc says as I cower on the very edge of the patio, as physically far away from the table as I can get without actually turning tail and running away. "I'm fine right here, Marc," I tell him, trying to keep my voice from quivering. I really am a weenie. Marc is instructing Greg how to do the whacking. This is not Marc's first rabbit. When he and Sophie surrendered their jobs and moved to the country from Paris with their three children, they committed themselves to a rural existence, albeit one that made prolific use of the *supermarché* outside Semur. Sophie is frugal and practical, a perfect French wife, tolerant of Marc's eccentricities. (Like his compulsion to buy up the abandoned farmhouses that litter this pocket of Burgundy since the mad-cow epidemic of the 1990s all but decimated local ranching.) She gardens in the summer, planting tomatoes that, she tells me sadly, sometimes don't ripen at all in the wan light, and jars and stores her crop for the region's long winter. They started keeping rabbits for the children, but always under the stipulation that they could be eaten at any moment. In fact, after the demise of the first rabbit, Lulu pitched a fit—not because she felt sorry for the bunny (Sophie assures me, she licked her plate clean after eating it), but because Marc had chosen one of *her* rabbits for dinner, which she thought colossally unfair. For whacking the bunnies Marc keeps a sturdy wooden paddle, about six inches long and an inch and a half thick with a four-inch-long handle. It looks uncannily like a fraternity paddle and belonged to his great-grandfather in Switzerland who, he informs Greg, designed it specifically to accomplish this task.

"You bring the paddle straight down the back, very hard, so that it hits the animal right at the base of the skull," he tells Greg. "Very hard. Right down the back. And then, *voilà*." I take it that *voilà*, in this instance, means "end of the road, rabbit." Indeed, the languid bunny is lifting its head somewhat, as if willingly presenting its vulnerable sweet spot like some sort of furry martyr. By following the line of its body, the paddle will connect exactly where skull and spine connect, dealing an instant, deathly blow.

"At the same time as I'm holding it?" Greg asks and I, who know him well, can hear that his voice is a little higher than usual, betraying his nervousness. Greg loves animals. He brushes our dog Doobie's teeth every Tuesday night, for Pete's sake, and is the only person I've ever known to scrub the bowl and change a beta fish's water on a weekly basis (resulting in possibly the longest living beta fish known to man).

"Yes. Very hard. Right down the back. *Voilà*."

Greg practices the motion with the paddle twice, and then time stands still and I don't know whether or where to look and my heart is racing and my finger hurts where I tear with my teeth at the quick of a hangnail and there is a sickening thwack and big, red drops of blood fly from the bunny's mouth and it hangs limp and bleeding from Greg's hand. The next few moments are gruesome as Marc says they need to get the blood out of the rabbit—"If we were making a civet we'd keep the blood to thicken the sauce," he tells me—and suggests that Greg pop out one of its eyeballs, an old-fashioned method he's heard of to drain the blood quickly and neatly. "You'll see: it should pour right out like wine from a bottle," he tells Greg. But dislodging the rabbit's eyeball proves to be nearly impossible using the little kitchen knife he has provided. (There is a nauseating sound of metal on bone as Greg digs into the eye socket. I am certain I will puke.) "Well, *voilà*," Marc says, resigned and disappointed, and sends me to fetch a bigger knife—I knew I should have brought a knife kit with me to France—to slit the rabbit's throat instead. Running pell-mell across the field toward our farmhouse, I can feel the adrenaline pumping. Now that the deed is done, a fait accompli, I am growing excited for my part of the butchering. In an instant, the rabbit has passed in my mind from adorable, cuddly, living creature, to food, and now that it is food I have purpose. I'm not sure exactly what this says about me. How humane am I if, the moment the creature is dead, I forsake all my misgivings about whether or not it is right to kill? What does it say when I am morally indignant one moment and salivating the next?

COULD YOU KILL AN ANIMAL? Despite my assurances to Marc that sure, sure, I could do it, there was never much of a doubt in my mind that I could not, even as much as I wanted to experience the complete journey of our *lapin à la moutarde.* I'll take responsibility for the death of the rabbit, because it was my idea to kill it and eat it in the first place. But when the phone rang and it came down to who would actually wield the paddle and suffer the actual sin, I punted.

And as usual, it was Greg, my husband of five years, who came to my rescue.

If Greg and I were two vegetables, I'd be something like a leek, a venerable member of the French table. The leek is spicy and robust, even a little showy—at least in America, where its role in cooking is usually occupied by the more run-of-the-mill onion. When cooking with leeks you might find yourself inspired to new heights of creativity. You might get a little whimsical with the seasonings, cast aside your hesitation about cooking with wine or using prodigious amounts of butter. But a leek can do very little without assistance. Greg, on the other hand, would be a potato. Earthy, stalwart, dependable. The kind of vegetable to put in the cellar to see you through hard times.

Here's what I believe in: divine intervention, fate, karma, kismet.

Here's what Greg believes in: planning.

These eighty days in France—there are one hundred more still to come—came about because when we combine the power of our two vegetables, we come out tasty and delicious as vichyssoise. Nearly six months previously, I had looked at Greg one night over the dinner table and said, "You know what? I think we should move to France." To which I am sure many husbands would have responded, "You know what? I think you should put down that glass of wine you're drinking." But Greg replied merely with an obliging, "Hmm," and days later began figuring out how we could actually make it happen.

He is the embodiment of my dreams.

Except, of course, when he's not, and then he can be the most maddening, frustrating, irritating, vexing, even—just the one time— heartbreaking man on the face of the planet. But I have come to ac- knowledge—especially over the last year, especially over the last eighty days—that I depend on Greg to do what I seemingly cannot. It is prob- able that if Greg were hit by a bus tomorrow, Indy and Scarlett would live a life of emotionally pitched chaos. They might eat meatloaf for breakfast and cake for dinner, and never make it to school with brushed teeth or matching socks. There would be elephant rides at their birthday parties, but I'd forget to send the invitations. On the other hand, if I were the one under the bus, they might not sob over Charlotte's loyalty to Wilbur, or notice the moon on enough successive nights to remark how beautifully it waxes and wanes. They might not wonder. I love my children so much, I am sometimes afraid I will smother them. Greg loves them so much, I fear they will never struggle.

○ ⌣

ONCE I RETURN WITH THE KNIFE it takes the two of us to finish off the rabbit as Marc guides us through the skinning process. Greg plays the part of a meat hook, holding the bunny up in the air by its hind legs, and I cut around the skin at the ankles and pull the fur down toward the groin, then make two slits to pull it away from the tail. After that, the rest of the coat slips easily off the body like taking a sock off a foot. (When Indiana sees the rabbit in the kitchen that evening he says, "Now it's all covered in chicken!") It's a little disconcerting to handle the skinned rabbit—which is now clearly meat—because it's still warm. I realize I have never touched meat that wasn't icy cold, or at least cool, from the refrigerator. I notice Greg flinching when he touches the flesh, and when I use the knife to open the thin, translucent skin covering the abdominal cavity and the intestines come spilling out, he goes certifiably green. "Are you okay?" I ask him. "Umm . . . no. I think I'm going to sit the rest of this one out," he answers, and recedes to a chair near where I had retreated during the killing. He stays there, chatting with Marc and only occasionally venturing a glance in my direction, while I remove the internal organs in one long, gory chain. I want to show Indiana, who had been very interested in the heart—"If you want to kill it, you should take out its heart, because that's what pushes the blood around the body, and blood makes you alive"—how it is connected to the lungs, with the liver and stomach and other guts interconnected, too. I save the intestines, too, the lower ones, because . . . well . . . they're full of little poop pellets. And there's nothing a five-year-old boy finds funnier than poop. After I trim it of its emerald-green bile sac, I set the liver off to the side because Marc tells us we must cook and eat it immediately. "Season it, get the pan very hot with a small amount of butter," he says, "and then just barely cook it on one side. Then, *tack,* turn it over and barely cook it on the other side. It should still be rosy pink inside. You can rinse the pan out with a little red wine vinegar and then eat the liver and the sauce with a little salad." Eating the liver of a freshly killed animal sounds satisfyingly pagan, like a giving-thanks ritual. I'm just glad Marc didn't insist that we eat it raw, standing on his patio, blood dripping down our chins.

～ ⌒ ⌒ ～

LAPIN À LA MOUTARDE IS A DECEPTIVELY EASY DISH. If you start with a whole rabbit, as we are, the trickiest part is cutting the rabbit into pieces. (This task is made even more difficult if you are doing so with a crappy "butcher's knife" from Ikea, which is all I have in the kitchen. It becomes a two-man operation. I situate the knife and hold it in place while Greg slams down on it with a cast-iron frying pan. Obviously, this is precarious. A cleaver is better suited to the task of hacking through bones.) The *cuisses,* like the thighs of a chicken, separate easily from the carcass when the tip of the knife is run around the knobby hip bone. Then you do basically the same thing with the front legs. Without its limbs the poor rabbit looks like a forlorn butterfly, with two flaps of muscle fluttering uselessly around the midsection. These mark the saddle, which is separated into two equal bits by cutting through the middle of the backbone (thus the necessity of the frying pan) after cutting away the rib cage and the tailbone (more frying pan). All told, the rabbit breaks down into six big pieces (by keeping the halves of saddle intact), or eight smaller ones (by dividing the saddle in half). Since we are six sitting down to dinner with Marc and Sophie, I opt for eight, knowing full well that Indy and Scarlett (well, possibly not Scarlett) will pick at their rabbit and devour the white rice I'm serving on the side. Since Greg abhors waste, I know he'll finish one of their portions. Marc is similarly indiscriminate about leftovers, and I'm sure he'll eat the rest. Which leaves Sophie and me with a *cuisse* apiece, plus rice and salad and bread and cheese, which, really, is plenty.

While we're hacking through the rabbit I ask Greg a question that's been on my mind all afternoon. "Was it hard to kill the bunny?"

"Well . . ." He pauses to slam the knife with the frying pan, being careful not to smash my fingers, then continues thoughtfully. "Not really. I was worried I wouldn't do it right, though, and that I'd just hurt it and that would be really bad."

"But, I mean, the will to do it. Was it hard? Because at the end, I couldn't even watch. And if I don't have the nerve to kill my own food, what right do I have to go strolling into a supermarket and buy what someone else has killed?" Pale fluid oozes from the bunny's shattered backbone.

"You don't consider all the skinning and gutting and stuff to be part of killing your own food?" he asks, dabbing at a tiny bit of blood that has splattered on my cheek.

"Once it was dead, I had no problem," I confess. "It was that moment right between life and death that was really horrible. I felt like I was going to pass out." I reposition the knife for the next cut and we hack through another bone. "Buying meat is easy. I kind of feel like everyone should have to kill something they want to eat at least one time, so that they always appreciate that something had to die so they could eat it. It's hard to feel that way in the grocery store."

"I like that we knew the rabbit," Greg says. "We helped feed it, Scarlett played with it, and when it was the right time, we helped it die. I think that used to be the natural way people lived with food. *I* was thinking that maybe we should start raising rabbits in San Diego."

"Are you serious?!" I trim the saddle flaps, neatening them.

"Yeah. Like, maybe we could have a rabbit farm and then you could go around and teach people how to cook it. It's environmentally friendly, easy to raise, it would be perfect."

"I don't know, baby. I couldn't even kill the one rabbit. I am positive I couldn't deal with being in the merchant-of-death business."

"Well, I'm just saying. There are all kinds of interesting things we can do when we go home."

With the rabbit dismembered, Greg goes back into the fireplace room to play with the kids, leaving me to finish the cooking. *Lapin à la moutarde* is a Burgundian dish because of the mustard used to season and marinate the rabbit. (Just fifty years ago, mustard was still a major crop of Burgundy, the regional capital of which is Dijon. But now ninety percent of the seeds that go into Dijon mustard are grown in Saskatchewan. As in Canada.) The first step is to salt and pepper the rabbit pieces and smear them generously with mustard. Since mustard is a mixture of powdered black or brown mustard seeds and vinegar, which is made from fermented wine (the other of the two crops that were introduced by the Romans that is still going strong in Burgundy), the acid begins to break down and tenderize the rabbit's muscles. Then the pieces are browned in butter, creating a rich, golden crust. Next, you take out the rabbit and add chopped onion and garlic and a little more butter to the pan and let them caramelize, then pour in white wine and scrape up all the delicious bits that are now sticking to the bottom of the pan. (Some of the best white wines in Burgundy come from Chablis, about forty-five minutes north of us, and I'm using a fine Chablis to honor our departed bunny.) After, the rabbit goes back in along with sprigs of fresh thyme (the flavor a lucky rabbit might have nibbled on while it was alive) and you put a lid on the pan and lower the heat. The rabbit braises and the wine bubbles and reduces and thickens until, about thirty minutes later, you have gorgeous, tender rabbit swimming in a lusty brown sauce. (Big, bold flavors are a hallmark of Burgundian cooking, the better to ward off the continental chill.) A little crème fraîche—a slightly soured, thickened cream—and a shower of chopped parsley are the finishing touches. *Voilà,* as Marc would say.

Cooking is how I decompress. While I'm chopping or stirring I'm paying attention to what's going on with my dish, but in a deeper part of my brain I'm doing some of my heaviest, most thoughtful thinking. I try to envision our backyard populated with hutches and little pens of free-range rabbits. Can you even have a free-range rabbit? Wouldn't that just basically be like setting them all free, what with the hopping and the burrowing and all?

In the other room Greg turns on the iPod and Lauryn Hill's voice fills the kitchen. "Strumming my pain with his fingers . . . Killing me softly . . . with his song . . ."

When the beat kicks in, Greg comes dancing into the kitchen. "Yeah . . . Yeah . . . One time, one time!" He does his best Wyclef Jean impersonation, which is really, really awful, considering that Greg is a six-foot-two-inch-tall skinny white guy with long, grizzled, curly hair and not much in the way of dance skills. He comes up behind me at the stove, nuzzles my neck, and does a few hip grinds, and then turns around and sashays back out the doorway and into the living room, where the kids are laughing.

"You're very funny!" I yell after him.

"I know I am!" he yells back.

I don't know if there's a rabbit farm in our future. There are one hundred days left of this trip, many more meals to eat, many more places to see, and I'll think about San Diego when it's over. But at this point, I'm just glad to believe that there is a future. Because six months ago when I said, "I think we should move to France," despite appearances it wasn't an act of flippant whimsy. It was more instinctual, and something of an act of desperation. Six months ago I wasn't sure that Greg and I even *had* a future. But since France is where we became WE many years ago, I thought it was where we should return, to sort out the mistakes and missteps of the past, to figure out how we had got where we were, and where—if anywhere—we were going.

CHAPTER 1

Having never been to Marseilles before, all I know about it is what I've gleaned from *The French Connection*, which I'll admit isn't much of a starting point.

Indy and Scarlett are bone-tired from our early-morning train trip from Brianny, dragging their feet, always three steps behind Greg and me as we roll our suitcases through the glass-and-concrete train station, which is actually both (marginally) cleaner and less seedy than I'd been led, cinematically, to expect—and with no obvious gun-toting drug dealers or strung-out hookers in sight, which is a bonus.

And so my very first impressions of Marseilles will always remain of what it actually isn't. And as it turns out, it isn't a lot of things.

Scarlett finally stops in her tracks. "No more walking!" she wails and throws herself face-down on the ground.

I double back and pick her up quickly, lest she contract anything nasty from the grimy tiled floor, and balance her precariously on my hip. So encumbered, together we lumber downstairs to the taxi stand, me cajoling Indy—who's now begging Greg, of course, for a lift—the whole way.

From the taxi window, rolling through the windy streets where litter blows down the sidewalk, you can get a pretty good look at what else Marseilles isn't.

For example, it isn't Paris, the only French city where I've ever lived. There the streets are grandiose. Marseilles's streets are, I hate to say it, plainer, narrower, a little ugly even, having been reconstructed in the 1950s after the retreating Nazis blew up most of the town. (It was high times for concrete and stucco.) And Paris is all gray and white. Somber colors, for sure, but when the sun is shining, those old stone buildings glow as if they were lit up from within, wrapped in lacy ironwork; and in the mist of a cold, wet winter, they are positively majestic. Marseilles's buildings are all chalk-toned pastels, pale and bleached. The trees lining the sidewalks are bare. We pass a bus on the road and our driver points to a grainy picture of Barack Obama plastered on its side, already looking confident and presidential on the cover of the weekly *L'Express*. The driver grins in the rearview mirror, flashing me a thumbs-up, the international symbol of "We like this guy." "He's going to win, yes?" he asks.

"We hope," I say, but without my usual enthusiasm. Marseilles just isn't stoking my optimism at the moment.

The city isn't the opulent, fleshy Côte d'Azur of my previous imaginings, either. For the most part, the women I see shuffling down the streets look nothing at all like Brigitte Bardot. They're all older. Grandmotherly types in black skirts wearing flimsy plastic shoes, carrying food in colorful plastic shopping bags. I elbow Greg, dozing with Scarlett on his lap. "No bikinis," I observe wryly.

"It's January," he retorts, yawning. But then looks around at the grandmothers and adds, "Thank God."

Our travels have officially begun.

On our way to the hotel the taxi drives through Marseilles's commercial port, swarmed with ferries and cargo ships, but it isn't as imposing or impressive as the one I remember in Genoa, another old Mediterranean city. And then we're passing through the old town, the Vieux Port, which isn't as crowded with wizened fishermen selling their morning catch as I'd heard it would be, either. There are just a few scrappy-looking boats, a few tourists taking pictures. "What time is it?" Greg checks his watch. "Nine," he answers. We've been on the road from Brianny for five hours—an hour to drive to the station in Montbard, four more hours on the train—and away from San Diego for seven days.

Just past the Vieux Port we finally reach the coastline, and it isn't the string of soft, white beaches or sublime cliffs that I'd imagined, either.

And now I am officially starting to freak out.

It's true that I have a habit of great, some might say impossible, expectations, but frankly, I have a lot riding on this trip. Because we're not just here to buy a car, though that's the reason we're in Marseilles. We're here because this is stop number one on a journey intended to save our marriage. We are recuperating from a truly awful, horrible year, and from what I think can fairly and empirically be called a betrayal. Besides some five hundred pounds in suitcases and a behemoth crate bearing Doobie, the family dog, we arrived in France a week earlier with a lot of baggage: several years' worth of bad, marriage-toxifying relationship habits to unlearn, some wounds to lick, and two small kids who are still a little gun-shy from a year in which the big, bad d-word—*divorce*—has been aired frequently and volubly.

But how we're going to fix things, exactly, well . . . actually . . . I still have no idea.

But a beautiful setting would surely help, right?

So, no pressure or anything.

The taxi zips along the corniche road next to squat, narrow buildings constructed right up on the cliff's edge, housing dive shops and pizza parlors buzzing with teenage boys. And as we fly past I can just barely make out glimmers of turquoise from the water beyond.

As we get closer to the hotel, the sidewalks are thick with strolling pedestrians: more grandmothers, the teenage boys, an awful lot of small children weaving expertly through the dense crowd on kick scooters. But amazingly, no one stands still and gawks, slack-jawed, the way I want to when there's finally a pause in the buildings and a low sea wall and before me spreads the full beauty of the clandestine sea.

It turns out to be stunning after all.

I hadn't even realized I was holding my breath, but when I see the water it all comes rushing out in a great big billowing sigh of relief.

O UR CAR CONNECTION—the eighty-one-year-old grandmother of a
friend of Marc and Sophie's—has made us a reservation at the
Hôtel le Rhul, directly across the street from the much more expensive
and much more famous Petit Nice. The Nice is a modern whitewashed
wedding cake right on the rocky *calanque,* replete with a swimming pool
and on-site babysitters and a Michelin three-star restaurant and a coif-
feuse. The Rhul looks like a sea captain's turreted, balconied fantasy,
especially on the inside.

In the interest of economy we are all sharing one room, and the kids,
as kids will when faced with a clean hotel room, immediately jump up
and down on the neatly made beds, strewing pillows and blankets willy-
nilly, while I scoot our luggage into the closet. For me, I'm ready—more
than ready—to touch the water. If the exhale was one of relief, my very
next inhale was like a rush of nitrous oxide, euphoric but disorienting,
too many thoughts and their attendant emotions racing into the void. I
am tense. Pixilated. The water, I hope, will make everything coalesce.
Considering our mission, it may even be like a baptism. Rebirth. "Okay,
let's go," I say, ready to dash back out the door again.

But Greg, as Greg will when faced with a plethora of leaflets, is taking
his time. "Just a second," he says, happily making piles on the rumpled
bed of the maps and literature requisitioned from the Algerian ladies
downstairs. "Let's get settled in first. No need to rush." He rifles through
the pamphets. Boat tour information: check. Map of the metro system: check. Sensing no immediate departure, the kids keep right on

jumping—it looks like we've lived in this room for days already—so I clear my throat a few times until I finally capture his attention, wondering if I'm truly growing less distinct by the second, even my voice diminishing, or if I'm just battling the leaflets' potent spell over him.

"What?" he gripes. "What's the hurry?" What, he can't he see that Indy and Scarlett are now practically kicking down the hotel room door, trying to bust out? Manic energy floods the hotel room. Doobie cowers between my legs, ears flattened.

"Dad, let's go-o-o!" Indiana whines.

"I'm ready!" I say. No need to give voice to my own urgency. The door is covered in thick black skid marks from the bottoms of their shoes. I grab Scarlett before she can aim another kick at the door, hoist her to my hip, and sling my purse over my other shoulder, jangling the hotel room keys enticingly.

"Fine," Greg says. "Just a second." He digs through a suitcase. "Now, where's Doobie's leash?"

Lord, it seems as if it takes an eternity until he's found it, snapped it on, and led us down the stairs and across the busy street, dodging whizzing buses and speeding scooters, and alongside the Nice to a stairway leading directly to the sea.

Scarlett flies from my arms as soon as we reach the bottom. "Let's go!" Indiana shouts joyfully, grabbing her hand, and together they rush toward the waves that slap against the sun-bleached rocks. A moment later he doubles back and starts shedding layers of jacket, sweater, and sweatshirt, like a little Swede rejoicing on the first day of summer. "It's hot here!" he announces in happy amazement. A pile of clothing—my own sweater included—grows quickly at my feet where I sit on a rock watching Greg skip rocks for Scarlett while Indy runs around in his T-shirt, slashing at imaginary ninjas with his plastic sword.

Slowly the knot between my shoulder blades relaxes as my fragmented, fragile calm resumes form.

During our week in Brianny, I had been so bombarded by satisfying everyone's immediate needs that I never let myself dwell on the monumentality of our move to France, no doubt why it finally all came rushing at me in the taxi. And maybe there had been an aspect of self-preservation in this, too. Keeping the monolith at bay. Because if I had stopped and thought, while standing in the green, grassy yard of the farmhouse, looking out over the lonely rolling fields and seeing the leafless, lifeless trees and the low, gray sky, I might easily have lost my nerve. ("Hello, Mom? Yeah. You were right: this was crazy. We're coming home.")

It was better to stay busy. So I unpacked our clothes and put everything away, which in itself took up the better part of about two days. And while Greg set up our computer in the freezing-cold office and started telecommuting to his job back home, I got to work acclimating Indy and Scarlett to their new room. We all had jet lag, the kind that turns days into nights and nights into days and makes three o'clock in the afternoon the single longest hour in all of human history. Slowly I got Indy to stop sleepwalking every night. And patiently, I broke Scarlett of her middle-of-the-night habit of padding softly down the hallway to our room and materializing, silently, by the side of my bed like a specter, scaring the bejeezus out of me when I sensed a presence and opened my eyes in the dark, strange room to find her hovering over me.

The first seven days of our trip were all spent solving all of our new life's little but pressing problems, like how to build a fire in the wood-burning kitchen stove without smoking out the entire farmhouse. (It turns out—if the wind is blowing strongly enough, which it does, seemingly nonstop—that it actually can't be done.) And occupied with these sorts of activities, Greg and I never even fought, although it's exactly under these types of circumstances that lately we have been most notorious for breaking down into a vortex of hot bickering and finger-pointing, self-pity and accusation.

Instead, unusual for us, we divvied up responsibilities as dispassionately as a team of Vulcans: Logically, who should take the first work shift of the day? Oh, you? Okay. And logically, who should watch the kids in the morning? Oh, me? Okay. And logically, who should be in charge of the fire and who should be in charge of dinner? Oh, you *and* me? Okay!

If these questions and their answers seem obvious, well, they didn't at the time to the two of us. This is the magic—and the promise, and the purpose—of Brianny: our own world, unsullied. Every decision a chance to begin anew, to prove to each other that we have indeed grown—well, are growing, at least—and are mutually committed to the brand-new, spanking-fresh start we have bought ourselves with the money we would otherwise have spent on our children's college educations.

And now, here we are, finally on the road, and here I am, on the water's edge, because even without the smoking stove (or the lonely fields, or the low gray sky), sitting around Brianny and staring at each other all day was bound to grow tiresome. Brianny is home, but France is the adventure. Besides saving our marriage there's only one other thing we have to do here, let loose on the autoroutes: eat.

Greg comes up beside me when I'm investigating a tide pool with Indy and Scarlett. He has the glad look of a profiteer. "Did you notice that the parking garage at the train station even smelled like piss?" he muses.

"That's what you are always going to remember about being in Marseilles for the first time?" I poke an anemone so that Scarlett can watch it shrink like a flower drawing in its petal-like tentacles. She squeals in delight and begs me to do it again.

"You shouldn't say *piss,* Dad," Indy scolds. "That's a bad word."

"I can say *piss* because I'm talking about pee, dude. I like pee smell." He rises to his own defense. "Pee smell is the smell of France." He fills his lungs deeply, nostalgically, at home here, then bends and reaches for a flat stone. "Watch this, sweetheart," he summons Scarlett. He launches it across the water's surface where it skips two, three, four times. Greg was born in France, in Paris, his mother a true-blue Parisian equal parts cultivated and cliquish, his father a mild-mannered American doctor finishing his residency. Before arriving at his new home in Virginia at age seven and starting first grade, expatriated for his father's practice, Greg had never even spoken English. He grew up in Montmartre, raised by his maternal grandparents until then, enjoying a French boys' privilege to splatter the cobbles at will with his own golden stream. "Like how the metro always smells like pee. Remember? I've missed it."

"Brianny smells like smoke," I say.

"Or like mud," Indy adds. "Because it rains so much."

"Yup. Like smoke and rain," Greg agrees, skipping another stone. At the edge of the tide pool Scarlett picks up a rock nearly half her size and chucks it, dousing herself in a cascade of salt water. Drenched, she begins to cry. "You know," Greg says, wiping her face with his shirt, "I think we'd better be going or we're going to miss the window for bouillabaisse."

"Is it noon already?" I look up, see the sun high overhead in the sky, signalling afternoon.

He checks his watch again. "Nearly two." Which is all I need to hear to start grabbing up all our shed clothing and dragging the bedraggled kids off the beach and back up the stairs toward the hotel. After all, there's only one other thing we have to do here. And it's time for lunch.

WE WERE MINDLESS OF TIME, so engrossed and merry in the sunshine, so happy to be warm and dry, you would think we'd never
seen the sun before. But I'll defend this behavior to anyone who mocks it:
After all, we are Californians. (Or at least the kids and I are natives.) Recently we have been exposed to both rain and cold. And it has been well
documented by people other than me that Californians—especially Southern Californians—have absolutely no idea what to do with actual weather.

But in France, lest we forget, lunchtimes are taken very seriously. A
restaurant does not even open its doors before noon, really more like
twelve thirty, and it is certain to close its doors, firmly and unapologeti-
cally, at two, not to reopen again until the civilized seven-o'clock dinner
hour. Walking in the door any later than, say, one forty-five is frowned
upon. You may be seated, but at three o' clock without fail, the waiter will
start giving you the eye. You would be wise never to arrive for lunch later
than one thirty if you are to maximize your waiter's good graces.

By the time we've dropped a salty, damp-smelling Doobie off at the
hotel room, we darken the doorway of Le Rhul's restaurant—dirty and
disheveled, Scarlett's sobs winding down into hiccups—at 1:55. And
right as we enter a clutch of other guests make their way past us out into
the sunshine, giving Scarlett's natty hair and Indy's half-drenched jeans
a disapproving once-over. I stare them down protectively and smooth
Scarett's flyaways with my palm.

The restaurant smells delicious, the scent of garlic and saffron making my mouth water.

"Bonjour, Madame, Monsieur," says the host. He stands stiff and erect at his station, very deliberately ignoring the high probability that we're going to try to talk our way into a table. He is all smiles, but he doesn't even touch a menu, fully aware of the time and our tardiness. He clasps his hands instead behind his back and rocks back and forth in his shiny black shoes, enforcer of the gastronomic code.

"Bonjour," Greg replies. *"Pour la bouillabaisse, s'il vous plaît."* He is on the offensive. This is good.

The host scans the freshly reset tables, clad in bright Provençal cloths, conveying both "Let me see what I can do" and "You idiot, it is too late!" I must say, it is a commanding performance.

Seconds tick by.

But Scarlett's tiny stomach is no slave to ettiquette. She grabs my face with her two hands and presses my cheeks so that I am forced to look her straight in the eye, not two inches away from me. "Mama," she says once she has my undivided attention. "I'm hungry!"

I look beseechingly at the host. Normally, I am tentative in these situations, adherent to code, which is why I was more than happy to let Greg do the talking. But the sunshine and salt air have me brazen.

"S'il vous plaît, Monsieur," I say in my best, plaintive, Sally Struthers voice. "The children are starving."

～◦〜

AH . . . BOUILLABAISSE.

Now, I—believer in mystical messages that I am—I wasn't at all surprised when Marc said that his friend's grandmother lived in Marseilles.

Of course she did.

Because Marseilles is the home of bouillabaisse, and bouillabaisse is all nattily entwined with how I fell deeply in love with French cooking in the first place. And it's also cooking, in a strange, roundabout way, that eventually got Greg and me into trouble, because the less I did of it—slipping deeply into an unintended, fretful, and self-perpetuating stay-at-home-motherhood that stretched from six weeks into nearly six years—the worse things between Greg and me became.

Here's what Greg was doing a lot of during that time: controlling things.

Here's what I was doing a lot of: letting him.

But back in 2000 it was all still wine and roses.

I was giddily unemployed when I met Greg, having just spontaneously quit my job as a science writer, surprising myself and my editor, incapable it turns out of loving quarks and proteins, weather patterns, and ocean currents enough to give them the gift of my mid-twenties. Our first date was in the early spring in San Diego, after we were introduced by a mutual friend. Greg was living and working in Paris at the time, but visiting his parents, who'd moved to my hometown, and even just down the road from my mother, when he was in the fifth grade. That our paths had never crossed before seemed fate. Over the span of just three breathless, time-ticking dates—the imminence of his departure the subtext of every look, kiss, and conversation—we drafted a future, and by the time I finally moved to Paris two months later, we just went right on ahead and moved in together. Date four: picking out curtains. In totality, it's an event that within my family—even though I was twenty-six at the time— became known as "the time that Amy ran away from home."

And then here's what happened: It turns out that Paris is adorned with food. Decorated with it. Towers of iridescent fish and festoons of jeweled vegetables in the *marchés,* wrought-iron escargots suspended in mid-glide over ancient storefronts, vines whittled into the wooden signs of wine shops. Greg's and my courtship rituals, too, revolved around hunger. We sat at cafés and ate *rillettes,* which are strands of salty pork suspended in its own creamy fat, and guzzled carafes of red wine. Strolled in parks eating yellow and pink cherries from a paper bag. We licked Nutella from each other's fingers standing in line for the movies eating crêpes at night, and in the morning, the crumbs of our buttery croissants fell onto the mussed-up bed sheets like snowflakes.

You've heard of musicians who see music? Colored swirls materialize around them and they can identify the melody and the harmonies by their complementary rainbow hues. Well, I began to *feel* in food. Weird as it sounds, after a while when I thought about Greg, I was just as likely to picture in my mind a plate of steak au poivre—hot and piquant, dripping with meaty juices—as I was to picture my boyfriend. My mother, on the other hand—sorrowful and sad on our trans-Atlantic phone calls, wondering *when* was I coming home—she was brioche: the taste of melancholy.

So I went to culinary school. Okay, correction: I wanted to go to culinary school. Very badly. (I'd always dreamed of cooking.) But characteristically and considering how I'd literally dropped everything to move to France, I was now both flat broke and, having overstayed my three-month tourist visa, facing deportation. I'd just reached that paranoid state where I was certain the gendarmes were giving me funny looks out on the boulevards. Greg and I went to dinner: my plight seemed less hopeless over pig trotters. "Well, how about I pay for culinary school?" he suggested. (Could he do that? Was that okay? What did that *mean*?) And then he plunked down nearly fifteen thousand dollars of his hard-earned savings (Savings! What a novel concept!), at once enrolling me in school, financing my legal, scholarly right to remain in Paris, and bankrolling my fledgling inferiority complex. "It's a remarkable gift, Greg," I said nervously. "It's an investment," he replied.

But until the May day when we made bouillabaisse, I actually thought that I had made a terrible, and very expensive, mistake.

Our Paris evenings invariably found us out on the postage-stamp terrace of our apartment on the Île-Saint-Louis, me giving Greg what he called the rundown of the "best of the worst" parts of my day.

"It's just not the same!" I moaned. "I don't feel the food! Does that make sense?" He would nod sympathetically and, depending on the despondency in my tone, head inside to pour me a glass of wine or make me a gin and tonic. "It's all . . . flat!"

The problem was this: on the streets of Paris I'd associated food with the city's messy, lusty life, but I found the classical cuisine of school highly codified and thus a little impenetrable and a trifle suffocating. In classical cooking, there is very little room for variation: either a recipe is something, or it is something else. If you cooked a tournedo (which is a slice of beef filet), for example, sauced it with a brown sauce of reduced white wine and veal demi-glace, and garnished it with an artichoke bottom filled with little nuggets of potato called *pommes noisettes,* you would have made a *tournedo châtelaine.* But if you cooked a tournedo, sauced it with a brown sauce of reduced white wine and veal demi-glace, placed a sliver of truffle on top, and garnished it with wedges of artichoke and little footballs of potato called *pommes cocottes,* you would have made a *tournedo mascotte.*

Chef would nod his head sagely when he told us these things and the rest of the class would gravely concur. The difference was very important . . . and completely incomprehensible to me. So much so that when someone brought in an old article from the *New Yorker,* asking "Is There a Crisis in French Cooking?," while the rest of the class erupted in shock and outrage, I kind of found myself thinking that . . . yeah, well . . . maybe he might be right.

I felt like an interloper, an unbeliever lurking amid the faithful.

But then one gorgeous spring day we made bouillabaisse.

Now, the soul of bouillabaisse is *rascasse,* a grotesque-looking rockfish that is as menacing dead—covered in a toxic slime that clings to its mottled red spines—as it is alive and swimming in the shallow waters off the Côte d'Azur, which the one I was cutting up on bouillabaisse day had been doing just the morning before. All around me in the chilly *poissonnerie,* French- and English-speaking students of our government-run school hacked the ugly, pugilistic brutes into thick chunks, blowing on their cold fingers and looking longingly toward the sunshine that streamed into the school courtyard.

Back in the kitchen—pot lids clattering, scented steam rising into the air—Chef gathered us near the passageway to the dining room.

"The traditional bouillabaisse accompaniment is rouille," he said. "It has a lot of garlic and is very h-h-hot and spicy." Chef loved to show off his command of the tricky fricative English *h*. "You spread it on croutons and dip them into the soup." He kissed his fingertips. "Delicious. *Alors*, before you begin, you must blanch the garlic three times. Otherwise, it will be too spicy. Too h-h-hot. *Alors. Vas-y*."

I was standing next to my friend Sandra listening to Chef's instructions and grabbed her arm as she started for the *garde-manger*. "Wait," I pleaded, perplexed. "Didn't he just say that it was *supposed* to be spicy and hot?" Sandra, more pragmatic than I—only twenty, she'd already cooked in three professional kitchens—shrugged.

And this wasn't the first confusing instruction of the day, either.

Which brings me to what bouillabaisse is.

So, imagine that you live in a city on the water, like Marseilles. Now, I want this to be realistic, so get over the idea that you live there in a beautiful, spacious apartment with a view of a pristine harbor or a glimmering bay. You don't. You're the wife of a fisherman. Your apartment is small, but clean to the point of antiseptic, because you are down on your hands and knees every day scrubbing it vigorously. (You hate the errant fish scales that fall from the clothes of your husband, the fisherman.) You wake up too early every morning, because he has to be on the water well before the sun rises, and you have to make him *pain grillé* and *café* and be sure that he has his rubber boots on and his knitted cap and is well padded against the maritime chill. You send him off with a kiss and a cuff.

When his boat docks back at the port around eight in the morning, you've been up for hours and you meet him at the wharf and set up a table with an old knife, the blade honed sharp as a razor, and wait for him to start tossing out the catch. You cut and you haggle and you sell the morning catch, and off to the side you set a few nasty-looking rockfish and toxic scorpion fish, the kind that the elegant ladies won't touch.

By the end of the morning, after the blood is washed off the port's stones and the boat is squared away, in addition to the trash fish, to your bucket you've added the scraps from your labor and the leftover fish that nobody wanted.

This all goes home and because you're tired, you throw just about all of it into a gigantic pot—if it was a slow day and you're lucky enough to have them, setting aside just a few delicate fish, like the Saint-Pierre with the spots behind its gills where it's said Saint Peter (the fisherman) once pulled it from the water. (It's a quick cooker; it'll go in at the end.) You add some tomatoes and fennel and seasonings, which you always have because they grow abundantly in the warm weather. Some good saffron (worth the splurge, and the most expensive item in the pot). Top it all off with cold water. Then you blast the heat so that the pot rattles and shakes from the fierceness of the boil, and you call it a day. You go sip a glass of Pernod. Maybe put your feet up. The kids are coming over and soon the apartment will be filled with the noise of generations—babies crying, children being scolded, husbands and wives arguing and laughing, everyone filling their bellies.

Whatever other recipe you may have ever read, and whatever else you have ever eaten, that is bouillabaisse.

Or it was.

And Chef's instructions for the dish that May day were about that vague. They pretty much amounted to pointing to a smorgasbord of fish and shellfish, a pile of potatoes and tomatoes and fennel heaped on one of the stainless kitchen roll-aways, and saying, "Go for it."

So, trembling, I made my first independent decision of the entire school year and I didn't blanch my garlic for the rouille. It was a sunny day, hot and beautiful, the kind that reminds me of home, and in the end, craving heat and spice, I just couldn't bring myself to do it. I mean, there are instances in which blanching garlic is perfectly reasonable. The bite of raw garlic comes from enzymes embedded in its tissues, released when the clove is ruptured or sliced. But if you blanch the garlic first, those enzymes are deactivated. So, when you pound the cloves in a mortar and pestle as you do traditionally to make rouille (or whirl them in a food processor, which is nowadays much more common), blanched garlic produces a flavor that is mellowed, closer to the sweetness, say, of roasted garlic, than the eye-welling punch that comes from raw.

Chef came around the kitchen tasting our rouille, which we'd spread as instructed on slices of toasted bread. Mine was a gorgeous rust-red. (Rouille, which rhymes with "ooh-wee," means rust.) It had four cloves of garlic pulverized with a roasted, peeled, and seeded red pepper, mixed with an egg yolk and seasoned with a little bit of saffron, salt, and a generous pinch of cayenne pepper. But when it came to emulsifying the sauce with olive oil—the same as you would do to make mayonnaise—I'll admit: I cheated. I called Sandra over for help, mayonnaise being my culinary bête noire.

Chef took a bite of my crouton and winced as if he'd just been slapped. "Meez Feenlay!" He skewered me with a look mingling exhaustion and frustration. "It is obvious—you did not blanch the garlic as I instructed. May I ask, why not?"

"Oui, Chef. You said the rouille was supposed to be spicy."

"Oui. Spicy. That is why we use the *poudre de cayenne*," he spat, unamused. "But this is not spicy, this is . . . is . . . offensive."

Normally, when Chef and I butted heads—which frankly was often, culinary school being both much more and much less than I'd expected—he would excuse himself from the confrontation with dignity, padding away on his silent, buffed white shoes. But this time—perhaps because we were so close to the end of the school year, perhaps because I had touched some Gallic nerve—he took my crouton and threw it disdainfully down on the floor, like a *mousquetaire* throwing down the gauntlet.

It seemed as though all the clamoring pot lids in the room suddenly rattled a little more quietly.

My insurrection attracted the interest of another chef in the kitchen, who came around the piano—the big, hot, hulking flat-top stove—to my station and picked up another of the croutons from my plate. He studied it curiously. Chef Royer, who taught the French students, had a reputation for dressing down students in strident, withering diatribes. I quaked as he raised the crouton to his lips and took a bite.

"*Mais vous êtes fous. C'est parfait,*" he said to Chef with a dismissive nod of the head.

I scanned the faces of the two big men anxiously, standing nearly toque to toque next to my station, hands on their hips.

"*Mais oui,* it is perfect if you don't want to taste the soup," said Chef with a cunning smile.

"Bouillabaisse is robust, strong, like a man from the Midi!" Royer declared forcefully.

I recalled that some weeks earlier, when the French students roasted a leg of lamb atop a *tian* of zucchini and tomatoes flavored with rosemary and garlic, Chef had told us that Royer was from the south and had spent most of his professional career cooking in Provence. Chef, I knew, was from the north—he had a weekend house in Normandy—and was a product of Parisian kitchens.

"The rouille must be equally *fort*!" Royer bellowed.

Chef took Royer's measure while a clutch of us students watched intently. Sandra's mouth hung visibly open. The French students twittered and tried to look nonchalant, but were flushed with agitation, faces pinker than when sweating over the piano. Chef's frown changed to an ingratiating smile.

"Okay. Okay." He shrugged indifferently. "We disagree. This is fine. *C'est la cuisine régionale, non?*"

Chef Royer backed off, smiling, and clapped Chef hard on the back with one big, broad hand. "*Oui, c'est ça,*" he said chuckling affably, the palpable tension in the room magically defused by the invocation of this word, *régionale*.

It was astonishing. Apparently, the seemingly yawning chasm between something being offensive and something being perfect could actually be bridged if both sides just agreed that the thing in question was of a regional character. It was the culinary equivalent of a laid-back California, "It's all good, man." If there had been a sound track to the moment, it would have been "Free Bird."

I was stunned.

And then, as the import sank in, excited.

So, you see, it was bouillabaisse that confirmed there was that space I'd imagined within French food, where dishes expressed the lives and loves of their creators, hope and longing made edible, so that you could know what someone's life was like because you could know what it tasted like.

And from that moment on, I began to study regional dishes, cooking feverishly at home on our hot plate. Peppering Chef with questions. Cornering Chef Royer in the hallway and pressing him for more details about life in the south. The peppers: Were they spicy? Or merely hot? France came alive, illuminated by food.

And when I'd exhausted every resource they had at the school, I even went to see Meg, my connection for English-language books at the Red Wheelbarrow, a little bookstore on a cobbled side street in the Marais.

"Well, you've read Waverly Root, of course," she said. I just stared at her blankly, chastened. "Elizabeth David?" Wordlessly, she piled my arms with *The Food of France* and *French Provincial Cooking*, two books from the late 1950s, and shooed me out the door.

That weekend, I dragged Greg to the Luxembourg Gardens and planted myself on my favorite bench under the chestnuts. I raced through David: genteel, urbane, a tremendous chronicler of French cooking, recipes that read like poems.

But Root . . .

Every dish in his retinue was like bouillabaisse: Promethean, symbiotic, storylike. Now, culinary school had done nothing to dispel my notion—born of seasonless supermarkets—that ingredients just appear as if by magic, nor to impress that there were any unwritten natural laws governing their use and combination. But in Root's France—the France of 1958, to be exact—there appeared to be a simple and organic, harmonious order to the kitchen—and between the land and the food and the cook and the eater . . . and thus the people and their lives?—that just about knocked my socks off, so little of either simplicity or harmony had I ever known.

~ ∽ ⌐

ON THE NIGHT OF MY GRADUATION, Greg and I sat atop the colossal millennial Ferris wheel erected on the Place de la Concorde and gazed out over the glittering lights of Paris. From such a vantage you could easily imagine France stretching far off beyond the lights, unruly, ancient, and a little mysterious. Two hundred feet up in the air, a strong wind blew in our faces as he nervously reached into his pocket and took out a cheap silver costume ring set with three brightly colored stones. "This isn't an engagement ring or anything," he shouted over the gusting wind as my heart pounded hard in my chest. "But I just wanted to tell you, I don't know where I'm going, but I do know that I want to go there with you!"

With shaking hands, he slid the ring onto my finger, a perfect fit.

In my entire circumscribed life right up until that exact moment, I'd never felt such a sense of limitless possibility. It felt like bubbles under my breastbone, like electricity tingling in my fingertips. My God, how I loved him! "Let's go everywhere!" I shouted back, the flavor of adventure on my tongue. "Let's travel all over this country! I want to see it all with you!"

"Whenever you're ready to take that trip, you just tell me! I'll make it happen!"

We sealed the deal with a kiss that night as the city shimmered and the bucket began its long, slow descent to the ground.

And seven years later, here we are.

CHAPTER 4

B UT AS REVELATORY AS THAT FIRST BOUILLABAISSE HAD BEEN, my first spoonful of the soup at Le Rhul—placed ceremoniously on the table before us along with a basket of oven-crisped croutons and a dish of rouille—actually makes me wonder why I would have ever, ever, *ever* have eaten bouillabaisse anywhere else. I put down my spoon and for a moment I just stare at it, entranced. I'd like to build a little shrine to that beautiful bouillabaisse.

Its color is deep russet, and the texture is quite thick and smooth, like a purée—the robust fishiness, the spicy flavor of garlic, the licorice of fennel, the sweetness of onions and tomatoes, a little smoke from bay leaves, a floral hint of dried orange peel, are all in there, amalgamated, concentrated. Outside the restaurant window the steady, bright sunshine glitters on the turquoise water and the soup tastes just like that. Just exactly like sun-soaked Marseilles.

When I finally emerge from my reverie, I look up and notice a look on Greg's face.

"What?" I ask.

He looks mildly horrified.

He inclines his head surreptitiously, indicating the rolling trolley set up off to the side of our table, set under a glass case containing a delicate model of a sailing ship. Having finished serving us our soup course, the waiter has resumed his ministrations. There's a large silver platter on the trolley, big enough to hold a Thanksgiving turkey, and on it he's assembling a golden, saffron-scented pile of glassy-eyed fish, their mouths agape. While we watch he heaps it higher with mussels, crabs, and floury potatoes dyed yellow as sunshine from the broth.

Greg looks around the restaurant and gulps, realizing that this couldn't possibly be the portion meant for some other table of ten or so people. (Besides ourselves, the restaurant is now completely empty.) Scarlett sits next to him in her booster seat, munching on French fries and squabbling with Indiana over whose turn it is to play with the little crab carcass the waiter has brought them from the soup. She loves to eat. Surely, she's good for a fish or two, right? He hits her up like a used-car salesman.

"You're going to eat a whole bunch of fish for Daddy, right, big girl?"

"Fish, yuck," Indy says, noticing the groaning platter. "I'm stickin' with the French fries." He crams another handful into his mouth and snatches the crab from Scarlett, who promptly reaches across the table and whacks him in the head with her spoon.

The waiter begins loading our plates with fish. Greg gamely picks up his fork.

Soon, it is like the parable of the loaves and fishes, where the fish keep multiplying to feed the hungry crowd. Except that we're only a meager crowd of four, and though Scarlett eats and eats, her belly is only child-size, and Indy, underwhelmed by fish to begin with, is no help at all. Yet there seems to be always more, and more, and more, and more fish. If you're the fisherman's wife, bouillabaisse is the meal that conforms to your instinct to nourish abundantly. A pot produces bowl after bowl of soup, always served first and separately, followed by plate after plate after plate of fish.

And when the waiter appears at our table for the third time and piles more firm nuggets of conger eel, two or three potatoes, a tiny crab, and some sea robin and more rascasse on his plate, Greg begins lavishing every bite with rouille. (The restaurant rouille is only mildly spicy and very slightly sweet.)

I notice it with something that feels distinctly like malice. "Don't you like it?"

Now, truthfully, I wised up early. And I know he's struggling. And also, I'm rather enjoying outwitting him.

This is supposed to be a ground rule of the trip: no more recriminations.

But this is not: deny thyself all opportunities for a little private, gleeful gloating.

See, the trick for two people consuming a bouillabaisse is to eat strategically. The slower one eats, the more the other one must, because the waiter will inevitably dart in and pile more fish onto any available plate real estate. Rookie Greg has been eating steadily while I've been nudging my fish around my plate, taking breaks to shepherd Scarlett to the bathroom, playing hangman in my notebook with Indy . . . Consequently, Greg has eaten at least twice what I have. And now, probably a cup or so of rich, mayonnaisey rouille.

"You don't like the fish?"

"I just don't really want to taste it anymore."

"Oh, you poor baby," I say, and though I try to disguise it, maybe he can still hear the escaped mocking in my voice because he gingerly brings fork to mouth and looks at me with hangdog eyes. With pursed lips I move a morsel of eel off to one side of my dish and scoot a chunk of potato over to the other. I can't help it: *serves him right,* I think.

———— ⌒◦⌒ ————

NEARING THREE O'CLOCK ON THE NOSE, we finally sit back in our seats, stomachs groaning, and survey the damage. The white tablecloth is speckled with yellow stains from saffron, as are my fingers, a halo around Greg's lips, and the bibs the waiter sagely suggested we wear. Our bottle of rosé from Toulon down the coast lolls on its side, knocked over by Scarlett, who draws in my notebook. She eventually grew curious about the crab, remembering a crab leg once savored at my mother's house, and tried unsuccessfully to suck the meat from its carcass. The shell lies vacant amid the rubble of French fries and ketchup on her plate.

"Can you take this to the monsieur?" Greg hands Indy a twenty-euro bill to get change for the tip. (Tipping in France isn't obligatory, but a small tip is becoming customary.)

"I'm going, too!" Scarlett throws the notebook to the floor and springs from her seat. She never wants to be left behind, and, anyway, Indy is usually much too timid for such a solo errand. They trot off in search of the waiter.

A minute later, while I'm drinking my *café*, they return empty-handed, Indy looking sheepish. "What happened?" Greg asks.

"He took it and said *merci*." Indy shrugs. He looks like he might cry.

Scarlett parrots the body language of his mortification. "Yeah. *Merci*."

Lesson learned: don't show up late for lunch.

REGARDING THE TRANSCENDENT BOUILLABAISSE at the Hôtel le
Rhul: lest anyone believe that instead of a chef there was a bona
fide fishwife cooking in the kitchen, which there was not, let me clarify.
In fact, let me waffle on whether there are still any fishwives bothering
to make bouillabaisse at all in Marseilles anymore, because maybe there
aren't. Maybe making bouillabaisse from scratch is just another one of
those things people only talk about doing nowadays, like sewing your
own kids' Halloween costumes.

Whether the fishwife still exists anymore in this day and age I really
don't know for sure. But here is what I do know: there is a rumor floating
around the docks that it is getting harder and harder to be a small-boat
fisherman in France. The fleets are consolidating, fishing's going global.
And drawing from my own recent history, I'll say that to be a small-boat
fisherman in France these days must feel an awful lot like being a married
couple with two kids living in the suburbs: it's hard to fight the sinking
feeling that your best days are behind you.

And man, I *hate* that panicky feeling because I know it all too well.
I've been there. Okay, truthfully, I'm still there, which is why I can look
at Greg struggling with his rouille and his bouillabaisse and not feel the
stir of compassion. But it's been worse in the past. By the end of 2006,
two kids deep into marriage—so far from the glories of Paris we were
living in a quasi-legal unpermitted bungalow in my mother's backyard
for crying out loud—I was awash with it, waking up most mornings in
a flop sweat, startled out of sleep the way a newborn jerks herself awake

and cries to discover that her exile from the womb continues. How had this happened? Once upon a time in what felt like an alternate universe, I rose happily before dawn to work in a restaurant pastry kitchen. But now I stumbled through an entirely different routine: get up early with Scarlett, the family rooster, incapable of sleeping past the sunrise. And now, all the coffee in the world's rain forests wasn't enough to make that walk to my own kitchen to make breakfast more bearable.

Wait. Does that imply that I was cooking? Because that, actually, would be a total fallacy. I didn't cook. I couldn't cook. It was the mother of all paradoxes. The more I ached to cook—to have a blade back in my hand again, to feel wrist and shoulders coordinating the neat flip and toss of a pan, to feel mastery and control the way I only had ever done when I was in the restaurant kitchen—the less I did of it.

An act of self-flagellation? Yeah, probably. (Along with Catholic guilt, it runs in the family.) But here's what I kept thinking, the thought that kept me stewing in that delicious bouillabaisse of indignation and self-pity: What, exactly, I wondered, was the point of cooking if I couldn't cook for real? By which I meant, if I couldn't leave home—slip away from the kids and the dog and my family and Greg and the chores and the endless messes—and cook professionally?

It felt perversely good to deny myself the pleasures of cooking. Homemade stock? Yeah, right. Bouillabaisse from scratch? Hah! Plus, added bonus, every meal I didn't cook gave me the opportunity to look straight across the table at Greg and think to myself, *You know what, buddy? This is all your fault.*

This is all . . . your . . . fault. It wasn't completely true, of course—I was complicit in our arrangement even if primarily through my guilt-driven acquiescence—but it might as well have been. The fact that I thought it with such pure conviction made it true enough. In my beleaguered mind at that dark point in time, he was no longer the love of my life but my oppressor, and the sadness of losing him turned me cruel and half mad. As far as I was concerned, the Greg I used to know had ceased to exist, because the same man who'd once promised me a lifetime of adventure, sitting together atop the Ferris wheel, who had invested in me and in our future by sending me to culinary school, had taken to arguing ever since Indy was born that I should give up cooking professionally—give it up!— and stay at home with the kids instead. "The mother is the cornerstone of the family, Amy," he said, and like that, I was caught as neatly as a fish in a net.

He wanted me to give up cooking? *Well, I'll show him,* I thought.

So I wasn't cooking, not really, but daily I still managed to serve up a tantalizing smorgasbord of guilt, resentment, and blame. They were my new specialties: the specialties of the house. Denied adventure, instead we all dined on drama, and wow!, that's a dangerous substitute.

And then, in 2007, came the episode of the tape, which started out so innocently I never dreamed it would nearly destroy us. The tape was little more than a housewife's escapist fantasy. A chance to luxuriate in the improbable, like reading *Vogue* in your sweatpants. I'd heard about this reality show on Food Network, the premise of which was to find new talent to host a cooking series. Far from problematic, the reality show itself sounded like . . . fun. Three weeks, solo, all expenses paid in New York City. And the winner's prize could be an extraordinary career slingshot, though I never dreamed that things would go that far. *Now,* there's *an adventure,* I thought. And in my mind, that's about as far as things went, standing alone in my kitchen, microwaving chicken nuggets for Indy.

You can see how by degrees I talked myself into it. What was the harm in sending in a tape? Sure, I knew that Greg, who treasures privacy, hated the voyeurism of reality television (actually, *despised* would be a better word), but it was just an *audition* tape after all. What, realistically, were the chances that I'd actually get on the show? And besides, if I did get on the show, it's not like I'd win. But if somehow I *did* . . . well, then wouldn't the outcome make everybody happy? No matter how he felt, wouldn't Greg have to let me give it a shot? See whether things could work out for us? After all, when we got married, wasn't that exactly what we'd promised we'd do for each other? And besides, was it *really* an iron-clad certainty that the life of a television personality was like a self-service buffet, open for public consumption? Wasn't it possible to be the exception to the contemporary rule: the one television star who sought *less* fame and *less* exposure rather than more? It was possible, right?

Several weeks later there were no gauges warning of an approaching marital meltdown, only idiot lights flashing, signaling we were already there. First indicator: total silence on the other end of the line when I called Greg at work to tell him—*Surprise, honey!*—that they actually loved my audition tape. They were casting me on the show! I now had a one in eleven chance of becoming a television chef. "Think of the opportunity, baby!" I parsed my arguments before he'd even uttered a word. "Heck, think of the money! We can finally move out of the backyard!"

Second indicator: probably several long minutes later when, blindsided, Greg finally stuttered something like, "Television? You want to be on television?" Foreboding pinged around my nervous system. My heart took a caustic dip into my stomach. And it got worse. In truth, among my own fears were many just like his own: What if we became grist for the gossip mill? Everyone's a critic and comments on blogs can get especially vicious and hurtful. What if we'd never have a normal, anonymous life again? What if that kind of scrutiny ruined cooking for me forever? But still, I had my hopes—and, gads, what could be worse than the stasis and uncertainty of our current life?—so even with a heart etched in acid, what I wanted more than anything was for Greg to hop back on the Ferris wheel and assure me that it would all be okay: we'd figure it out together.

But, unfortunately, there was not a single encouraging word he could think of to say to me. Instead he sank footings into the bedrock of his opposition and commenced building us a roller coaster, the construction rumble audible as a low groan into the receiver. "Well, I like our life, Amy. I know things are tough, but I still don't want to be married to Rachael Ray, either!"

I could have shouted into the phone, *I don't want to be Rachael Ray, either! But I do want . . .* MORE. And if I had, I don't know, maybe things would have gone differently, the coaster's track a single up/down instead of the gut-churning twister it turned out to be. Just as the imminence of Greg's departure had once spurred our declarations of love and fidelity, maybe the looming possibility of such a radical change in our lives would have compelled us to talk openly and honestly, without judgment or blame, about our life as we were currently living it. As a couple we have a long history of doing things *because*: like falling in love, or culinary school, or how we'd eventually gotten engaged because I was pregnant with Indy, acquired a permanent address because I was pregnant with Scarlett. But out of wounded pride and long habit, I stayed silent. "Don't you think you should have gotten that kind of thing out of your system before we ever got married?" he went on. The words stung like a slap—the implication, real or imagined, that he wouldn't have loved me if he'd known I could harbor such an aspiration, the way it flew in the face of the reality of our shared history, even the reality of me as he should have known me. I cradled the phone like a stone, ready to hurl it across the room: as the saying goes, hell hath no fury like a woman scorned. From that moment forward, we were senseless, locked into a high-stakes game of chicken regardless of whatever reservations we shared: he'd made me a cook after all and damn it, I was going to cook on television now whether he (or I) liked it or not.

So much for Ferris wheels.

SO NOW HERE'S WHAT I CAN'T STOP MYSELF FROM WONDERING, the kind of thought that plagues me. The fisherman's wife—membership in the Marseilles fishing fleet is one of those things that used to stay within families. So if you married a fisherman, it's probably because you came from a fishing family yourself. As in, you knew what you were getting yourself into. What the life was like. You knew the bad points—the hours, the scales—but you also knew the very good points, like the way he'd kiss you good-bye every morning. Or the way you'd work together on the dock when his ship came in. Or the bouillabaisse.

Well, okay, and so now what? Pardon the pun, but does she ever feel—as I do when I'm being honest—as if she's been the victim of a serious bait and switch? I'm no idiot: I knew that marriage was going to take work. But I also thought that in marriage, Greg and I were going to come out greater than the sum of our two respective parts. Instead it feels as if the very worst parts of ourselves have lately been running the show—my guilt and crippling anxiety, Greg's militant aversion to disorder—browbeating jejune optimism into subordination. I hardly recognize us these days.

But back to the fishwife: Does she lie awake at night worrying about the future? Whether she even wants to be a fisherman's wife anymore without at least some of the upsides she'd been promised? I feel terrible for her because I know she can see that things are going downhill fast. Not only is their cost of living up in Marseilles, threatening to put them out on the streets, but the *rascasse,* the soul of bouillabaisse, is getting harder and harder to find, which means that now, of course, everybody wants the damn thing. Which means that suddenly it's valuable, the little bugger, and that she can't even keep it aside for her family any longer and call it a trash fish. No way. Not now that one of those nasty, tasty little things—victim of its own success, or of global warming, or pollution, or whatever (the scientists aren't sure)—could buy gasoline. Or couscous (the Marseillais version of fast food, a specialty of the North African immigrants who have been swelling the city's population steadily since the 1960s).

So what does the fishwife do? Does she start stuffing euros in a mattress? Plan her escape? Send out for brochures on retirement communities on the Costa del Sol? Find a sugar daddy with a penchant for black-clad Mediterranean grandmothers?

Or does she just content herself with the couscous?

Here was Greg's final thought on the issue of whether or not I could go to New York to be on the show: "Over my dead body, Amy."

Here's what happened: I went off to New York anyway.

~ ⌒ ~

ALREADY VERY WELL TIPPED, the waiter approaches our table with a leather folder and lays it deferentially next to Greg's empty wine-glass. *"Prenez votre temps,"* he says, backing away. But he keeps standing there . . . attentively . . . waiting.

Greg opens the bill and studies it for a few protracted seconds, then pulls out his credit card and places it inside the folder, and hands the whole thing off to the waiter.

"Wow." He whistles low through his teeth as the waiter retreats to the kitchen.

"Wow?"

"One hundred and twenty euros," he says. "And that was just for the bouillabaisse."

In the maw of silence I'm pretty sure we're both calculating how quickly our paltry savings is going to drain away. Realizing how, one day, the kids will probably ask us, "What happened to our college money?" And we'll have to tell them the honest truth: "Sorry, guys, we ate it."

It's at moments like these that I find myself once again surveying Greg with jaded eyes. The room drains of color and the strident chorus in my head picks up its refrain: *And this is all your fault, buddy.*

~ ⌒ ~

NEW YORK WAS A DISASTER. It was worse than a disaster: it was a living nightmare.

Imagine this: You're there. It's stressful. It's . . . surreal. Celebrity chefs and gorgeous, I mean really gorgeous, gleaming kitchens, and nearly a dozen other incredibly talented, charismatic individuals, all

cooks, all of whom are considered your peers, and you are all cooking together. The producers and directors are kind, friendly, and generous; the
atmosphere is more camp than cutthroat. There's nothing to fear here:
It's just work! You're cooking again! And on top of all that, you're doing
really well! You're actually distinguishing yourself, thriving on the competition. You, who haven't felt successful in years, are enjoying . . . your
success! And even beginning to wonder if . . . hot damn . . . you might actually have a shot at this thing. In the studio, also formerly unimaginable,
this notion is no longer worrying. One celebrity chef, someone who is
practically a household name, even compliments you on your seasoning
abilities. You! Who could help it? Your heart does a little dance. Blushing with pride (and a little embarrassed) you think you might remember
the moment forever. And then another one tells you that you're a natural
on camera. A natural! Mentally you start cashing the paychecks. Sign-
ing the cookbook contracts. The days press on and the longer they keep
you, the more vividly you can imagine bringing the kids with you to the
city when you tape episodes of your own show. There is *nothing* to fear
here! You'll take them to Chinatown, you think. And they'll love Central
Park. You can all move out of the backyard! Maybe you'll all move to New
York! It is a whole new world!

And then the phone rings.

Actually, a bunch of phones start ringing. All over Manhattan, it
seems, cell phones are going crazy. And, lucky girl . . . it's all for you.
Because your husband, back home alone with the kids, is losing it. It
would be funny if it weren't also so terrifying. The man never loses it and
I mean now he is genuinely *losing* it, caught up in a frenzied panic all of
his own, terrified that he's being dragged kicking and screaming into a
world of your making in which he has absolutely no interest while also,
for the very first time ever in his kids' lives, being faced with the prospect
of having to work and still do single-handed dad duty while you're off
filming, and he is trying, with all the power of telecommunications, to
break down the almighty fortress that is the lockdown surrounding con-

testants of a reality show. There is everything to fear here! And he can't even reach you, which is *weird*, so he's calling producers and directors and cast nannies. He's even discovered the chilling power of a threatening fax. And he's got a message for you, oh deluded wife, tormenter who thought she could escape the real world—where he lives—and go off and play on television: you've left him no options. If this is what you want—fame, celebrity, vainglorious self-aggrandizement—well then, he wants a divorce.

I thought those were the worst words I could ever hear, and words I'd never hear, not from Greg. Not so long as we retained even the memory of wind in our faces on top of the Ferris wheel.

I was the last to go, the very last person eliminated before the two-personal finale, and the whole way home from New York, sobbing into my Bloody Mary, concerned stewardesses checking to make sure, was I all right?, this is the thought I couldn't stop myself from thinking: Sabotage? How had we ever arrived here?

⁓ ᴐ ᴄ ⁓

THE WAITER BRINGS GREG'S COPY OF THE BILL while I sit growing red-faced and fuming at the memory.

"I just can't believe that it's one hundred twenty euros for soup," he says, scrawling his signature.

Despite our pledge of no more recriminations, I look at him across the table and for an instant, I really, really wish that I could just make like Scarlett and whack him right in the face with a spoon.

"Yeah, well, *rascasse* isn't cheap," I mutter.

⁓ ᴐ ᴄ ⁓

OF COURSE, the bouillabaisse across the street from Le Rhul at the Petit Nice is even pricier. "Why don't you and Scarlett go play some more," I suggest after lunch. I'm still silently seething. Greg has his sweater back on and just looking at him all bundled up, just a stupid little thing like that—that we're outside again and that it's hot and that he's still wear-ing his sweater—is making me irrationally angry. I know I need to cool off before I go and say something I'll regret. "We'll find you guys in a bit, okay?" My smile is as insincere as a fishwife's handing over her last *rascasse*.

Together Indy and I walk around the Nice, checking out the pool, admiring the lobby. It's all very posh. Very sophisticated. Indy is im-pressed. "Why didn't we stay here?" he asks innocently. *Stupid, stupid, stupid Greg*, I fume.

Finally, we find the restaurant, and while Indy admires his reflection in its highly polished floor, I read from the menu. Of course: Chef Gérald Passédat doesn't do bouillabaisse. He does "bouille-abaisse," an auda-cious interpretation that has won him three Michelin stars. And there it is: specialty of the house. I translate the description for Indy. It sounds like nothing the fishwife would ever even have recognized: delicate sliv-ers of lightly cooked fish, an emulsion made of the strong-tasting shell-fish known as *violets*, something that the chef calls "nectar" of rockfish. Foam.

"Want to try it?" I tease, but Indy just rolls his eyes and pulls me back outside toward the stairs and back down to the beach.

THE WINTER SUN SETS EARLY but we all play for a while longer there on the waterfront before we go keep our appointment with the grandmother for the car, and this is what I keep thinking about: back when the *ras-casse* wasn't so expensive, back before bouillabaisse took refuge in the restaurants, there were passionate defenders and opponents of this, that, and the other variation. The best bouillabaisse on the planet was the one that your mother the fishwife made, and to suggest otherwise was to invite the kind of spider monkey throw-down usually reserved for prison mess halls and biker bars. There was no foam. Perhaps, in addition to simplicity, what was once glorious about one's family bouillabaisse was the loyalty that it commanded.

And that in particular is what sticks in my mind as the sun journeys toward its vanishing point on the horizon: today, in a fickle world, loyalty, especially to something like food, can seem quaint. But loyalty, I'm willing to swear, well . . . that may be the greatest treasure that we are rapidly, and to our peril, devaluing.

CHAPTER
6

THERE'S A GAUDY STRIP MALL RIGHT ON THE MARSEILLES waterfront, down the way near the towering Corbusier-designed apartment complex, separated from a white sand beach by a traffic roundabout
anchored by a cheeky reproduction of Michaelangelo's David. (The Marseillais, post Nazis, have a more practical attitude toward antiquity.) And
that night, in the grocery store there, all hell breaks loose.

It took me the rest of the afternoon to regain my composure, a con-
certed effort to just relax and enjoy the kids that proved as good as a
workout. By nightfall, surprisingly, I was ravenous again. "Dinner?"

"Let's buy groceries," Greg suggested prudently. "We'll take the car
and eat in the hotel room tonight; it'll be cheaper." Ah, yes. Cheaper.

The grocery store scene was typical, Indy and Scarlett running wild
in the aisles until Greg scooped up Scarlett and I grabbed Indy by the
hand and dragged him off with me to go look for bread. "If you're a good
girl you can have a treat," Greg promised wiggling Scarlett.

"Can I have those pink kitty socks?" she asked, eyes wide. They
were standing in front of a display of Hello Kitty items. Scarlett adores
cats.

"You can have the kitty socks."

Sometime in between her ecstasy over the pink kitty socks and our
hasty, apologetic retreat from the store back to our seventeen-year-old
but not-two-hours-new-to-us Peugeot 106 Kid, Scarlett must have felt her
tummy rumbling. But being two, and maybe fearing that Greg wouldn't
buy the socks after all, she said nothing. And so we were all equally sur-

prised when she turned her head daintily to the side and barfed all over the dairy aisle.

"Go get the guy," Greg ordered and Indy and I ran for the front of the store.

"How do you say puke in French?" Indy wondered.

"Boo Boo, I have absolutely no idea."

There was more barfing in the car, totalling the grandmother's carefully preserved denim upholstery. There was barfing on the stairs of the hotel. As we raced for our room carrying our little spewer, the Algerian ladies emerged from the office and peered anxiously through the banister. *"Vomit,"* one of them muttered and went to fetch a bucket.

"Médecin?" the other asked us.

"No, it's okay. I'm sure she'll be fine," Greg said.

The woman raised an eyebrow but went back inside her office: it was none of her business.

"No doctor?" I fretted. Generally speaking, in all other instances save illness, by long-standing tradition I am the calm one with the kids. But Greg's dad being a doctor, in the face of illness he is calm by association, while I am a wreck. "I swear she's got typhoid or something."

"She's fine," he assures me.

But there was even more barfing as I changed Scarlett from her smelly clothes and dressed her in pajamas. With a wet washcloth I tried to wipe the worst of it from her matted hair, my normally clamorous spitfire too lethargic even to complain.

"Is she okay?" Indy asks me, worried, curled up on the twin bed shoved up against the far wall. Doobie dozes at his feet, beneficiary of my distraction, flaunting an earlier admonishment to stay off the beds.

"She'll be fine," I say and go wring the cloth out in the bathroom sink, but I know I don't sound convincing and he doesn't look convinced. I can't stop myself thinking about our own pediatrician, now five thousand miles and four time zones away. Damn: it's Saturday. Even if I call, I'll just get the answering service.

It is a long evening.

But, eventually, not without gallows humor. Right around ten, I am finally beginning to unwind, even singing the praises of the bathroom bidet—who knew it was the perfect size and shape for a puking two-year-old?—when Greg's belly gurgles ominously.

By eleven he is doubled over on the bathroom floor.

"Rouille," he groans as I watch aghast from the doorway, remembering guiltily how merrily I'd observed his earlier torment. "Too much rouille . . ."

"Oh honey, I'm sorry," I say, passing him the wet washcloth, though Greg's gastric distress travels down, never up. "I never meant for *this* to happen."

At one in the morning, he comes out of the bathroom all pale and sweaty and lies back beside me on the bed, where I am pinned flat beneath a very hot and fidgety Scarlett.

"Any better?" I ask hopefully. He looks terrible and I feel awful, like it's me and not a cup full of rouille that's to blame.

"Tell me again what you love about bouillabaisse?" he says, throwing a hand over his forehead in a gesture of surrender. We speak softly so as not to wake Indy, but Doobie, roused, shuffles sleepily and jumps off the bed, threading our discarded clothes and plunking down on the floor at Greg's bedside with an annoyed huff. He lays head on paws and resumes dreaming.

"Okay. Well, people wrote poems about it," I whisper in the soothing tone of a bedtime story. "They called it the golden elixir. And there is a legend that says it was even invented by Venus to lull her husband, Vulcan, to sleep while she went off for a little wah-wah with Mars. Isn't that cool? I love food that comes with legends."

"My bowels are writing a poem about bouillabaisse. Wanna hear it?"

"Disgusting, Greg."

"Sorry. Okay. Well, how about this," he says, clearing his throat quietly.

There once was a dish from Marseilles,
Made from tiny little fish from the bay.
I couldn't be sicker
From this golden elixir.
Dear God, make the pain go away.

"Or I've got one," I say, smiling in the half-light. The moon through the shutters falls in bright bars across the bed, and I compose in my head. "A haiku . . ."

So potent, so strong,
Tangled fishes in red soup.
Why hate my husband?

There's a pregnant pause, then Greg laughs uneasily in the darkness. "You really do hate me right now, don't you?"

Taken aback, I stammer incoherent denials, just making it worse.

"No, I know," he stops me. "But whatever. It's there, I can feel it: at the very least, you still don't like me very much."

Scarlett's panting breath is a counterpoint to the sound of the crashing surf. A long quiet stretches between us, broken only by the sound of the waves, a metronome to measure how long it takes me to find the right words. We are in taboo territory.

"I'm still just . . . angry," I finally admit.

"All the time?"

I sigh. "It comes and goes. Depending on which part of it all I'm thinking about."

"So, couldn't you maybe skip ahead to one of the parts where I wasn't such an asshole?" It's a gentle appeal.

Scarlett snorts loudly in her sleep. Through our skin I can feel her heart beating as fast as a hummingbird and I wonder if that's normal.

"Do you really think she's okay?" I ask.

"Sure. She's just got whatever Marc's kids had before we left. Or something she caught on the plane. She'll be fine. Kids get sick."

"So it's not something she picked up on the floor of the train station?" I'm trying for levity and to change the subject, convinced that at this point we'll be better off if we can just stop talking. "It's not like a PCP trip or something? Because I have never seen a two-year-old puke so much."

"Maybe," he chuckles, following my lead. "But probably not."

"Do you think this is all going to be too hard on them?" My mother, who had seven kids, has always said that life is just a bunch of transitions, and what's hard about children is that kids hate transitions. (I'm adding my own corollary: What's hard about children is that transitions make them barf. Repeatedly.)

"I think this is the reality: sometimes this trip is going to be beautiful, and sometimes it's going to be hard. But I'm glad we're here. Don't start changing your mind about that." He takes his hand from his hot forehead and gropes blindly for my mine, finds it on the sheets beside him and gives it a tight squeeze.

"What if something happens to us?" Lying worried in the dark, I've been hearing my mother's airport admonishment echoing in my head all night long: "Bring them all home safely, Amy."

"You're getting ahead of yourself there, babe," he answers, and then grows quiet, fallen back asleep.

CHAPTER

7

Greg's cousins, Danielle and Michel Nicaud, live in Aramon, a little village outside Avignon that is named for the type of grape that everyone in Languedoc—the just-next-door-to-Provence wine-producing region—used to grow. And according to our map, the A7, the autoroute back home to Brianny, passes right through Avignon. So when Scarlett wakes in the morning, springs from my bed, and demands breakfast—sweet relief!—we give them a call to see if we can visit on our way home.

"*Bien sûr*," Michel says. "Of course. Come for dinner."

There's a funny story about those Aramon grapes. Well, maybe not funny, but relevant. I'd spent a sleepless night, and not just because of hot, writhing Scarlett, or my guilt, or Greg coming and going noisily from the bathroom long into the wee hours. I couldn't sleep because all night long I was brooding, asking myself this question: Is there really such a thing as a fresh start?

The Aramon grapevine was a workhorse—disease-resistant, high-yielding—that's why everyone in the Languedoc planted it. The grapes and the light, cheap *petit rouge* they produced were a fact of daily life, which, for years, was simple. It was simple all over France. As late as the 1960s, about twenty percent of all French workers were employed on a farm or on a vineyard, but that number is down to less than five percent today. As with the fishwife in Marseilles, it was work you were more or less born into. And while the work was grueling, as with the fishwife in Marseilles, at least you knew from experience what to expect from such a life: the hard work, yes, but also the rewards—a pastoral existence tied to the rhythm of the seasons, a close-knit community within the rural villages, a day of rest on Sundays and, it can't be understated, even a certain menu: all of Root's well-documented regional dishes, dependable flavors that reinforced ideas of continuity, solidarity, familiarity, and security.

Sadly, war was another fact of daily life for much of Europe during the nineteenth and twentieth centuries, which is one reason in the early 1990s a core kernel of European nations, France among then, signed the Maastricht Treaty calling the European Union into formal existence. The EU was Europe's fresh start: by linking and strengthening their political and economic destinies, the Union aimed to render war obsolete on the European continent.

But there were inevitable large- and small-scale consequences to the EU, and among them is what in France has become known as *la crise viticole,* the winemaking crisis, and the rise of a militant, sometimes violent faction of dispossessed winemakers in Languedoc called the Comité Régional d'Action Viticole, or CRAV, many of whom were once Aramon growers. Because when you aggregated all of the winegrowing regions of the EU there was simply too much cheap wine being produced—too much supply, too little demand—and so the price of those cheap bottles plummeted even further, taking down with them the livelihoods of many Languedoc producers. Simply put, Europe's fresh start spelled disaster for any Aramon grower who couldn't afford to make a similar fresh start—to reorganize and replant and start making a smaller quantity of higher-quality wine. Ask an Aramon vintner if there's such a thing as a fresh start and he might say this: sometimes, one man's fresh start is the end of another man's way of life.

There are a lot of good reasons to be invested in the past. But for now, if Greg and I have any hope of our own fresh start, I've got to figure out how to stop living there.

"I'M HUNGGGGRRRRRRRYYYYYYYY!" Scarlett wails.

I crane my neck peering into the backseat. The Kid, befitting a French car, is very petite. Scarlett's American car seat takes up sixty percent of the backseat, easily, and Indiana is crammed into the other corner, knees tucked up under his chin, staring out the window looking miserable. Doobie shares his distress: ears down, he's flattened like a floor rug below Scarlett's kicking feet. "How can you be hungry? You just ate!"

"If you can call hot dogs eating," Greg mutters.

I look at him askance, a fresh wave of irritation cresting. "They were *your* idea," I hiss. We'd scarfed a stand-up lunch at a crêpe stand in Aix-en-Provence: long, skinny hot dogs tucked into soft, chewy baguettes. Adequate, but not a meal to linger over. "It's not my fault that we're broke," I mutter under my breath.

"She didn't eat her hot dog," Indy tattles.

"I'm hungry! I'm hungry! I'm hungry!" Her cries resonate in my kidneys; a hail of kicks to the back of my seat.

"What'd she do with her hot dog?" I ask Indy, catching his eye in the rearview mirror. Outside Aix we left the autoroute for a smaller national road through the countryside. Trimmed plane trees lining the side of the road flash by us, looking like upturned hands cupping the sky. There are narrow, dusty-green cypresses and groves of olive trees but only a few scattered buildings. Few signs of civilization.

"She fed it to the pigeons."

"Nice," I snort. Scarlett howls hungrily. "Can't you do something, Greg? I'm driving."

"And I'm reading the map. She's fine."

"You should have brought snack bags, Mom," Indy nags. Helpfully.

"We're going to eat as soon as we get there, big girl," I cajole Scarlett. "Danielle is a wonderful cook. You'll love her!"

The first time I met Danielle was back during culinary school, back when she and Michel were still living in Paris with their children, Chloé and Thomas. Greg's parents were visiting and we all gathered at the

Nicauds' for dinner. She made *nems,* like crunchy spring rolls, filled with duck confit, and rabbit sautéed with rosemary and sun-dried tomatoes, a tender mâche salad to go with a plate of pungent cheeses, and an apricot tart, the crust so buttery and crisp it shattered when you touched it with your fork. Gratefully, I kept my mouth full so as not to reveal my paltry French, the grammar of a five-year-old.

"Maybe she'll make us ratatouille," I say, mouth watering.

"Like the movie!" my baby squeals.

"Uh-huh. Or a daube. That's even more delicious."

"What's a daube?" Indy asks suspiciously.

"We're in Provence now," I explain. "A daube is a special dish from here. It's got meat all cut up and cooked for a long time with garlic and onions and carrots . . ."

"I hate onions . . ."

"And herbs and tomatoes and olives . . ."

"I love olives!" Scarlett yells. She keeps right on kicking my seat, but happily now.

"Or maybe she'll cook a gigot," I say. "Roasted lamb, lots of garlic, with potatoes . . ."

We've entered the suburbs of Avignon, which look remarkably like the suburbs of any midsize American town. There are big-box stores and big, crowded parking lots and families pushing big carts loaded with big-screen televisions and tiny little refrigerators to their SUVs. (Although here, you call an SUV a "cat-cat"—a *quatre-quatre,* a 4 × 4.)

"I'm not so sure she'll cook," Greg says, directing me through the suburban streets and back toward another national road. "We just called this morning."

"Well, a *grillade,* then. Michel likes to barbecue."

To marry into a French family as a foreigner has been, in my experience, to willingly embrace a potential minefield of social customs. Like at that first dinner with the Nicauds in Paris, to which I showed up, the girlfriend, feeling awkward about my finances and my French, eager to be accepted by the family I feared suspected me of golddigging, carrying a fairly expensive bottle of Bordeaux, only later to be informed by Greg that this was a faux pas. ("If the bottle is too nice, you embarrass your host," he explained. "And if it isn't very good, you embarrass yourself." Why hadn't he told me this earlier? "It's always better to bring chocolates," he concluded.) First and foremost among these familial customs is to always respect the sanctity of the family gathering, which is really just the same thing as saying to respect the sanctity of the family meal, because a meal is *always* the focus of a family gathering.

Scarlett looks worried.

"Don't worry, baby," I reassure her. "Of course she'll cook." I sniff confidently. "As if . . ."

Aramon is gorgeous. The creamy stone houses hide behind buff-colored rock walls, looking as if the whole village has been bleached by the strong Provençal sun. The Nicauds live in a sixteenth-century row house just beyond the village square, so we park and Greg gets out our suitcases while the kids run after Doobie, who makes a blessed racket going down the gravel road, barking and lunging furiously at the leisurely stretching cats atop the garden walls, overjoyed to be out of the car again. The air is perfumed with lavender. Just as I'm wondering which of the plain, unmarked wooden doors to knock on, handsome, silver-haired Michel opens one.

"*Bienvenue, Robin des Bois!*" he says, spying Indy, who's brandishing his bow and arrow from Aix. Chuckling and giving each of us the times-four cheek kisses that are the hallmark of the south (I miscalculate and stop at two and there's some awkward bumbling as we try to regroup), he escorts us into his home's softly lit, elegant interior.

Upstairs, Danielle breezes through the living room. "Do you know," she exclaims, greeting us with another round of kisses, "you are the first of the family to see us here! *Bienvenue!* Come in, come in!"

Within minutes, she has whisked Scarlett from my arms and is carrying her around the house like a doll, smitten, while Michel pours aperitifs at the kitchen counter. "I had so little time with Chloé and Thomas when they were little," she says ruefully, "but I'm looking forward to when Chloé has a baby. Then I'll be like your mother, Greg, a doting *grand-mère*." She bustles around the rustic pine table next to the kitchen, removing candles and flowers one-handedly and setting it with two plastic plates and cups. *"C'est jolie, non,* my table? Do you speak French?" she asks Scarlett, who answers with a coquettish smile. Danielle jiggles her on her hip, soliciting a peal of giggles. *"Alors,* Amy, we'll feed the children first and then we'll eat, *non?"* I look around the tiny kitchen, hopeful for signs of dinner. A pot bubbles on the small gas stove next to a microwave and a stack of cooking magazines. It's steaming, but emits no enticing smells.

Michel hands me a beer-and-tequila drink and sits beside Greg on one of the overstuffed sofas arranged around a wall-mounted flat-screen TV near the dining table. "But we're not in Paris," he reminds Danielle. "How is your mother?" he asks Greg, raising his glass. *"Santé."*

"She's fine. *Santé.* Is that where Chloé's living now? Paris?" Greg asks.

Michel nods. "She and her partner run a restaurant in Montmartre, close to Uncle DD and Mamie's old apartment." DD is Greg's mother's brother, a widower and now habitual bachelor, living within sight—just across the courtyard—from the apartment where he was born.

"We hope for a baby soon," Danielle confides. "And then, Michel, we'll go to Paris and help." She hands me Scarlett, freeing her hands to finish dinner, and I go to call Indy to the table. He appears from the garden still brandishing his bow. "Did you see a barbecue out there?" I ask quietly, but he shakes his head no.

Once hands are washed, Danielle sets a bowl of hot pasta on the table in front of the kids. "In Provence we use a lot of *l'huile d'olive,* Amy, but the kids like butter, *non?"* she asks, piling pasta on the plastic plates. "And I put some Gruyère."

Scarlett beseeches me with big eyes, her bottom lip quivering. "Where's the meat, Mama?" she sniffles.

"*Qu'est-qu'elle veut?*"

With a sharp nod I try shushing Scarlett. "Nothing," I say. "It looks delicious, Danielle."

Scarlett's eyebrows knit in a scowl as she scrutinizes her plate of pasta, disappointed. "I wanted olives," she grouses. Indy happily slurps his noodles.

"Olives?" Danielle empties a few plump black Picholines into a bowl from a jar in the refrigerator. She sets the olives in front of Scarlett, laughing. "She's a *gourmande, non*? A good little French girl!"

∽ ◦ ◡ ∿

AFTER THEY EAT, I bathe the kids in Danielle's big marble tub and kiss them good night in her spare bedroom. In the living room, Greg and Danielle chat while Michel pours yet another round of drinks. I slip in beside Greg on the sofa with a fresh glass in my hand, the alcohol starting to make me feel a little loose. My French flows faster, much to Danielle's amazement, as we talk about the last time we were all together.

"I've always wondered, Michel," I screw up my courage to ask. "Did you like that bottle of Bordeaux I brought?"

"We haven't drunk it yet," he answers, winking. "It was a little young. Soon, though, it will be *parfait*. It's a very nice bottle."

"Do you still cook, Danielle?" Greg asks. Embarrassed, like he's read my mind—when are we eating?—I pinch his leg, but Danielle doesn't seem at all offended.

"*Pas beaucoup*," she says matter-of-factly. "The kids are gone and we both work too much." Sharply, suddenly, she catches her breath and makes a clapperboard of her hands. "But you!" She rounds on me, flush with excitement. "*Alors!* Now you are the cook! The famous cook! DD told us everything! How could I forget? We were so happy for you! How is your show?"

My hand on Greg's knee begins to sweat. He shirks my sidelong glance and sips his drink, then studies the dregs in his glass. I'll be fielding this inquiry solo.

"No more show," I say breezily, a tone to change the subject. "How did you cook the rabbit that night, Danielle? Sautéed, right?"

But she dismisses my dodge with a curt wave. She looks confused. "But you did win, right? DD even said they gave you a new *quatre-quatre*."

Greg is absorbed in contemplation of a napkin on the coffee table. So . . .

"Yes," I tell her simply. "I won." That's it, the whole story: five months after I was eliminated, one of the finalists pulled out of the competition, caught up in one of the kinds of made-for-TV scandals that seem to plague reality shows and please their viewers. In June I was reinstated as the second finalist, Greg walked out on us again in protest, and in July the viewing public, unaware of any behind-the-scenes drama, voted me the winner. A fittingly fairy-tale ending, if by then it hadn't become so evidently unsurvivable. Danielle works out the puzzle and Greg keeps his enigmatic quiet, which is what usually happens whenever this topic is broached by outsiders, even though what we're doing here now expresses a decision that, ultimately, *I* reached all on my own: no more television. Move back to France. Save the family.

Michel saves us all. "Actually, we did hear a little about your troubles," he concedes, setting his drink on the coffee table as the doorbell rings. He rises to answer it. "But it's better now, *non*? You're traveling with your children and you are putting the past behind you. That's the way to do it. New memories chase away a sad history." He pats Danielle's arm affectionately as he sidles to the stairs.

"I'm sorry. I thought you were in France for the television," she mumbles. "But you quit." It's a statement now, not a question. A brisk shake clears her head and she plucks our glasses from the coffee table. They are placed on the kitchen counter and she returns to the sofa with another mystery. "And the car?"

"Sold it," I answer, and offer, "That's how we're paying for this trip." Greg stares at the coffee table like he half-expects it to get up and walk way.

"So then, you are just here driving around and eating? That's all?"

"Pretty much," I conclude. Tipsy from three drinks on an empty stomach and with another little angry buzz at silent Greg building, I'm all at once tempted to yammer like a fishwife, but Michel, thankfully, reappears at the top of the stairs. To my total astonishment, carrying four Domino's pizza boxes.

"*À table,*" he commands. "Dinner."

CHAPTER
8

LIKE EVERY CHILD OF DIVORCE, I am an expert on its sad, lonely aftermath. I was just five when my parents split, and my younger sister, Casey, was two, coincidentally the same ages as Indy and Scarlett when Greg and I separated the first time, a fact of which I was well aware.

When I was nine or maybe ten, my dad appropriated my grandparents' American Clipper motor home and started hauling us kids on summer trips up to the California redwoods to go camping. If Michel is right and new memories really do have the power to drive away a sad history, then that was how we tried to do it, the three of us: by literally driving. On the long stretches headed north from San Diego, Dad behind the steering wheel, Casey and I would conk out for hours, lulled by the droning motor and the vibrations of the unrolling road.

Similarly, Indy and Scarlett surrender to sleep time and time again on the ten-hour drive northward to Brianny.

So only Greg and I are awake to see the clouds swell over the hillsides, and the landscape change—becoming mountainous, rugged, and green—as we leave the sunnier south firmly and definitively behind and re-enter Burgundy.

It's just Greg and me laughing when we realize we have no idea what exit to take to get off the autoroute. (It might be the first laugh we've shared in months.)

And just Greg and me noticing that in Burgundy, the exits from the autoroute are few and far between.

Eventually, it's just Greg and me apprehensively studying the brown road signs that pictorially describe the attractions of the surrounding areas. One shouts out for Époisses—the cheese—way before we think we've neared Époisses the town. Which is important, because Brianny is just south of Époisses.

And when a sign finally appears saying that the next exit is for Semur-en-Auxois, the village right next to ours, it's just Greg and me sharing a sigh of relief.

The darkness around Brianny is total, the only illumination from the gazillions of stars that pierce the frosty night sky.

In the driveway, before we take the sleeping kids upstairs, it's just Greg and me holding each other tightly under the light of the universe.

G REG'S MOTHER WASN'T AT ALL SURPRISED ABOUT THE PIZZA.
Greg called to tell her about our visit with the Nicauds. "You
have to realize," Ghislaine said dismissively, "Danielle and Michel are
very healthy."

It is one of the things that I adore about this woman, with whom I
have a sometimes-complicated relationship, that she actually thinks
takeout pizza is healthy.

Because you eat less of it . . .

Naturally . . .

Because it's takeout pizza . . .

Which isn't really food.

Confession: Ghislaine isn't much of a cook, either. Although our family gatherings do always involve eating, these days, if we're in San Diego,
the meals are more likely to be reheated and come from Costco. And
when Jim and Ghislaine are in Paris visiting her brother, then the food
comes from her favorite traiteur down the street from their apartment, or
from Picard, a prolific chain of supermarkets specializing in frozen foods
that may be single-handedly remaking the cooking habits of the French.
Here is just a short list of some of the things you can buy chez Picard:

- PORC À LA MOUTARDE
- CANARD AUX CÈPES
- FOIE GRAS DE CANARD CRU AUX FIGUES
- BOEUF AUX CARROTS

- BLANQUETTE DE VEAU
- BOUILLABAISSE
- FRITES
- CROISSANTS
- CRÊPES AU CHOCOLAT
- TARTE TATIN

You can find frozen versions of regional specialties like *daube Provençal* or *pommes Sardelaise* or *aligot de l'Aubrac* or *ravioles de Royan* at Picard and there's even a special section called "*Cuisine Evasion,*" which sounds suspiciously like it should translate to "Avoid Cooking," but which actually means something like "exotic dishes" and is comprised of entrées like moussaka, couscous, *poulet au curry Thai,* fajitas, and even—incredibly—frozen sushi rolls.

The prize for winning the Food Network reality show was six episodes of my own series, which I titled *The Gourmet Next Door.* I originally intended for the show to focus on French dishes but the producers preferred that we take a broader approach. But nonetheless, in one of the first episodes I made an endive gratin—tender spears of steamed endive wrapped in ham and topped with Gruyère and a béchamel sauce—that was an old family recipe passed down from Greg's mamie.

Guess what else you can buy at Picard? Yup. *Gratin d'endives au jambon.*

"*ALORS,* THERE'S NO PICARD IN BRIANNY," Sophie sighs. "Pity."

I've hounded Sophie, but in the week we've been back in Brianny, this is the first I've caught her at home. Usually, I pick my way across the frozen tundra from the farmhouse only to have Marc inform me that "the wife . . . ah, yes . . . she's gone to her Arabic lessons," or, "She's fetching the children from their karate," or some such. I like Marc, although I find his big booming enthusiasm a little . . . intimidating. Sophie is quite nearly his opposite. Marc is balding and short (although much taller than me) and a bit round, and likes to dress in what he ironically labels "country gentleman" attire: meaning long-sleeved plaid shirts (invariably with patched elbows or a button or two missing) and baggy faded jeans cinched with a hefty western-style turquoise-and-silver-buckled belt. For a man of means, he's a populist in dress and at heart. Sophie is almost as tall as Greg, elegant with her gray bobbed hair and leopard-print glasses, and subdued. Deprived of my sisters, pining for female companionship, I've been hoping to get to know her better: I wouldn't mind another woman to talk to. Someone who can relate to the plaguing questions of marriage and children. Someone to commiserate with. But we're hardly there yet, shy novices at the rituals of friendship. She pours me another cup of coffee from the French press and reaches for one of the madeleines I've brought from the patisserie in Précy-sous-Thil. They're not particularly good, the madeleines. Dry.

"Really? You would shop at Picard, Sophie?" I dip my own dry madeleine into the coffee. Better, but not great.

Refined Sophie's snort is incongruently graceless. "If the nearest boutique wasn't in Dijon? Yes. Of course I would, Eh-mee." We speak in English. Marc was pleased for the opportunity for Sophie and their children to practice English with Greg and me and our kids, but she hardly needs the exercise. Her English is much better than my French, owing both to Marc (half Swiss, half American, raised in Europe) and to her former career as a publicist for the museums of Paris. "They have some very nice *produits* chez Picard." She dunks a madeleine diplomatically. "Sometimes, when we are being in Paris, I pick up the *sauce béarnaise* because this sauce, Eh-mee, it is very difficult to make and I am keeping it in the freezer for dinner parties." I find her allegiance hard to fathom and even harder to reconcile with my hopeful caricature of Paris-eschewing Sophie as bastion of the old ways. Mother France.

She seems uninterested in the part. But before I leave, as I'm shrouding myself again in coat and scarf in front of the fire for the frigid trek to the farmhouse, Sophie retreats to the kitchen and returns with a battered madeleine tin. "Here," she says with a friendly grin. "The madeleines are always better when you make them yourself."

ALONG WITH, well, everything else, it's the fact of the sauces at Picard that drives me most crazy. "Meat and sauce," was how Brad, an old culinary school friend, tidily summarized French food. "Meat and sauce and potatoes." I'd argue his point but it's an apt description of simple French cooking, which evolved from a basic three-step dance: sauté a piece of meat, deglaze the pan with wine and add stock to make a sauce, then reduce. (And garnish with potatoes.) Vary the type of meat (or fish), vary the wine and whether you add shallots or peppercorns or tomato concassé or herbs or what have you to the pan, and you've got a whole range of quick bistro dishes. (The word *bistro* may even mean quick, having come from the retreating Russian soldiers besieging Paris in the nineteenth century, who wanted a last meal in the restaurants before they dashed off. "Bistro! Bistro!" they are said to have shouted, by way of urging on the kitchen.)

But if you don't intend to make sauces, quick or otherwise, at home, then you've no need to learn to do what is perhaps the most beautiful thing in the whole repertoire of French cooking: you don't need to learn how to make stock.

(And a clarification: there's no stock in a béarnaise. Just egg yolks, shallots, wine, tarragon, and a heart-stopping amount of butter.)

Stock is a microcosm of French home cooking: an everyday ingredient—a scrap, even—elevated to the realm of art. And it all begins with bones: at home generally chicken bones, though you can make duck stock and lamb stock and veal stock and fish stock—anything with bones to provide the gelatinous ingredient necessary to give the stock body and, in a sauce, to let it thicken. Depending on whether you want a light stock or a dark stock, those bones can be fresh and raw or roasted first in the oven until they're the color of umber and sticky and caramelized all over their surfaces. (If you've roasted a whole chicken for dinner, it's also perfectly acceptable to make stock with that carcass once you've picked it clean.)

Next, you add the *garniture aromatique*—chunks of carrot and an onion sliced in half studded with a single clove, and usually the greens of leeks. Some insist on peeling the carrot first, but for a home-cooked stock, topping and tailing the carrot—the kitchen term for chopping off both root bit and stem bit—is fine, as is leaving on the onion's skin. (This also gives the finished stock a nice amber color.) A few cloves of garlic, unpeeled, go in next, and then you top the pot off with fresh, cold water.

Finally, you make a bouquet garni—an herb bundle. You can wrap the whole thing inside of a leek leaf if you like, tucking in sprigs of thyme and parsley stems and a single branch of rosemary, and then tie it all up with kitchen twine. And if it you tuck the bundle deep down inside the chicken carcass, the rib cage holds it neatly in place while it's cooking, making it that much easier to fish the whole thing out and discard it at the end.

But most important is this: never salt your stock until the very end of cooking (and most cooks will say never, ever at all), because as the stock bubbles and boils, all of the flavors in the pot become concentrated, including any saltiness you've introduced prematurely.

The other essential element of stock-making is to skim. The stock should cook slowly and gently, churning from the bottom of the pot like bubbles coming up in a water cooler, and during the first stages of cooking, all of its impurities rise to the surface. It looks nasty, like a thick, foamy layer of greasy, gray scum, and you have to ladle it away until the clear, amber stock below is revealed.

Although I stopped making stock at home when Indy was a baby, in Brianny, I've begun again, in part because I'm trying to reclaim cooking, in part because given the weather, the time barrier between France and San Diego that impedes phone calls, and the rareness of finding Sophie at home to talk to, frankly, there's little else to do.

Two frigid weeks on since coffee with Sophie, Greg arrives home from the school drop-off, an errand I've been scrupulously avoiding for reasons I'm too embarrassed to admit, even to myself. He leaves his muddy shoes by the wood-burning stove and glides across the warm kitchen in his woolen socks. "Smells good," he says, plunking down at the table.

I pull a pan from the oven: the carcass of the same generous chicken we've been enjoying for the past couple days—roasted the first night, meat scraps baked into potpies topped with puff pastry the next, and now browned and destined for the stockpot. I've given it twenty minutes in the oven at high heat, surrounded by carrots and onions to give the whole stock a deeper flavor. "How were the roads?" I ask him. They've been icy and treacherous of late and the Kid has old tires.

"Slick." His nostrils quiver like a bloodhound's, keenly detecting a single sweet note amid the layers of the kitchen's savory aromas. "What else do I smell?"

I take down a plate of madeleines from their cupboard cloister. The little cakes are still warm: two eggs beaten with a few spoons of sugar, scented with vanilla, then mixed with a scant amount of flour and made tender with melted butter folded into the batter at the last minute. Sophie's right: nothing compares with homemade madeleines. He takes two and they disappear in fleeting bites. "Don't eat them all," I scold as he reaches for a third. Greg still eats with the greedy haste of a ravenous child. "Save some for the kids."

"Is it a good day today?" He nicks another anyway and pauses in the doorway, cake in hand, en route to the freezing-cold office at the back of the farmhouse, ready for work.

Is it a good day? I know that by this, what he really means is, do I *like* him today? "I made you madeleines," I answer benignly, tossing him a fourth. He smiles and heads for the office, whistling.

Actually, though, I don't like him much at all today, a conundrum which I'd love to discuss with Sophie but, *commes toujours,* she's nowhere to be found. Try as I might, distracting myself with books and stock and playing with the kids, it's been a forlorn few weeks. The weather is hideous: icy, windy, wet. In the mornings, I cower in bed until Greg looks out our bedroom window and gives me the weather report. ("Brace yourself, babe," he says by way of delivering the bad news.) I haven't seen the sun in weeks, not since we left Marseilles. Skimming the stock a little later in the morning, I have to laugh—a half-hysterical sound that echoes around the kitchen—when I realize that that is exactly what I feel like: scum. Perhaps loneliness and isolation work on a person exactly the same way as a slow boil does on stock, one's impurities bubbling steadily to the surface.

Mom has a different theory.

"Maybe it's PTSD," she says, her voice deadly serious. When we can, we Skype late at night. Midnight in Brianny is only early afternoon in San Diego, and she's just finished half of her school day. We chat through the short window of opportunity between her mornings teaching high school and her evenings teaching adult school. Mom has held two jobs for most of the years of my life.

"PTSD?"

"Post-traumatic stress disorder."

"*Mom . . .*"

"I'm serious, Amy. I told you this wasn't going to be easy. I know you wanted to be able to just *run off* to France . . ."

"We didn't run off to France, Mom." My blanket snug against the office chill is a protective shield rebuffing the tug of memories. I draw it tight.

"It's PTSD, Amy," she states firmly. "Don't you remember how *terrified* you were?" she adds ominously. "Remember the grocery store?"

Remarkable how effectively she breaches my defenses. God, I wish I didn't remember. The final episode of the reality show had just aired, taped in New York the week previous, Mom and Casey, Aunt Rosemary, and my sister Diane cheering me on from the front row of the live audience. (Mom beforehand proudly chatting up the Food Network brass backstage and regaling the producers with tales of my childhood cooking misadventures—the guacamole pies and cookies made with pow-dered strawberry milk.) Under blazing lights and to the sound of a drum roll there'd been a balloon drop and confetti and then teary hugs and high-fives between my vanquished costars, and while the camera circled the pack it had taken every ounce of my composure just to muster an ap-propriately happy expression for the moment when it stopped panning the crowd and zoomed in on me for an ecstatic close-up of the winner's face, one that wouldn't betray my mind's braying of its startled, stupefy-ing realization: *Oh my God, I'll have to tell Greg!*

The day after the taping, Mom and my aunt and sisters and I flew home to San Diego, but on the day of the grocery store incident, I'd just gotten back from a second trip to New York in less than a week. I'd watched the finale there all by myself, alone in a hotel room with a stiff drink and a certainty of impending disaster, waiting to tape a morning-after victory lap on *The View*.

I can't remember what, exactly, Greg and I were fighting about on the way to the grocery store, what the specific catalyst of this particular fight was—we woke up, went to bed, brushed our teeth, and ate and drank furious with each other; it took nothing to start a screaming match—but it continued into the store, where we ran into Ghislaine in the produce section. The children flew into her arms like refugees. "I'm leaving with her," Greg thundered. "I'll be in the car, Mom." Ghislaine looked at me lamely, pityingly, disentangled herself from the wailing kids, left her cart, and followed him. Indy and Scarlett stormed at me—Why had I let them leave? Where was Dad going?!

Where was Dad going?! Where *was* Dad going?! Within ten min-utes, I was a frazzled mess. The kids yanked at the car doors—*Open them, Mom!*—and I couldn't find my car keys anywhere. I searched my purse. Did Greg have them? I dumped the contents on the street: lipsticks, receipts, junk, toys, wallet, my notebook, no keys. Had I dropped them somewhere? I went through the pile over and over, certain they had to be there. Lipsticks, receipts, junk, toys, wallet, my notebook, no keys. Indy tried to help me. Scarlett cried. Wild eyed, I zoomed around the store searching, on the verge of hysterics—where were the fucking keys?!—when an older woman approached our cart and placed a timid hand on my arm. "Are you Amy?" I stared at her, confused. Did I know her? Did *she* have my keys? "Oh, you are! You're Amy!" she cried, certain she'd recognized me, which was stunning since at that moment I would have been hard pressed to identify myself. "Honey, it's *Amy*!" she called to her husband. "Oh my goodness, congratulations! We're all so proud of you! And we voted for you, of course . . ."

In the end, I abandoned the car in the parking lot, called Mom, and had her come pick us up. She's had a hard time forgiving Greg.

"It's not PTSD, Mom. It's probably more like . . . seasonal-affective disorder or something."

"Well, maybe Greg's controlling the weather."

She's so serious, so ridiculously on my side, it's comical. *"Mom . . ."*

"Well, it just seems like the more miserable you are, Amy, the happier he is."

Which is kind of true, but I won't believe the two are actually related. Greg springs out of bed in the morning. I slink. Greg keeps himself busy all day. I've been so bored—is bored really the right word? Stultified? Numb?—I feel like I'm collapsing like a black hole into my own stillness. What I should be doing is planning another trip but instead, I've been spending a lot of time in the bathtub, making my way quickly through Marc's library. (The man has eclectic taste. And I owe him money for a circa-1970s compendium, *Everything About Cats,* that I've been letting Scarlett scribble in.) Lately, I've been reading the autobiography of Zelda Fitzgerald.

Did you know she went crazy?

Okay. I knew that, too. But what I didn't know or appreciate was how painful it would be to read an account of someone slowly losing her mind, poisoned by a genteel cocktail of love and thwarted ambition. And what I absolutely didn't know was how certain reading it would make me that I am currently losing my own mind. It's a hideous form of appropriation, borrowing someone else's real-life misery. I decide not to tell Mom—it would just convince her that she's right, that I'm traumatized—but lately, a few times I've gotten the shakes so badly, I've been afraid my heart would stop. And then, because I've been afraid that my heart would stop, I get afraid that I can't breathe. And I don't trust my vision, either. Sometimes, I even think I'm seeing things—like starbursts and halos—which is the true reason I've been avoiding driving the car. My discomposure is humiliating, so I'm disintegrating in silence. Every morning I offer Greg, who wouldn't mind sharing the driving duty, a different excuse: I'm tired, I need to write an e-mail . . . In actuality, I'm just certain that if I get behind the wheel, I'll see stars and wind up dead, or be overcome and befuddled and wind up wandering around the countryside, lost. When Greg's working and the kids want to go somewhere, even if he offers to drive and drop us off, I still make up a hundred more reasons why we can't to hide this other shameful truth: that I am petrified to be by myself with them lest something happen to me and they are left to handle my breakdown all alone, without me there to shepherd them through it.

I also don't tell Mom this: that with their uncanny, umbilical sensitivity, they both seem to know this. The other day, Indy and I were sword fighting in my room while Greg and Scarlett colored in the cat book downstairs. And when I pretended to stab Indy through the heart and he pretended to die, I threw my sword to the floor dramatically and raised my arms to the heavens.

"No, God!" I hollered. "Take me instead!"

And then I fell back upon the bed, eyes closed.

A moment later, I heard muffled sobbing and opened one eye a sliver. And then Indy threw himself passionately across my chest, bawling: "I thought you were really dead!"

It took me a good hour to finally assure him that I was actually (*ahem*) okay.

So I don't like reading *Zelda,* but I can't put it down, either.

I keep hoping for a happy ending.

S CARLETT REQUIRES TWO BOOKS, A KISS, and three pacifiers to go to bed at night. Indy needs a story and a glass of water. Since arriving in France we've added prayers and good-night wishes for everyone we miss at home and the list grows longer daily. Indy misses his preschool teachers and our next-door neighbor whose name he never actually remembers and his bike and all of his buddies from the old playgroup and their moms. Scarlett—influence of the cat book?—misses all of the cats at Mom's house. We go through them all by name: God bless Mew-Mew and Ping-Pong and Tiger and Merry . . .

Finally, I close the door to their room behind me and creep quietly into the hallway.

Their room sits at the top of the creaky stairs, right across from the bathroom. Back when this part of the farmhouse was more of a barn than a house, it used to be a grain storage. Marc converted it into a bedroom and just above the stairwell there is still a nook carved into the thick stone wall, fronted by a tiny, purposeless glass window. Before we arrived, Sophie placed a small statue of the Virgin Mary there, and during the day the statue faces out into the hall. But each night, before I put myself to bed, I enact my own ritual: "Watch over my babies," I say to her, and then I turn the statue inward to face into their room. I like to think that under her protective gaze, their sleep is peaceful and untroubled.

In my room, the purring fan billows hot air from the downstairs fireplace and the Kinks croon softly on the iPod, barely audible above the rain pelting the windows and battering the roof. This particular storm

has wailed for three long days now, more gently by day and always fero-
cious at night, a devilish assault. I've measured its length in madeleines: a
batch a day, three more batches since it began, Greg and the kids happily
gobbling up the treats I churn out to keep my own demons at bay. Greg is
on his hands and knees on the floor inspecting our mattress with a flashlight, the sheets and comforters strewn haphazardly. The room looks like
it's been ransacked. Perhaps six cold, lonely weeks have at last taken their
toll on him, too. He looks frantic.

"What are you doing?"

"I think we've got bedbugs," he mutters and trains the flashlight beam
into the crevices of the stone wall behind our bed. "They could be anywhere. Google says they look like lentils, but I still haven't found any."

(Two mornings earlier, Greg, scratching compulsively at the breakfast table, discovered a constellation of tiny red bumps on his stomach.
"What is it?" he'd asked nervously, his faith in my divination touching if
totally misplaced.)

Instinctively, I back away toward the hall and survey his progress
from the theoretically safe vantage of the doorway. "Sophie and Marc
don't have bedbugs."

He rocks on his heels and lifts his shirt, revealing his chest now dot-
ted with tiny red bumps. An angry accumulation rings the new black-
bird tattoo over his heart, the site of which is, as ever, a shock. "Well,
just look at me," he moans. "They're on my back now, too. And on my
arms. Look!" He strips away clothing, showing me the welts. "They're
always there in the morning and I don't get any new ones during the day,
so it has to be happening at night. That's when they eat." That's Greg's
brain for you: irrefutably logical, although sometimes arriving at an
answer that seems just too far-fetched. Bedbugs? How about a delayed, but
impressive, stress response? (Memo to Greg: Me, too! Me, too!) I'm certain it's nothing more, and annoyed that he probably won't even acknowledge the probability. I could walk away, leave him to his plight and his
ransacking of the bedroom, but he looks pathetic, scratching his scab-

bing skin, flinging the bedclothes around in desperation. In the name of the tremulous goodwill that has been timidly building between us—his sardonic weather reports, the way he lets me linger in the hot bath without once pointing out how much water I'm wasting—I sit down and grab his arm.

"Well, then, let me see them again." The bumps are small and red but to my uneducated eye undistinguishable from any other type of rash. Knowing he'll balk at psychosomatic suggestions, I offer reasonable alternatives. "Could it be allergies? Maybe the new laundry detergent?" He shrugs pitiably. It's not my forte, but I revert to logic: "If it *were* bedbugs, wouldn't they eat me, too?" Unbidden and despite my incredulity comes the image of our inanimate, supine bodies covered in scurrying nocturnal scavengers. I spring from the mattress, shuddering, and Greg resumes his examinations without me.

Shrouding myself in a cast-off blanket, I head for the office, pressing my ear to the wood of the kids' door on my way down to check for signs of stirring, but remarkably, despite the gale blowing outside, they dream on. At the living-room window I watch the storm rage, moonlight illuminating the whipping tree branches. What a night.

In his building-block repurposing of structures to make the farmhouse, Marc got creative. The office is actually a separate stone building that was annexed by means of a sloped, tiled, windowed corridor from the living room. Formerly it was a root cellar and most of the time it's still as cold as a refrigerator. I dutifully Google bedbugs and read e-mails in my thin covering, shivering. There's a new one from my mother.

We had quite a conversation again today and you are now probably asleep or tossing and turning trying to figure out how to make things better. Maybe you need a nanny or someone to help you? Or you can always come home . . . I am largely preoccupied with worry and frustration that this still isn't going the way you want it to. At times it is so frustrating, I know. Every day with little kids is hard. I want to fill in that help for you so badly, yet here I am, stuck at school. I am missing you and wanting to help. I don't know what to do. I am just counting the days until we arrive for Easter. Only a few more weeks now . . .

Greg appears in the doorway. "Hey," he calls softly, "come see. It's snowing." Snowing?! There is yet a part of my brain that notes his excitement and thinks, *Heck yes!* Go watch the falling snow! Whoopee! But he has uncannily picked the exact moment when I was just settling in for a good homesick blubber. "I hate snow," I grumble, and then lay my head down on the keyboard and sob, missing my mother, hating the snow, hating Zelda, hating the country, hating bedbugs . . .

He freezes in the doorway, then enters and rubs my back soothingly while my tears bathe the laptop. *Melt,* says my placating brain. But like Zelda's, my mind is divided against itself, and the cantankerous half is louder, unyielding, and humorless: *Why is he so manipulative! Aren't you entitled to a good cry now and then! This place is so stupid!*

"Just leave me alone, okay?" I sit up, blotchy, red-eyed, and peevish. Goodwill? To hell with goodwill. Misery loves company.

The road map tops a stack of my books next to the computer, just where I'd left it when we unpacked from Marseilles. Greg fingers it cautiously. "So are we going somewhere or what?"

"Why don't *you* plan the trip, then?" I retort snidely.

He doesn't take the bait immediately. Instead he drops the map and retreats to the living room. I hear him open and close the grate to stoke the fire and then he reappears in the doorway.

"Easy," he says in a tightly controlled voice, "because if I do, then you'll get mad at me and call me a dictator. Isn't that how this goes? I'm the bad guy because I control everything. So if I do anything, I'm taking over. But then if I don't, then I'm the asshole and poor you, you have to do all the work, right?"

I smile at him sweetly, venomous. "No, baby, you're just the asshole, period," I sneer.

He turns then and stalks out of the office and with satisfaction, I can hear him pacing in the living room: it's what he does when he's upset. "And you're already taking over anyway!" I yell, fury bubbling up from the wellspring where my sadness retreated. By the twisted logic of righteousness, I feel I deserve to fight. I don't *want* to be the only one feeling terrible: it isn't fair. "It's just like with the firewood!"

Although it's a familiar line of attack—my everything-is-relevant, everything-is-related brand of marital warfare—he returns looking confused. "What are you even talking about?"

"When the firewood guy dropped off our firewood, remember? And there was this huge, gigantic pile of firewood out there in the middle of the yard. And you . . . You dove right into the middle of it and you took all the biggest pieces!"

"You're mad because I carry big logs?" Incredulous, annoyed, he walks back out the door.

"Aaaaggggghhhhh!" I could scream, or throw things after him, I'm so frustrated. Doesn't he get it? It isn't logs, or bedbugs. "NO! It's that if there were any justice in this world, *I* would be the one flourishing here and *you* would be the one who feels like shit! But no, you work, you drive the kids, you make the fire, you take care of Doobie, you carry the big logs, and all that's left for me to do is work around the edges, like I'm some sort of lesser-evolved human being or something because I can't keep up with you—you're so goddamned *balanced*! Man, do you know what I actually *liked* about the Food Network thing? That you finally seemed human! A total dickhead, but human!"

"You don't give yourself enough credit," he says stonily from the doorway. "No offense, but you know what you get from your mother?" Under the map was *The Food of France*. He flings it into my lap, where it sits like a stone. "Two great traits: martyrdom and a total aversion to accountability. Plan a damn trip. I am *deliberately* not taking over. This was your idea."

The kitchen door opens and closes and Greg heaves a load of wood from the shed into the basket next to the wood-burning stove. The grate of the fireplace opens and he drops in a heavy log that will burn all through the night and leave embers for the morning.

"So, do you want to go home?" he asks when he finds me sitting, arms folded tightly over my chest, shivering from anger and cold, glaring. "Is that what you're talking to your mother about? You're giving up?"

"I want a divorce."

He deflates in the doorway like a popped balloon, and slumps to the floor, defeated, remaining on the office stoop, head in his hands. He rocks back and forth and speaks slowly from between his fingers. "I . . . can't do this anymore, Amy . . ." This is the first time it's happened in France, but we've each wielded this weapon against the other many, many times before, the genie out of the bottle. The ugly, coercive, wounding threat.

But what if it backfires? "Can't do what?" I bellow, at once livid and petrified. Every time I throw that punch it rebounds on me, a wicked, coiled cross hook of conviction that he doesn't love me the same way that he used to: What if he seizes the opening and divorces me? I *don't* want a divorce. I just want things to be . . . normal. How—*when*—will things ever be normal again? When will I stop worrying whether he feels stuck? Whether now we're just staying together for the sake of the kids? If that's our current *because*—we're still married *because* we have kids? God, it's a mountain of fear and uncertainty with no discernible track either up or around it. So I'm reduced to these reckless attempts to blast a shortcut right through its granite heart, fearing landslides in the aftermath.

I no longer feel like screaming: I feel like crying again. "No. I don't want to go home. And I *don't* want a divorce. But I'm a mess, Greg."

"No kidding," he says, but not unkindly, considering. We fall silent listening to the wind's teakettle whistle through the roof tiles. "But why do you have to be so . . . mean?"

I kick the map at his feet, sighing. "Because I'm stuck, Greg. I have absolutely no idea where to start and I think maybe this road trip idea was crazy. It's all just too damn big. The trip, the kids, money, us . . ." He spreads the map open on his lap and inspects its colorful spiderweb of roadways. "And then, on top of it all, you're so happy here and I'm so not: it seems like the more miserable I am, the happier you are."

"Wow, I hate it when you do that," he says, exasperated.

"What?"

"Make two things related that aren't at all. It's like when someone takes a car to the mechanic, right? And you say, 'The transmission doesn't work.' So the guy fixes it, and then you get the car back, but you call him back right away and you say, 'But now the AC doesn't work!' There's no cause and there's no effect, Amy."

"Well . . . that's what my mother said," I mumble.

"God, can we ever have a conversation about our relationship without dragging your mother into it? Do you really think I would want you to be miserable?" he demands, sounding astonished.

"I don't know what I think anymore," I cry. "I am tired of thinking, Greg! I *hurt* from thinking!"

"Well then, stop it! Do you remember in Marseilles? When I said maybe you could try remembering some of the parts where I wasn't such an asshole?" He lifts up his shirt and points to the bird. "Do you even remember *why* I got this?"

I was doing dishes the August night when he came home with the tattoo. All was not well. In a week's time, I was flying to New York to film my first six episodes of *The Gourmet Next Door*. Too much was at stake—Indy, Scarlett—and we'd decided—or I'd decided and Greg, magnanimously, hadn't tried to sway my decision—that they'd be the last six, too, regardless of whether they wanted to pick up the contract, and I was as riled and itching for a fight that night as I'd been this. Consequently, I'd been more disdainful than touched by the gesture when he showed me the freshly inked bird and said, "This is for you. I know what we said before, but if you want to keep your show, Amy, keep your show. I've got to let you fly."

I'd smirked cynically. "A meaningful tattoo: how easy this must be for you."

"Look," he says now. "You're only helpless if you can't help yourself." He sets the map, open, on the desk and starts to leave. "Don't try to do everything at once," he coaches gently. "Just do something."

"Are we just staying together because of the kids, Greg?"

He pauses in the doorway. "I'm not."

His footsteps overhead rattle the floorboards while I sit for a long while, shivering, reading Root with the map open in front of me, figuring things out.

CHAPTER
❦ 11 ❧

Perhaps the most important contribution made by Waverly Root to all of food writing was his butter/oil/lard theory, the alternate history of French cooking that rewrote my entire thinking on the subject during school.

Essentially it is this: that all of France's disparate flavors were once a mere happy by-product of geography, and thus of the type of available fat in which they were cooked. Buttery dishes came from regions with good and ample pasturage for cows. But where the soil was poor, instead people raised pigs and geese, both of which, even on a diet of meager scraps, grow plump with fat that can be rendered. And finally there's olive oil, like Danielle said, the predominant cooking grease of Provence.

Now, climate is a function of geography, and so it is interrelated with the fats and how and what people eat, or at least it used to be. Root's wisdom worked out nicely: where it's bitingly cold and you need extra calories, conveniently the food (butter- and lard-based, mostly) tended to be heavy and rich. But where it's warm, like in Marseilles and Provence, the local food is olive oil–based, fish- and vegetable-centric, and naturally light.

Root was a Chicago newspaperman who first arrived in Paris penniless and jobless in 1927, like Hemingway and others of the expat crowd lured by the city's bawdy siren song and the promise of good food and romantic adventures. (Seemingly, that's why everyone goes to Paris.) The first time around, he stayed for thirteen years, and he would later write in his autobiography, "It took a world war to send me home."

He returned to France after the close of hostilities in World War II and published *The Food of France* in 1958. The book explains and supports his theory and gives an unparalleled history of the nation and its dishes, but it also exposes the response of a keen, creative, and disciplined mind when faced with a daunting task. France is the size of Texas: it is a big country. It is the forty-third largest country in the world and, if you don't count Turkey, straddling both the European and Asian continents, it is the largest in all of Europe. There is, obviously, a lot to be eaten.

Faced with this enormous challenge—to explain to a lay audience what, at the time, was still the world's most revered cuisine—Root posed his butter/oil/lard theory, an extraordinary, but ultimately simple, solution to the problem of bigness. There was no telegraphing of editors: PANIC STOP TOO MUCH FOOD STOP IMPOSSIBLE TASK STOP! Whatever doubts he may have harbored as to his fitness for the task, or the plausibility of even doing it successfully, he set his shoulder to it, staunchly refusing to succumb to the monolithic mindset and its accompanying paralysis, the murk clarified by his commitment to taking on the fabled cuisine one single dish at a time, the map taken apart and respectfully rearranged as a composite of regions, mini countries, shaped by cooking fat. When this dawns on me—not what he did, but how—I am struck by his genius. Just before I call it a night, here is what I realize: *The Food of France,* for all that it's about the food of France, could easily have had this alternate—and for me, this personally instructive—title: *How to Eat a* SMALL *Country.*

❧

WHEN I CLIMB BACK UP THE STAIRS TO OUR ROOM—fortified by my revelations and my unlikely kinship to my hero and his labors, sworn to be kind—Greg's in bed. On *my* side of the bed. I walk into the bedroom and there he is, grinning sheepishly, argument seemingly surrendered, the cheery yellow duvet wrenched tightly under his chin.

"I've thought about it, babe, and this is the *only* way," he says.

"No way! *Greg!*" I toss the book and launch myself on the bed, tugging at his blankets, laughing. "Forget it!" I shriek. He pretends to fight me off and I pretend to be overcome: we're play-acting forgiveness and it feels good, satisfying, even if it does mean that I'm intended as bait.

"No, you were right! You were right!" He tugs the duvet even tighter. "The only way we'll know for sure that it's bedbugs is if they eat you, too. I think they're living on my side. So . . . good night!" He rolls over, mirthful, facing away from where, if he's right and I'm wrong, the bedbugs will soon be feasting—on me—and feigns sleep, a devilish grin still tugging at his lips.

And, damn him, he actually does sleep as soundly as a baby all night long, while I, sacrificial lamb, toss and turn and squirm uncomfortably until I finally fall fitfully asleep, my dreams plagued by gigantic, horrific, blood-sucking, car-driving insects.

But at dawn, when I spring out of bed and race into the lamp-lit hall to inspect myself all over for bites, there are two bits of good news:

One, I knew it: I am totally, completely, one hundred percent unscathed. Hallelujah!

And two: I think I finally understand how to get this trip rolling.

S TRASBOURG IS FREEZING. Strasbourg makes Brianny look like the
Bahamas. Strasbourg is colder than the coldest place I have ever
been in my entire life. Ever. But our very first night there, stuffed full of
choucroute from S'Muensterstuewel, a mouthful of an old butcher shop
turned restaurant right next door to our hotel, I could have walked outside in the frosty cold air for hours, high on my own gastric juices and the
memory of steamy sausages.

Here's something I've at last admitted: Brianny *is* smack in the center
of the freezing-cold heart of continental France. And while that means
that there are, potentially, weeks and weeks (and, oh God . . . weeks?)
of bad weather ahead of us, it also means that we're within just about a
three-hour drive from the majority of the other freezing-cold regions of
France and their internal-fire-stoking cuisines.

Like, Alsace: capital, Strasbourg.

Strasbourg is an exceedingly pretty, lacey, gingerbread-architectured
city consecrated to the glories of the pig, a fact of which, if you are in
doubt, is upheld by its street names, by the omnipresence of charcuter-
ies, by choucroute, and even by the name of the square where we ate that
impressive first meal: Place du Marché-aux-Cochons-de-Lait. Place of
the Suckling Pig Market.

We took an early reservation and the waiter led us through a nearly
empty dining room decorated in a cheery rooster motif to a booth near
the front window overlooking the busy square, set with a white table-

cloth and yellow linen napkins. Close by, the cathedral bells were peeling loudly.

"*Bon appétit,*" he said, leaving us to our selections.

Indy scanned the menu anxiously. "Why are all the words so long?" he fretted. "I'm not eating anything weird, Mom."

The menu *was* intimidating, Alsatian-French (like the Alsatian region) being a hodgepodge of German and French influences, the results looking as if in the end they couldn't decide and so just mashed both words together and called it a day. The most heralded annual event on the Strasbourg calendar is the Christmas market, called the Christkindelsmärik. Navigating by street names in Strasbourg has reminded me of when Greg and I traveled in Japan: there, we tried to memorize the look of just one character in a place name; here, I try to remember just the sequence of the first four or five of fifteen to twenty or so letters. (And as in Japan, we've spent much of the day lost. Fortunately, Strasbourg is a charming city in which to be lost.)

Greg closes his menu and places it on the table. "Well, you're in luck, dude," he said. "They've got spätzle."

Indy is becoming a veritable connoisseur of what he persists in calling the "junior plate"—a name he poached from a restaurant in Semur-en-Auxois, the menu of which featured that odd substitution for the proverbial *menu enfant*—and his junior plate selections to date have consisted almost entirely of *croque monsieur,* French fries, ham, and variations on a theme of hot, buttered pasta. So no surprises, he adores his spätzle. (He has his own name for his favorite pastry treat, too—a chocolate éclair that he has dubbed a "chocolate wiener.") He slurps down a whole bowl of the ropey, twisted egg noodles while Greg and Scarlett and I tackle the choucroute.

The dish is a true snout-to-tail extravaganza, arriving in a giant bowl piled deep with tangy, juniper-berry-flavored sauerkraut and topped with nearly every conceivable bit of the pig, most of it converted into sausage form. There is earthy *boudin noir,* made with the pig's blood, and pale *boudin blanc* made from bread crumbs and milk mixed with the pig's finely chopped and chervil-perfumed organs. Stomachs groaning, Greg and I split the *quenelle de foie,* a savory poached dumpling made from the pig's liver, and Scarlett commandeered the dish's single thick slice of *poitrine fumée*—possibly the world's most delicious bacon—plus she ate forkful after forkful of sauerkraut. "Taste, Indy," she urged, offering a mouthful. "It's like pickles."

He watched with a look of unmitigated disgust. "How can you eat that?"

He's the only one among us who's not a bit surprised when she's as sick as a dog again the next morning. Comatose from choucroute, I hadn't noticed when she crawled into my bed sometime late in the night and wrapped her tiny body around my head, like a cat curled up on my pillow. So I awoke in the morning to the din of the again loudly peeling cathedral bells with the uncomfortable impression that I was wearing a heating pad as a hat, only to discover that it was actually a feverish Scarlett.

"One hundred two degrees," Greg announces, shaking the thermometer. "Looks like you and I are staying home today, baby girl." Her face is pale and sweaty, her lips dry, and she rolls over on the bed and promptly falls back asleep. Poor thing.

Indy pouts. "I want to stay, too." He knows it'll be a day of movies on the portable DVD player for Scarlett, and it's testament to the biting cold that he's willing to sit through countless princess tales if it means he doesn't have to put his jacket back on and go outside.

"Or," I try to entice him, "Dad can take you back to the rides." Strasbourg teems with children, most of them so thoroughly bundled against the cold, only the color of their garments gives away their gender. At the town center there's a merry-go-round, a cotton-candy seller, and a go-cart track all doing a brisk business despite the fact that it's two euros a go. We've already dropped twenty euros or so there ourselves. (Our economy, too, is on ice.) There are also numerous playgrounds around town and large, well-fed swans gliding on the waterfall-churned canals surrounding Petit France, the *quartier* where the city's millers and tanners and fishermen used to live. (Note to parents: a large, well-fed swan is not nearly as afraid of your children as your children should be of it.) It's our last day in Alsace and while I want Indy to have fun, I haven't completely surrendered Zelda: I'm still skittish at the thought of being all by myself with him. Greg will have to do the rides. Sure, wandering around and getting lost was charming when we were all together, but if I'm all alone with Indy . . . . well, that's a different story entirely. I can already feel my pulse racing.

"This is my job, Greg," I insist doggedly. "I'll stay."

But he grabs my purse and propels us toward the door. "That, my dear, is the dumbest thing I've ever heard," he says, smiling. "Have fun."

"No, seriously, Greg," I protest. What if I can't find our way back to the hotel? What if Indy falls in a canal? What about the *swans?* "I think I should stay." Oh God, my heart's thunk-thunking loudly.

"Let's *all* stay here," Indy interjects. Bless him.

"You're going," Greg says firmly. "It'll be fun."

Indy glumly pulls on his jacket. "Can I at least take my sword?"

I sidestep Greg and shift blankets on the bed. "Of course you can, Boo Boo." Disturbed, Scarlett sighs in her sleep and rolls over. The sword is tangled in the sheets beside her. "You can't forget to change her diapers, Greg," I fuss, fetching the sword and fumbling excuses. "And if she's got a fever you've got to keep her hydrated. Did we bring the Tylenol? Don't you think I should stay? Here, Indy." He catches my clumsy toss and slouches in the doorframe.

Greg's eyebrows furrow mockingly. "Which of the two of us is better at dealing with illness?" Damn. He's got me. "Now, stop being tragic and listen to me." He waggles his fingers like a ventriloquist speaking through a dummy. "*I am cold. I don't want to walk around anymore. I want to stay here.* So, would you please leave me in this nice, warm, cozy hotel room

with the sick kid while you guys go freeze your butts off again? Please?!
She's going to be fine, Amy. I know the Tylenol dosage. I've got this."

He hands me my purse and gives me a kiss as he pushes me out the
door. "You're going to be *fine*," he whispers. I fidget nervously with my
purse strap while he grabs Indy's knit cap from off the bed and squashes
it on his head. "And you," he warns. "Watch out for swans."

Exiles on the square, Indy and I stare at each other warily, his sword
hanging limply by his side, a standoff he finally breaks, shoving his free
hand deep down into his jacket pocket and rolling his eyes. "*Soooo . . .*"

I grab his arm and off we march. "Who died and made you a teenager?" I mutter.

The square is just off the riverfront—the river Ill (how appropriate),
which encircles old Strasbourg and meets up with the Rhine outside of
the city. A stream of people heads around the corner to a small parking
lot on the water and we fall in with the crowd. It disperses into a bustling
marché, tables and tents, the vendors wrapped in layered scarves and
jackets, wearing thick hats and gloves against the biting cold. I lead Indy
by the hand through the market. He drags his feet, takes just a half a
step to every one of mine, and we make our way in fits and starts. *Look,
kiddo,* I feel like telling him, *I don't want to be out here any more than
you do.*

You wouldn't call Alsace particularly pretty. Outside its fairy-tale
cities—like Strasbourg and Colmar, Riquewihr and Ribeauville—the
land, fertile as it is, is now largely given over to factories: giant smoke-
stacks churning great gray plumes of steam into the chilly, damp air.
Alsace hugs the German-Swiss border and is a hub of affluent, industrialized northern France. The few farmers left grow hops for beer or cold-
hardy Gewürztraminer or Reisling wine grapes, or potatoes, which still
sprout prolifically even in the short growing season. Driving to Strasbourg along the national roads, just as in San Diego we see roadside signs
for homegrown avocados, every hundred yards or so we'd come across a

hand-lettered sign at the end of a driveway advertising, PDT ICI—*pommes de terre,* potatoes, here. And potatoes are all over the market, too. We stop in front of a table piled high, holding so many it looks like the output of the entire state of Idaho except that only a few of them resemble the big brown russets of my experience. They are every shade of cream and golden yellow, pink as a blush or brown as clods of earth.

I channel my mother: "Never knuckle under to tyranny when faced with a child's adversity: make it a game," she says. "I know," I suggest brightly. "Let's practice your reading." I blithely ignore the ensuing melodramatic eye rolls, pointing to a hand-lettered sign affixed to a box of egg-size potatoes with thin, light-colored skins. "How about that one? Can you sound it out?"

His eyes barely flicker in the direction of the sign. "It's too *long.*" (MONA LISA, the sign reads.)

"All right." Another box is heaped with potatoes shaped like knobby fingers. "Then how about these?" RATTE, the sign reads. (These, by the way, are truly extraordinary tubers.)

Lest I prolong his obvious torture, he stares at the sign, lips moving silently, letter by letter. "Rat?" he reads. "That's stupid. Why are they called rats? They're *potatoes.*" And . . . cue eye roll. His scowl is fierce, his face all but hidden behind the knit cap jammed low on his forehead and a lock of his growing-longer-by-the-minute hair that is hanging in front of his eyes. He's at that stage of growth where lately, those eyes seem two times too big for his face, hazel in color and fringed with dark lashes just like mine. They're normally soft, sweet doe eyes, but now they glitter with rage. He looks at me as if he would like to bite me, or maybe just whack me with his sword. His body is tense, his free hand balled in a tight fist. *Oh, my little apple,* I think. *How close you have fallen to my big tree.*

"This is good practice for school, you know."

"We don't *do* this in school," he answers petulantly.

"Oh, yeah? Well, what *do* you do?"

"Cursive."

By this I am genuinely surprised. "Wow . . . cursive? I didn't know that."

For a split second, he almost smiles, relishing my proud astonishment, but then remembers how much he *hates* me. "What do *you* care about my school," he yells. "You never even come there. Only Dad does. Dad drives me to school and Dad picks me up and you *never* do." Suddenly, inexplicably, he turns and sprints across the market and down the stairs to the riverbank, leaving me bewildered among the potatoes. Startled, I take off after him. At the bottom of the stairs there's a running path where Greg and Doobie walked the previous night. Despite the cold it's swarmed with joggers, their breath condensing in little clouds as they huff and puff their way through the icy air. I dodge them, chasing Indy, and finally, snagging him by the back of his jacket, whip him around. He brandishes his sword as if he's ready to duel to the death.

"Do you mind telling me *what* you're so mad about?" I fume. "Don't you *ever* go running off like that! What if I lost you?"

"When are we going home?" he demands.

"Tomorrow!" I shout.

"No. I mean *home* home! When are we going *home*?"

Aha. So that's it. I should have guessed this would eventually come up. We've explained over and over to the kids: we're going home in July. I could say now, "It's February, we're going home in July," but frankly it's all just words to him. All he'll hear is that we're not going home—back to his life and his house and his friends and the rest of his family—*now*. He can comprehend the ambiguous passage of that much time little better than Scarlett can and she, I think, is fairly convinced that we *live* here now—like, permanently. I'd overheard her talking to her stuffed animals a few days earlier playing in her room and she was telling them, rather bossily, that the kitty cats at Mamie's house all lived in the *other* world. This whole trip: it can't make much sense to them. But how much to try and explain? For Indy: what's the right amount of burden to heap on a five-year-old? If I have one gripe about the aftermath of my parents' divorce—and I don't have one, I have hundreds—it's how my mother made me her confidante. The details of her suffering, her longing for my dad, her pain and his duplicity, these kept me awake at night. I regret with all my heart all the hard words and the spasms of rage the kids have already witnessed, but that damage is done. I'm inclined now just to stick with the facts, if I can.

"We're going home at the end of the school year," I tell him.

"But I don't *want* to go to school anymore," he howls. "I *hate* school."

"I understand, Boo Boo." And, man, I really do. Not even his teacher speaks a lick of English. In the beginning, Lulu gamely served as his translator but Lulu, I suspect, has lately grown weary of the responsibility. I wouldn't want to be in his shoes. "Is anything else bothering you?"

His bravado starts to melt. "Nobody wants to play with me."

It isn't a shock, but it's still heartbreaking. Nearly every afternoon I find him at the kitchen door, pulling on his jacket and boots, his sword in hand, and he tells me he's going next door to see if Marc's boys are home. Then he runs across the yard and stands hopefully at their glass library door, knocking politely and waiting, counting to ten before he knocks again, waits, and then he comes home to me, head hanging.

"What else?" I prod gently. My gut tells me there's still more.

His eyes brim with tears and he speaks so softly, I can barely hear him. "I'm afraid Dad will leave again," he says.

I should have seen this coming, too. "Oh, baby." Oblivious to the joggers, I drop to my knees and wrap him in my arms to rock him back and forth. How naïve was I to think—hope?—that in the war between Greg and me, he'd suffered only collateral damage? And that a trip to France with Mom and Dad—poor kid, leaving so much of his life behind—would serve to make everything all better? "Just the facts" . . . right. He's my son. When has "just the facts" ever been good enough for me? I'd quizzed my mother relentlessly—when is Dad coming home?— never really believing her when she answered, "Never."

"That was really scary, wasn't it, baby? I remember how scared I was when my daddy left." He nods almost imperceptibly, still alone with his fear. "Look at me." His eyes are red-rimmed. "He's not going to leave again, Indy."

"How do you know?"

"Because that's why we're here," I answer. "And that's why you have to go to school and I have to get my act together and plan more trips for us." Staring straight over our heads, clutching her iPod, a jogger nearly collides with us and I straighten up as she sprints away, aghast, glaring at me over her shoulder—"*En plein milleu!*" she hollers—and pull Indy to the side of the path. "Tell you what: Do you want to go get a chocolate wiener?"

We climb the stairs and walk back through the *marché* and now he clutches my hand tightly, dragging his sword behind him. There's a handful of pâtisseries near the cathedral and we stop in one to buy his éclair. "Now let's just walk," I suggest. I need more time to sort it all out in my own head. How do I assure him that his world won't fracture again without exposing him to too many of the rifts—my character flaws, Greg's character flaws—that weakened our family in the first place? He has a right to a few more years of believing—wrongly—that his parents are perfect. I head for the square where the rides are and Indy downs his éclair, licking most of the chocolate off the top first, sticking his tongue in the hole to lap out some of the cream. His face is smeared and he looks up at me and grins, contented. "Do you know why I'm not doing television anymore, Indy?" I ask him.

"Because Dad won't let you?"

Youch: so much for shielding. I shake my head no. "Because it wasn't real, dude. I was all excited," I tell him. "I couldn't wait to be in New York. Your dad and I, we'd kind of worked things out a little about my show—maybe . . . your dad had gotten his tattoo—and they made me a beautiful kitchen so that I looked like I was a real mama cooking in a real house. But you know what? I was cooking all day long and there were all these really nice people there making me look young and pretty and helping me make the food and taking my picture and stuff, but then I realized: it wasn't real, and for me, it would never be real, because you guys weren't there. There were like a hundred people all around me"—at this he laughs—"but not you guys. And I wanted you guys the most. I *hated* that your dad was right, but I realized he was: if I stayed on TV, a lot of the time—probably most of the time—I was going to have to be gone, missing you guys, pretending to be a mama cooking dinner. And I kept thinking, 'Boy, I wish I were just in my own house cooking for Indy and Scarlett and Dad right now.' Do you understand what I'm saying?"

He swallows the last bite of éclair. "Maybe . . ."

"I will never want to do anything more than I want to be with all of you," I tell him. "I thought maybe I needed all that excitement, but it turns out that I just want a real, happy, normal life—an interesting life, you know, a few things different than before, but still just a real, normal life. Get it?" Of course he doesn't. This is heady stuff for a five-year-old. I don't think I'm crossing the line, but it's obvious much of this monologue is for my own benefit: I haven't said these things out loud before. "But in real life, moms and dads do make mistakes, dude. Sometimes, pretty bad mistakes."

"Like Dad leaving?"

I stop walking and nod gravely. "Like Dad leaving. But he feels terrible about it, Indy. He really does. He loves you and Scarlett and he loves me." We start walking again. "I know that, but I've still been pretty mad at him ever since, because when he left he scared me really bad, too. Dad and I used to make each other brave, Indy. That's what trust is: being brave. We never used to be scared of anything, so long as we were together. And that's why we're all here now, kiddo: we're just taking a little break, learning how to be brave again."

"You make me brave," he says, squeezing my hand, and my heart just melts like warm butter. On some level, yes, we are staying together because of the kids, to preserve these kinds of moments and to preserve their trust, their willingness to believe in other people's courage and best intentions. But not "just" because of the kids. I think "just" *would* be insurmountable. Unfair, and insurmountable. But Greg said it, albeit indirectly, and I believe it: there's more to us than that. Always has been. Dispelling the hangover of worry is just going to take work is all, like purging the liver after a bender. But what did Root teach me? No shortcuts. You just put your shoulder to it and get it done, right?

We've reached the rides and I dig out my wallet.

"You make me brave, too, kiddo. But right now we still have a lot of worries left, you and me, don't we?"

"Yeah . . ." He's somber again.

"Are you tired of thinking about them?"

Eye roll. *"Yeah."*

"Me, too! So here's my plan: from here on out, so that I don't get stuck thinking about all my worries anymore, I'm just going to eat, and I'm going to cook, because those are two things that always make me happy. Okay? Now your turn. What makes you happy?"

He rolls his eyes again, but he's back to my sweet, joking, sarcastic son, and he cocks a finger, pointing it straight at me. "Mmm . . . Duh . . ." he says.

I sweep him into my arms and then nuzzle his soft cheek. "Seriously, who *did* die and make you a teenager? I love you, too." I put him down—so glad he's still not embarrassed by these lavish, public displays of affection—and pass a bill through the ticket window. I hand Indy our sheaf of tickets. "Real life is messy, but it is still way better than pretending. Now, let's go have fun."

AFTER STRASBOURG, all the potatoes in the ATAC look a little . . . paltry.

To explain food shopping in Brianny first requires an explanation of Brianny, including first and foremost that Brianny is basically just a single street, which is why our address is simply *route de Saulx*, with no house numbers or any other indicators. We live on the outskirts of the village, on the part of the road that is heading in the general direction of the hamlet of Saulx. And the no-numbers intimation is that, since there aren't many people living here, if you live on the *route de Saulx*, the postmaster must know you by name.

Brianny has a mayor and therefore a *hôtel de ville*, or mayor's office, but it is currently undergoing renovation to accommodate low-income lodgers, reflecting a new French law that requires all towns and villages to provide such affordable housing. The mayor has therefore been bumped to a small stone building just next door, but this doesn't seem to bother the mayor much, because he's primarily a farmer. (Although Marc warns me that I should use this term discriminately, lest I inaccurately romanticize: "There are no French farmers in Brianny," he says. "There's only one actual farmer living here, and he, like me, is Swiss.") To clarify: if the mayor isn't actually a farmer, well then, he primarily does something on his property that requires him to wear muddy boots both in and out of his office, where we've been several times, sorting out the paperwork officiating my extended stay in France. (Greg and the kids are citizens: I'm still skirting legality.) And whatever he does, my money's on that something involving cows. They're everywhere.

There are no shops in Brianny of any sort. Not even a village baker, which once upon a time in France would have been scandalous. There is still bread *service*, though, compliments of Ramon, who drives a bread truck for a *boulangerie* located over in Vitteaux. He makes deliveries three days a week. "How do we get him to stop?" I queried Sophie, and she advised me to hang up a sign so that he would know we wanted him to start honking outside our gate on delivery days. So I did, and what it said kind of cracked me up, considering the mental anguish I'd been punishing myself with. PAIN, SVP, it read. Which means "bread, please," but looked like I was petitioning for a greater share of the world's troubles.

For groceries, you drive southwest to Précy-sous-Thil, or northeast to Semur. But in either place, your choice of grocers is largely limited to the ATAC, Intermarché, or Maxi Marché, and they're practically interchangeable.

We have become weekly ATAC people, mainly because the drive to ATAC—located outside Semur's city walls—is the prettiest, including crossing the river via a single-lane stone bridge before heading up toward Montigny-sur-Armançon. From Montigny, Sophie favors a shortcut through the forest before rejoining the D970, our rural road, but we prefer to skirt the trees: the roads can get a little slick and dicey in the forest.

You can buy just about everything at ATAC. Inside, shoppers segregate neatly into two types. First, there are those who use the shopping carts, which are particularly intriguing to Indy and Scarlett because they're unlocked from a long queue in the parking lot by means of a special coin that dangles temptingly before them from my keychain. Now, nonscientifically, I have observed that the cart shoppers are usually women, like me, and that particularly they are women trailing children in their wake. (Although their children are much better behaved in the grocery store than are mine: theirs stay within steps of the cart, mine dart away screaming for cookies and chocolate croissants.)

And then there are the shoppers who bring a single woven basket of their own with them into the store. I've grown particularly curious about one of them: an older gentleman who always appears dapperly dressed in green corduroy knickers, woolen socks, a windbreaker, and a tweed cap, looking like he just stepped out of a daguerreotype.

Cart shoppers usually fill their entire cart to the brim, and the contents, because I snoop, lean heavily toward frozen entrées (reminding me ruefully of Picard) and other processed food items that come packaged in boxes and jars. On an average day my gentleman's basket, on the other hand, is typical of that of the basket shopper: two bottles of Côtes du Rhône, cat food, a few potatoes, and cheese. I find his restraint intriguing.

"I think *we* should get a basket," I inform Greg, and so on our forty-first day in France—notable for the funky smell of compost being liberally spread upon the fields, a harbinger of spring, I hope—he comes home from the school drop-off with a lovely picnic basket woven of light-colored cane.

"Okay?" he asks me. "It was all they had at the *droguerie*."

"It's perfect!" I rhapsodize.

But at the ATAC that afternoon, we immediately identify a problem. Semur used to have a variety of food shops: a *boucherie* (now vacant and all boarded-up), a *crémerie*, a *primeur*. The scene has now dwindled to just a handful of pâtisseries and a single charcuterie specializing in *jambon persillé*, a magnificent Burgundian specialty, nuggets of flavorful ham suspended in garlicky, parsley-replete aspic. And because there are so few stores now in Semur, ATAC is like Costco: everything available, from cheese to toys and garden equipment, including an aisle of little china dishes and pots and pans and silverware. On the aisle with the dishes there is a precariously stacked pyramid of blue and white café au lait cups for just a euro apiece, and because they're cheap and cute I automatically grab two—envisioning coffee with Sophie—before realizing that they'll take up valuable real estate in my basket. I put them back with a sigh and move on to meet Greg in the wine aisle.

Another problem.

"Score," he says, coming toward me with four bottles of 2003 Châteauneuf-du-Pâpe, normally a super-pricey vintage. "They marked them incorrectly. These were mixed in with the 2004s," he says happily; 2004s go for pretty cheap. Together we fumble with the basket, trying vainly to situate the four bottles, but soon have to acknowledge the futility: we can have food or we can have four bottles of wine, but not both. Muttering about the injustices of life, I return two to the shelf.

It is evident: basket shopping requires some deliberate and purposeful circumspection. The kind, perhaps, not best cultivated amid the temptations of the *supermarché*. (And this isn't even the worst of it: there's a whole other breed of French supermarket we haven't even encountered yet, called a *hypermarché*. The name alone makes me frantic.)

Home again with just a box of pasta, the wine, some apples, eggs, a hefty bag of carrots, and a box of cereal I had to carry out wedged under my arm, I go see Sophie, who, luckily, is still at home, but getting ready to dash back out the door again on another of her mysterious errands.

"Just use the cart, Amy," she twitters when I describe my peculiar predicament.

"There's got to be a better way, Sophie."

"There is, but this is not the nineteenth century anymore," she says. "Who has time? The grocery store is convenient. The only village nearby with the little shops anymore for the good little shopping is Saulieu."

I'm not totally over my fear of driving, but since our tête-a-tête in Alsace, I've made sure I at least tag along on the afternoon pickup, a small act of conciliation that Indy was sensitive and gracious enough to appreciate. (My first day in the passenger seat, he climbed happily into my lap and showered me with kisses before buckling himself into his seat in the back.) So after we pick them up from school, Greg and I consult the map and drive thirty minutes south to find Saulieu, a quaint village of tidy stone buildings surrounded by the mistletoe-swagged trees and emerald pines of the Morvan forest. (Backlit as they are in the bare trees by the dim wintry sun, Greg thinks the great balls of mistletoe look like Christmas decorations.) And in Saulieu, we quickly learn the secrets behind basket shopping.

Step one: ditch the well-intended picnic basket in favor of a roomier and less-rigid *couffin,* like a tote bag woven of palm fibers. ("Are you offended?" I badger Greg. "Not at all," he replies.)

Then make the rounds, starting at the *boucherie,* where a gaggle of elderly women will cluck over your purchases and winnow them down to the essentials: sinewy meat for pot-au-feu (a multi-night wonder), a well-aged saucisson (to eat sliced with bread, cheese, and salad), and a dark slab of calf's liver. (Which, jabbering and pointing at Indy and Scarlett, they *insist* is necessary for growing children. Indy studies the crimson mass and grimaces in disgust, but tries to be polite. Scarlett, however, makes them all rock with laughter when the butcher translates: "I even like blood!" she tells them.)

There are two *primeurs* selling produce in Saulieu, and I follow the crowd to the less-posh one where a wild-haired saleswoman with a wart on her nose like a witch selects the nicest of the button mushrooms for me, several slender endives, a few onions, and a bag of potatoes, and puts it all into my basket along with a tangerine for Scarlett—at the moment hiding behind my knees (*en cause* of the woman looking like a witch)— whom she declares *très, très mignonne.*

And then our final stop is Fromagerie La Fouchale, catty-corner across from the old Café de Paris.

Greg pushes open the door and a gust of warm air greets us smelling deliciously of fresh grass and barns. And then the white-coated Madame and Monsieur Dodane appear from the shop's deep, cool recesses, summoned like a couple of high priests by the tinkling of the door chime. I immediately adore them both, if for nothing more than their pink cheeks and their matching quiet, meditative demeanors. Greg and I lock eyes: he is smitten, too.

The shop is less a store than a temple to cheese, with illuminated wooden shelves running like altars along its length, and I speak rather shyly as I question Madame about her cheeses.

She walks slowly around her shop, pointing solemnly at the *fromages fermiers,* the farm cheeses specific to the region and produced locally that she and her husband seek out for their intense flavors and for their makers' dedication to old-fashioned production. Some are virtually nameless, like a creamy white, crumbly, aged cows'-milk cheese that floors me with its tart, nuanced flavor and that she shrugs and calls simply a *fromage grande-mère.*

"C'est la goût d'autrefois," she says: It's a taste of another time, when everyone in the country made his own cheese at home.

"People don't make cheese anymore?" Greg asks and she looks askance. "People eat *pizza,*" she says, like that's saying enough.

Other cheeses on her shelves are small production versions of Époisses, a fetid coral-rinded cheese with a smooth exterior and a powerful, almost liquid center. (When it is melted over boiled potatoes and generous chunks of *jambon persillé,* it may be my absolute favorite taste of Burgundy.)

Madame Dodane speaks of her cheeses maternally, sometimes picking up a small morsel and stroking it lightly with her fingertips as she describes its unique flavor.

Under her tutelage, the amount of cheese, fresh butter, yogurt, and raw milk I buy would send someone with lactose intolerance into hysterics just looking at it, but as I walk out the door—practically genuflecting and saying over and over again, *Merci! Merci! Bonne journée!*—I know it is but the first of many subsequent visits.

"That place alone was worth the drive," Greg says as we pile into the Kid.

The secret of basket shopping? Keep it simple. Buy only a little and only the best, stretch it and make it last. Until the drill of convenience is replaced by the thrill of having the old ladies in the butcher shop greet you by name.

CHAPTER

~❧ 14 ❧~

ANOTHER COUPLE OF LONG WEEKS LATER—the kids on an extended school holiday celebrating or commemorating what, exactly, I'm not sure—and the general whereabouts of our neighbors has become the subject of great, curious debate around our house.

Considering the amount of time that we four spend at home wondering *what* to do to entertain ourselves—besides building the fire or, if it isn't freezing or raining (or both), traipsing down to the fields to inspect the stream that runs along the fence line, looking for crayfish scuttling in the mud—it is baffling how *much* of a life Marc and Sophie seem to have. ("Of course they like living in the country," I remark as Greg and I wash the dinner dishes one evening. "They're never *here*.")

Indiana bursts through the kitchen door just as I'm pulling an apple crisp from the oven. "They're home, Mom! They're home!" he shouts in a tumult of excitement. "Can I go see the kids?"

I wave him back out the door and grab a kitchen towel to wrap up the hot crisp, surprised by my own elation. However much better things here are—and they are much better: steadily, incrementally, day by day, better—the homesickness is ever present. It is something apart from Greg and the kids, this longing for my family, and it's constant, like a toothache. It's a longing for familiarity, I think, and even though Marc and Sophie are hardly yet our intimate acquantainces, I'm so excited to see them you'd think Indy had just announced the spontaneous arrival of my entire clan come to visit. If it's pathetic to invite ourselves over the minute they reappear . . . well . . . I don't care.

With Scarlett on my hip I scoot out the door behind Indy, hollering for Greg to finish working and follow us, the crisp in my hand so as not to show up both uninvited and empty-handed.

The wood-burning stove in the library burns brightly and the room is cozy and warm and soothing. Indiana, Lulu, and Marc's towheaded boys, Joseph and Julien, have already disappeared into the playroom, where a loud and raucous game has ensued, but Scarlett, released, promptly scuttles toward Lulu's room and her vast collection of dolls. Marc and Greg discuss cocktails and Marc pours fingers of whiskey and mixes me a gin and tonic. All feels right with the world again.

"Where is Sophie?" I ask, settling into the tattered leather sofa in front of the stove. The room wavers as the fire's flickering light dances over the coffee table in front of me, a sheet of glass placed atop a battered old trunk piled with art books and a bowl of peanuts that Marc sets down.

"Ah, yes. Sophie. The wife is doing a jewelry class with a friend of ours in Semur this evening, making Indian jewelry or something, I don't know. It's a mystery. But, *voilà*. And what have you four been doing?" he asks. He topples into his armchair and scoops up a handful of peanuts.

We tell him a bit about Alsace and at the mention of charcuterie, he pops back up like a jack-in-the-box and hustles out of the library and into the winter kitchen under the stairs, leaving Greg and me to sip our drinks and exchange amused, puzzled glances.

He returns with a paper-wrapped package that he places diffidently on the coffee table. "You must try this." The undone wrappings reveal a small ham with a caramel-colored skin. He pulls a Swiss Army knife from his pocket and begins cutting slices. "Taste," he commands, leaning over the table to hand me a sliver.

The meat is smoky and not too salty, with an aftertaste that is, surprisingly, reminiscent of lemons. At least I think it's lemons: it's so unusual, I'm having a difficult time placing the flavor.

Marc is delighted: he's scored a culinary *coup*. "It's pine and juniper. From the Jura in the mountains. Did I tell you we were going to the Jura?" He hands Greg a morsel.

Being sort-of Swiss, Marc is a natural mountain man. His family originated in the Savoie farther to the south, and he is partial to the region and loves to pontificate on the vagaries of history that denied the Savoyards their rightful homeland—splitting it instead between the Swiss, the French, and the Italians. (I say sort-of Swiss: Marc cherishes a rather romantic idea of himself as a man without a country, neither truly Swiss nor French nor American.) He is also very fond of the Jura. But it is news to us that they have a cabin there up high in the mountains along the Swiss border, a mere three-hour drive from Brianny. ("It's falling down, really, and you have to hike in and there are wolves. But that keeps things exciting.")

Marc refers to his myriad properties as "bolt holes"—places to disappear to out of necessity or inclination—and his general air of mystery is such when he says it that it seems wise not to question what, exactly, might ever engender that necessity, lest you get lost in a tangle of typically French conspiracy theories. But Greg is intrigued by the idea, I can tell. He has this drifty look in his eyes as Marc describes his Jura bolt hole.

As we finish our ham, Marc regales us with tales of the high mountain meadows, the brilliant cascading waterfalls, and the swift-running streams of the Jura that make his heart race. "Oh! And the food! It's nothing to speak of, really," he says. "It's very simple. Fish from the streams, of course, but mostly pork, cheese, and potatoes. But very good." He rubs his hands together again, contemplatively. "I shouldn't," he says, seemingly to himself. "No . . . Yes . . . *Yes* . . . One moment."

The playroom provides connecting passage between the two halves of Marc and Sophie's sprawling house: on its one side, the old farmhouse and the family bedrooms, the library, and the small winter kitchen; and on the other, a whole other house, practically a second residence, that Marc designed inside the shell of one of his old stone barns. It has an open, airy downstairs kitchen, a pair of bedrooms, and a loft-like upstairs room with a massive window overlooking the fields and the far-off Butte de Thil. Those big rooms are impossible to heat with wood fires and they are essentially abandoned from November to April while the family hunkers down here in the cozy library. Marc disappears into the playroom, where the kids' game still rages, and passes into the frigid kitchen on its other side. He reappears cradling a small wooden box like a treasure.

"It's a Mont d'Or," he confides, eyes glittering with veneration. He removes the lid, revealing a pale pinkish cheese with a surface still quivering like gelatin from his traversal of the house. Its smell is earthy and powerful. "You can only get this in the winter and spring, because it's only made from September to April from the cows that climb the Golden Mountain to graze. Now, the proper way to do this is to open a little hole in the center and pour in some white wine, then heat it up and gobble it with a spoon." Marc closes his eyes and smacks his lips in gustatory ecstasy. "*But* . . . it's delicious just like this, too. *Regard*." With a small spoon he digs into the cheese, which oozes and drips as he brings the voluptuous mouthful to his lips.

"Boom, boom, boom, boom, *BOOM!*" he bellows, quaking from head to toe in appreciation. "So good! Don't tell Sophie we ate it. You . . ." He thrusts the spoon at Greg. "Taste."

Greg dutifully procures a mouthful. He closes his eyes and for a moment quietly savors the cheese, then hands me the spoon. (I am reminded, particularly by the reference to the Golden Mountain, of other evenings with Greg before the children arrived, passing around other clandestine pleasures.) A flavor deep, damp, and incredibly fungal spreads over my tongue.

"Isn't it marvelous?" Marc asks.

Indeed.

"And so, where to next?" he wants to know, which starts a round of lively chatter as we discuss Root and the cuisines of the cold climates and all of the places we've considered visiting while the weather is frigid.

By the time the last of several cocktails has been drunk, the Mont d'Or secreted away where a miffed Sophie will eventually find it with a gaping hole in its middle, and the apple crisp devoured by adults and children alike in lieu of dinner, Greg and I have concocted a somewhat boozy plan for the upcoming weekend: we're off to the Jura.

CHAPTER 15

MARC SWORE WE WOULD LOVE SALINS-LES-BAINS, but then, I'd like to fault Marc's unbridled enthusiasm, raising my expectations to ridiculous heights. Or maybe it's that we're still new at this and haven't really found a rhythm for our wanderings. Or have set off on this trip half-cocked, fueled by gin and a highly fungal *fromage*. But whatever it is, before we've even unloaded our bags into our somewhat shabby room at the hotel, I sort of hate the whole town with an almost instinctual dislike.

Here's what Greg had to say about the hotel room, decorated in shades of pink and green that were probably once, when freshly painted, cottage-cute, but that now look, well, fungal: "At least it's cheap."

"This whole place is a dump," I grouse. Marc's favorite charcuterie is nowhere to be found, just tattoo parlors and tatty secondhand shops. ("It's just there, right on the outskirts of town," had seemed like a perfectly viable direction at the time, two or three gin and tonics deep into my evening.) Indy grabs my hand and squeezes, as if with the pressure of his presence to remind me of my pledge: eat, cook, stop worrying, and have fun. I will myself to climb out of the funk and relax, but Salins is making me feel . . . hopeless. It's as cold as Strasbourg and about one-tenth as charming, gangs of sullen-looking teenagers lurking in the doorways. They look like they'd rather be anywhere but here, which makes me understand the statistic: that the high-mountain towns are dying faster than any other part of rural France, young people fleeing just as fast as they can, leaving behind an aura of decrepitude as tangible as the mangy bric-a-brac in the *brocantes*.

Scarlett growing heavy on his shoulders, Greg trudges quickly down the dirty broken sidewalk dragging Doobie—who sniffs every car tire, every doorway—by the leash. Indy and I must hustle to keep up. My steps are long—the better to get . . . wherever—so Indy trots to keep pace with me, eyes downcast, skipping over cracks in the sidewalk, muttering under his breath, "Step on a crack, break your mama's back." But he suddenly stops and points skyward. "What's that?" Good Lord! The sky is brilliant cerulean blue!

"Wow!" I brighten. "Boy, we haven't seen *that* in a while, have we?"

"I think he means the hang-gliders," Greg calls over his shoulder, Doobie now dragging him toward the corner and an as-yet unmarked, unsniffed bush.

"Oh. Yeah." I grab Indy's hand and we jog behind.

High, high above Salins, the gliders are soaring on the same ripping currents that here, down in the valley—the town nestled between two fort-topped, jagged-peaked mountains bristling with skeletal beeches and evergreens—get funneled directly into our faces between the soot-stained formerly private mansions fronting the main road. Gloom returns. I'm so tired of being cold.

"Babe, I think it's time to call it quits," Greg says, halting at the corner. We've walked back and forth nearly the length of the town twice now, which isn't saying much—it isn't a big town, despite history. Salins was once wealthy beyond measure from its salt mines, and powerful, since salt revenues were so important to the French monarchy. Looking for the charcuterie, I've been distracted by the inscriptions etched into the façade of the *hôtel de ville,* adjacent to the town casino and the thermal baths. There's an intriguing dichotomy of history on display there, one of a "how quickly things can change" kind. An inscription from the mid-eighteenth century, signed by Louis XV, one of the last of the French kings, thanks the town for its contributions to and participation in the construction of the *saline royale,* the royal salt mines built nearby at Arc-et-Senans, fed by an innovative network of canals that transported the region's salted groundwater to the factory for extraction. You can just imagine how happy the hard-worked laborers of the salt mines were for the king's grateful shout-out because right next to it, there's another etched stone, this one dated 1792—"in the fourth year of the Republic"—and it lauds the town's citizens for their patriotism and loyalty to the Republic. And the Republic, of course, dates from the 1789 Revolution that guillotined the monarchy and, along with it, all of its despised taxes, among them, the *gabelle,* an infamous one on salt.

"We're never going to find it," Greg says.

"I don't care," I grumble. But I do: we were going to buy *morteau,* a smoked sausage, specialty of the Jura. It's supposed to be delicious and I'd decided, at right about the time we checked into our shabby hotel, that *morteau* was going to make me like the Jura, make the teenagers look less forlorn, the town less tragic, the mountains less doomed.

"But on the bright side," he indicates a shop across the street, "when all else fails, there's always wine." The shop is cheerfully lit, with a display of glowing green glass bottles in the window. He crosses the street and I trudge gloomily in his footsteps.

A silver bell tied to the door tinkles and a tall, young woman dressed neatly in a blazer and skirt comes out from behind the counter to greet us.

Lisette, I will come to believe, reflecting over the next couple of days, is prototypical of the mountains: practical and clear-eyed. Within minutes, she has Doobie under a table, snoozing happily on a warm rug, and the kids coloring pictures and munching contentedly on crackers, the crayons and crackers materializing from a cabinet beside the groaning wine racks. Besides the desk clerk at the hotel, I concede, she's the first citizen of Salins we've actually spoken to, and she quickly refutes all the attributes I'd assigned to the town, being neither morose or forlorn. She's a passionate devotee of the Jura wines, which are as defiant of easy or quick classification as the Jura will turn out to be.

Lisette selects a handful of brochures from a wall rack and shows us a photograph of green-skinned grapes. "*Alors,* this is the Savagnin," she begins. "The native grape of the Jura."

Winemaking in the Jura began early, was already centuries old by the time a young Louis Pasteur (raised south of Salins in the Jura town of Arbois) began experimenting with heat sterilization to help out the local vintners, who often lost barrels to spoilage. Unlike in Burgundy or Bordeaux, where the land slopes softly, in the Jura geography is extreme, all peaks and valleys, dense forests and alpine meadows, and the climate is equally mercurial: both warmer in the summer and colder in the winter than in either Burgundy or Bordeaux. It is a seemingly inhospitable environment for grapes, and the fact that Savagnin is a slow ripener—sometimes lingering on the vine as late as December before it's ready—makes the wines of the Jura all that much more unlikely.

I take a sip from a glass she's poured of Savagnin—clear gold—and gasp. Greg swirls and sniffs his own, raises it to his lips, tastes, and his eyes bug out, shocked. The flavor is *exactly* like walnuts. It tastes hardly at all like wine, a rare gustatory illusion. "That," he says, "is the weirdest thing I have ever tasted."

"Yes, some people cannot abide by the flavor," she muses. "You're expecting one thing, you get another—some people do not like to be fooled." She pours us each another glass, this time of a blend of Savagnin and Chardonnay, which ends on a sweet, smoky note, like honey and wood smoke, the nuttiness much more subdued. Then she pours straight Chardonnay. "For those who crave familiarity," she says, smiling.

These aren't your typical dainty wine-shop sips. And she keeps encouraging us, "Taste, taste." Nearly three full-size glasses of wine in, I'm feeling a little lubricated when she places two more bottles on the table, one squat and rotund, the other thin and elegant. "They look like Marc and Sophie," I hiccup.

Inside those bottles rests the true reputation of the Jura, she expounds: our dumb luck, this expert tutelage. The first is *vin jaune,* the other *vin de paille,* both testimonies to the triumph of patience over expediency. *Vin jaune* (literally, "yellow wine") is sweet and mellow like vintage sherry; it is the product of straight Savagnin that is left to age in its barrel until a quantity has evaporated and a thick layer of frothy yeast has formed over the top. "For how long?" Greg asks.

"Seven years," she answers. "Strictly. If it is not, then it is not *vin jaune*. And this one," she pours a thimble of *vin de paille,* "is ancient. Since before the Romans, it has been made in the same way." *Paille* means hay, and the grapes are laid out on straw mats to shrivel and dry in the sun before pressing, so that their juice is extremely sweet and concentrated. "I can't give you so much, eh?" She smiles. "It takes kilos and kilos of grapes to make just one precious drop. This one is *très cher.*"

Later, she wraps up three bottles for us—a plain Savagnin as a gift for Marc and Sophie, another for ourselves, plus a bottle of *vin jaune* to be kept for a future celebration. Greg surveys the brochure rack, eyeing a picture of a rust-and-white cow grazing languidly in a grassy field. "You know what would go great with this wine . . ."

"Qu'est-ce que vous cherchez?" Lisette asks. In English it means, "What are you looking for?" But the precise translation is one of my favorites. It always sends a funny little shiver up my spine: "What are you searching for?" Such a beautiful, loaded question.

It's such a potent overture that for a second I'm awestruck again by the monolithic *why* of our trip to France. But I indulge it only for a moment. And then I dutifully give her the next best, truthful answer, the one Greg was obviously implying anyway. "Cheese," I state simply, collecting our packages. "We're looking for cheese."

⌒◡ ⌒

MOST PEOPLE HAVE HEARD OF CHARLES DE GAULLE'S FAMOUS QUIP regarding the impossibility of governing a country that has more than 246 different cheeses (the cheese count as of 1962, which is when he said it). In one witty sound bite, he described both the French character—

opinionated almost to a fault—and the country's emblematic, cherished relationship with its *fromage.*

So it's a surprise to many—it was a surprise to me—to learn that cheese is one of the foods of France that is the most threatened by modern life. In fact, in 2007, a cheese called the Vacherin d'Abondance—a raw-milk cheese similar to Marc's beloved Mont d'Or—quietly disappeared off the face of the planet when the very last person who bothered to make it, a little old lady in her eighties, hung up her apron and retired. Compared to before, there is a sincere lack of interest in cheesemaking these days. Those sulky teenagers lurking in the Salins doorways? Yeah. They're not dreaming of scraping a living milking cows and making cheese in an isolated village high up in the mountains.

The Vacherin wasn't the first cheese to disappear, nor will it be the last one, either. None are immune. Even true Camembert, perhaps the most famed of all French cheeses, has been threatened, though in its case the culprit isn't flagging interest but rather industrialization and the insidious twin forces of standardization and securitization. Essentially, here's what's happening: big agribusiness and their imposter *supermarché*-targeted mass-produced *fromages* would like nothing better than to hijack a price-inflating A.O.C. label. But if they manage it, they will have perverted a system designed to protect imperiled agricultural traditions, like cheesemaking. Appellation d'Origine Contrôlée—A.O.C.—is only awarded to products verifiably produced in a traditional manner, and it keeps many a small-scale operation in business.

Like that belonging to Monsieur Perdrix.

His cellar is humid and dimly lit and smells acrid from the fermenting cheeses on the groaning racks lining the walls like bookcases. Monsieur, a man with a deadpan sense of humor about the rigors of his lifestyle, walks slowly, meditatively, between them, stopping now and then to buff the oily perspiration off of a cheese with a soft cloth. Indy and I and a family of Parisians follow him, the Parisians peppering him with questions. ("Does he work every day?" "The cows aren't unionized.") He makes *comté,* an A.O.C. cheese not currently in any danger, a million wheels of it still produced every year in the Jura, hundreds of them currently ripening right here in this cellar. It's considered a cooked cheese, *comté*—the curds are heated during the cheesemaking process—and that plus the aging (which produces the acrid smell) exempts it from two of the biggest issues that may be dooming raw-milk cheeses: spoilage and contamination. Supermarkets fear both. Uncooked raw-milk cheeses, those disappearing the most rapidly, are anathema to inventory and the red herring of public health menaces.

Monsieur's paternal attitude makes me think of Madame Dodane in Saulieu, the way she lovingly touches her cheeses when she talks about them. He, too, is hands-on, which suits his profession: the cheese wheels have to be turned daily and hand-washed with brine. Between jokes he has a lot to relate about tending his *comté,* and he's got a thick accent to boot. It's hard enough to concentrate without Indy tugging at my sleeve the whole time, demanding, "What? What?" (The Parisians have a bespectacled boy with them a little older than he is. The boy's face is rapt with attention and I guess Indy feels a little sidelined.) Monsieur's been making cheese since he was just twenty-two—he's seventy now—and not only is he funny, he could teach a college course on cheesemaking. For Indy's benefit I stammer a translation: how they use veal stomach to coagulate the curds, and how the whey runoff gets fed to pigs, and how the cheese has to have a certain amount of holes and how the holes can't be too big or too small (the Parisians positively crack up when he says this, but I, obviously, didn't get the punch line). But Indy persists, yanking my sleeve anyway. I finally rebound when Monsieur won't notice, breaking off to quip an answer to yet another of the Parisians' seemingly endless questions. "Dude, seriously? You care this much?"

"Well, did he finally say? Where are the cows?"

Oops. That's my fault. When Lisette suggested that we that visit Monsieur's *fruitière* (medieval farmers considered the life-sustaining cheese to be the "fruit" of the milk), I'd assumed that we'd see the whole cheesemaking process in live action. "Want to milk a cow, Indy?" I'd asked, to which he had the most enthusiastic response I'd seen from him yet in France, practically sprinting out the door and back to the hotel and the Kid. To live in Brianny is to be perpetually surrounded by cows, but none that you're allowed to actually touch. Cows, cows everywhere, but not a one to milk.

But I now know two things that Indy doesn't: one, that we are here way too late in the day to see the cheesemaking (it happens at dawn), and two, that there are no cows here. (In my translation I deliberately skipped over that part.) Instead, Monsieur's son Gilles is responsible for picking up their milk in the morning. *Comté* can only be made cooperatively. It takes the milk of thirty cows just to make one cheese, so they work with eight local farmers and get milk from their herds of rust-and-white Montbéliard dairy cows, the same breed as was on the cover of Lisette's brochure. Even though his is a small family operation, just to make the quantity of *comté* that he does in a single day—about eight to ten gargantuan wheels—Monsieur Perdrix would have to care for hundreds of cows, and frankly, he doesn't have the time. He's a cheese advocate, a disciple of *comté,* and he'd much rather spend his "free" afternoons squiring guests like us around his *fruitière,* showing them the cellar and the big copper basins where they cook the curds, doing his spiel, indoctrinating people into his passion.

"I'm sorry, Indy," I confess, cursing assumptions. I was rather looking forward to the milking myself. "There aren't any cows."

Monsieur doesn't speak English, but he's had children, and he knows a tantrum when he sees one. He tussles Indiana's hair playfully, startling my boy in the middle of an aggrieved and empassioned foot stomp. "Ah, I'm taking too long again. *Désolé,* Madame," he apologizes. "My wife says I go on too much about the cheese, but—*pffftt.*" He grins broadly. Indy suffers the hair ruffling rather than risk a showdown with me, no matter his unease with the barrel-chested man's attention. I'm just grateful for the intervention. "I bet you're ready for some *goûter,* eh, *jeune homme?*" Monsieur wonders. "Shall we all go have a bite?"

"Want some cheese?" I paraphrase, earning two thumbs up from Indy, international symbol for "yes, please," cows forgotten, mom forgiven, and he scoots out the cellar door. He isn't much of an eater, but he has certainly always liked cheese.

My family reassembles in the tasting room, which doubles as a boutique. Monsieur passes batons of his delicious *comté* and invites us to taste the difference between a *doux,* soft and sweet after the minimum four months of aging; a *fruité,* gaining in intensity after a full year in the cellar; and a *vieux vieux,* which is sharp, with two years' worth of salt crystals that shatter between my teeth and a nutty, caramel flavor.

"Mmm. That one's definitely the best," Greg declares, and follows Monsieur to the counter. They wrap a thick slab to go with our wine. Indy watches them thoughtfully, several batons of cheese growing moist in his hands. The first few were purloined bashfully, but he'd soon been hot on Monsieur's heels, indulged with as many as he liked.

"Do you think he gets to eat as much cheese as he wants?" he asks, voice garbled by a mouth full of *fruité.*

"So, now you want to be a cheesemaker?" I tease. "I don't know about that, Indy. I'm pretty sure it gets awful lonely up here."

He's affronted dignity personified. "I'm already lonely, Mom," he attests and hooks a thumb toward Monsieur at the cash register. "At least this guy gets cheese."

ON THE WAY BACK DOWN THE MOUNTAIN, I consider what I'd liked most about Monsieur Perdrix.

When I could get a word in edgewise, and once I'd figured out the French for it, I'd posed a question. "Is it rewarding?" This was my motivation: eventually, although the mere thought of it currently makes my teeth chatter (what if we screw it up again?), I'll have to decide what's coming next for me professionally, and I have the vague idea that I would like to do something meaningful.

Given the odds against his imperiled profession, I would have expected a degree of self-satisfaction in his answer, but instead, all Monsieur Perdrix had to say was this: "What do I know but cheese?"

~◦~

THE WEEKEND'S LAST STOP IS AT ARBOIS, a lovely town of red-roofed stone buildings that glow golden in the afternoon light. It is the wine-making hub of the Jura, surrounded by vineyards and populated by wine shops and caves for the various winemakers and all manner of fine restaurants. Streets lined with arched, covered passageways emanate from its center square, where a limestone fountain gurgles. On the road leading toward the river and the *hôtel de ville* is the Hôtel Restaurant Jean-Paul Jeunet, where Jeunet—a native of Arbois with glossy dark hair and a handlebar mustache—has won two Michelin stars for his gracious upscale-rustic dining room and for dishes like foie gras with caramel sauce and oysters poached in *vin de paille*. (The restaurant is a hot reservation during the annual Percée de Vin Jaune, when wine connoisseurs from around the world convene for the release of the new vintage.) On another road, leading toward the home of Louis Pasteur, a restaurant serves monkfish cheeks in *vin jaune*. The plight of cheesemakers has me cynical: I'm reminded of Beaune, the Burgundy wine town where we'd paused for lunch en route to Salins. There, too, the chefs had appeared engaged in a spectacle of culinary one-upmanship, brought on by the wine and the money that comes to town seeking the wine. My indecision bristles like Jeunet's mustache.

"Yes . . . no . . . you've got to make up your mind, Amy," Greg insists. He's drawn dog duty again, and with the kids showing the first signs of the downward spiral my aunt Rosemary calls "the hungry coo-coos," seeks escape. Doobie'll wait out lunch in the car.

"They're too fancy," I fret. "Where's the mountain food?" Post *frui-tière,* we had hiked along an astonishingly turquoise river that put me in mind of Marc's and Root's words on the Jura, and the promised delicacies of its fast-flowing, crystal-clear waters. There's a time and a place for everything, but now I don't want any precious dishes. Thus we wander studying menus, the kids spiralling, and Greg trailing me hungrily.

"How about this one?" he pleads. "Or *this* one?"

"What happened to you not taking over!"

At last he breaks for the car anyway. Which is how, ultimately, apologetically, *he* found the restaurant I grudgingly had to admit I would have picked myself if I had seen it first, the Restaurant des Arcades, hiding in plain sight, a single sheet of paper taped to a wooden door in the shadows—itself opening onto a passageway leading to a courtyard leading to *another* door leading, finally, to the restaurant's unfashionable peach-and-white dining room. The sheet of paper announced plainly, in bold capital letters:

TODAY WE HAVE FROGS.

I have prepared frog legs—*cuisses de grenouille*—before. They usually come a dozen or so skewered together on a stick, the dainty little legs like appendages of the stick itself. It is a restaurant trick to make frog thigh lollipops by disconnecting the frog's leg at the knee and then stripping and shoving the meat surrounding the tiny femur bone down into a neat little knot where the hip joint would be. You then toss them gently in flour seasoned with salt and pepper, and sauté them very quickly in butter, never overcooking them or else the nuggets of flesh become tough and chewy. But I have never seen frogs like those that arrive at our table, tangled together in a red ceramic chafing dish placed over a candle. These are not lollipops. Nor full little can-can kicking legs.

"Where are their heads?" Indiana asks, bewildered.

Probably because they are the only things missing.

Inside the dish is a jumble of decapitated frogs, their small bodies no longer than three inches each, and complete with front and back legs and two morsels of flesh stretching along their delicate backbones—frog tenderloins. The meat is snow white under the thinnest of crisp, golden crusts speckled with minute bits of chopped parsley. I smell garlic and my mouth waters. Near us, there is a family of six—three teenage daughters and one teenage son—sitting quietly at a round table nestled into a corner of the restaurant. The waitress brings them four immense dishes of frogs and the whole family begins to eat with gusto, sucking on the bones and making a pile of the clean carcasses like we would at home with a bucket of chicken wings.

Greg pours me a glass of wine—Trousseau, a light Jura red—and we relish our frogs, chuckling when the kids finish their junior plates of ham and play with the skeletons, making them hop across the table in a macabre tableau of early spring. Behind our table, two elderly couples out on a septuagenarian double date gossip loudly, and it's irresistible to eavesdrop. "We used to eat a lot of snails," one woman says to her friend. "But now we eat more frogs. They're less fattening."

Her husband is discoursing on their apparently good-for-nothing son. Repeatedly he punctuates his diatribe, *"Sac de couilles!"*

"What does it mean?" I query Greg, reaching for another frog, but it's actually Indy who's laughing his head off. "What does it mean?" I grill him.

"It means balls, Mom," he snickers, grabbing his crotch like a tiny Michael Jackson impersonator. "You know? Like your nads?"

"Nads nads nads nads!" Scarlett whoops and they practically fall off their chairs onto the floor in hysterics.

"How do you know that?" I interrogate Indy when he resurfaces, face red and shiny with hilarity. He looks at me like I am the stupidest person on the face of the planet.

"From *school,* Mom."

"Guess we shouldn't worry so much about school after all," Greg says, sucking the meat from a tiny bone. "Seems like he's learning all the important stuff."

THE KID REEKS OF GARLIC AND CHEESE on our way home to Brianny. Just outside Arbois, Greg—who isn't wearing his seat belt—speeds past two motorcycle policemen, who flare their sirens and promptly pull us over.

"Here's the deal," Greg proposes with a sly glance over his shoulder at the policeman fast approaching. Surreptitiously, he fastens the culprit seat belt. "We don't speak French."

"Greg!" I hiss. "We can't—"

"You want to pay the ticket?" He shushes me with an upturned eyebrow. "It's the ticket or dinner." Politely, he rolls down his window when the policeman arrives, but what then transpires is a performance so brash, I'm dumbstruck and probably couldn't speak French even if I hadn't been admonished not to. My native Frenchman pretends not to understand a single word being said, just smiles idiotically and nods gamely, successfully exasperating the hapless cop, who finally looks to me, the blushing passenger, for support.

"Madame?" But even though I feel like I've just swallowed a handful of sawdust, as instructed I only smile abashedly. Nobody here but us Anglophones!

"*Ceinture!* Seat belt," he even tries in halting English. "You," he points to Greg, "no seat belt."

"Yes, seat belt," Greg repeats, plucking the band across his chest, grinning like a fool. "I always wear my seat belt."

Outwitted, the poor cop finally returns to his motorcycle. Like hell is he going to stand on the side of the road with us for an hour, negotiating our transgression, playing the "you-no-wear-seat-belt," "yes-I-do," game. He puts on his helmet. Greg turns and smiles at his coconspirators in the backseat. "Victory," he whispers.

The cop throws a leg over his motorcycle. "Forget it," he says to his partner. "Stupid Americans. Let's go." With a wave and a curt nod they drive off. Scarlett claps. Greg scans the selections on our iPod and picks one.

"Ready, family?" he asks as the strutting rhythm of the Bee Gees' "Staying Alive" pulses out of the Kid's speakers. "I give you . . . our theme music."

Under cover of blaring disco he turns to me as he steers the car back onto the road. "See?" he wheedles. "I'm not always the bad guy you think I am." He smirks, anticipating a punch line. "Guess what I was going to play?"

Greg's always had a fondness for raunchy, profane old-school rap, so I can guess which song he's talking about now, and I keep my stern face only by biting hard on the inside of my lip. We could have gotten into real trouble with those cops! Lying to police officers? Uh . . . bad idea!

"Come on, enough with the good-cop-bad-cop routine," he puns. "Live a little. What's the song?"

"Fine!" I buckle, giggling. Honestly? It was a thrill. "N.W.A., right?" I whisper so the kids can't hear me. " 'Fuck da Police'?"

"That's my girl!" Greg cheers, and away we go.

M Y HUSBAND HAS A NEW HOBBY: CHOPPING WOOD.
Our farmhouse abuts the one of Marc's two gargantuan barns
that didn't get converted into living space, the one that he still uses in
a barnlike manner. It's filled to the rafters with what from a distance
looks like debris, but what on closer inspection turns out to be an endless assortment of furniture, knickknacks, books, odds and ends, giant
pots and urns, the rusted frame of an ancient Mini Cooper that Marc
swears he could restore to working order, garden equipment, wine-
making equipment, laboratory equipment, tools, and cracked and peeling oil paintings. The barn is silent and dusty, inhabited by owls. For
some reason, long, thick draperies hang haphazardly from the rafters,
some nearly sweeping the tops of the piles of furniture, and they give the
barn the atmosphere of a souk. Greg likes nothing better than to prowl
through the barn. He lugs home oddities that he thinks Marc won't miss:
a threadbare tapestry to warm the stone floor in front of our fireplace,
a chunk of heavy limestone to wedge in front of the kids' door to keep
Scarlett from escaping at nap time. (Futile: she escapes anyway. She's as
wily and determined as a cat burglar, that one.)

Greg's morning routine has gone like this: drop the kids, come
home, work for a while, break to explore the recesses of the barn, collect
firewood from our shed, stoke fire, work, snack, work, roshambo to see
who'll pick up the kids, etc. Except that recently, he noticed that we've
nearly depleted our second load of firewood. (This is because we keep
the house heated to a temperature that approximates San Diego in July. It

is frequently so warm in our bedroom at night, I've been tempted to pull out my yoga mat and do a little Bikram. But only tempted.)

Concurrently, he noticed that stacked against the side of Marc and Sophie's house, just outside the barn, there are hundreds of massive, hulking logs, each five to six times or so the size of your average piece of firewood. You could carve child-size statues out of these logs. "Ah, yes," Marc said of them. "For when we are desperate."

"Can we have a few?" Greg asked, and Marc showed him where he keeps his ax, and the table-size stump in his front courtyard where he splits rails.

So now each mid-morning, after his hour or so in the barn, Greg chops wood. He strips down to his bare torso and centers a log on the stump, swings the heavy ax, and cleaves it cleanly in two. Then he splits the two logs into four, and four into eight, stacks them neatly, and carries them back home to our woodshed. He then arrives in the kitchen shirtless, dirty, sweaty, and hungry, usually just as I'm prepping lunch, readying for when the kids get home. And there seems to be a lot of muscle flexing involved as he makes his way to the sink for a glass of water. More than, say, is generally required for the actions of taking off one's shoes, opening a cabinet, and turning a spigot.

"That's a good workout," he finally says, preening one Tuesday, admiring a bicep as he curls the glass to his lips. He sets it empty on the counter and comes up behind me at the stove where I'm pan-searing pork chops. "Good thing, too," he says, giving my ass a firm squeeze, admiring the sizzling chops over my shoulder. I notice with a start that the handful of flesh he has nabbed is . . . ample. He pats his taut belly as he walks out the door toward the shower. "With all this good food we've been eating, I was getting a gut."

Confession: I like to prowl the barn, too. And among the things I've secreted home—books, crockery for the kitchen, ancient utensils that I have no idea how to use but that intrigue me with their complexity—there's a bathroom scale. But I didn't put it *in* the bathroom. I hid it under my bed, instinct guiding me. *Look,* it told me. *It's bad. You* know *it's bad. Why torture yourself?*

I've never really been big, though in college, living on a junior plate-esque diet of beer and pasta and chicken strips, I felt like I was huge. But pictures confirm that I was then merely, at worst, *solid.* During the shows, stressed and unhappy, I was even thin to the point where some bloggers obsessed about my health. (One could assign said bloggers the attributes of compassion, and concern, if they hadn't expressed their concern thus: wrote one, "She's so emaciated and flat-chested, I can't stand to look at her: she looks like a breast cancer victim.")

Let's just say I have since rebounded. And then some. Normally, to convert kilos into pounds I multiply by 2.5, which goes a little over (1 kilo = 2.2ish pounds), but even sparing myself the increments and multiplying by a straight factor of two, when I finally step on it, according to the scale I am *way* over the weight I claim on my driver's license. It's a good thing those cops didn't ask to see it. Lies upon lies upon lies . . .

Which isn't exactly surprising. I *haven't* done Bikram and *I'm* not chopping wood. Other than making infrequent hikes to the creek, at home I'm bascially sedentary, and that's something I've never been before. And choucroute and cheese and bouillabaisse and madeleines and pork chops and potatoes and wine (lots of wine), well . . . they take their toll. One would imagine that on our road trips we do a lot of walking—and we do—and that that would mediate the worst effects of over-consumption, but after all, the pace is set by a two-year-old. We're not sprinting or anything.

Though illness is usually heralded by weight loss and not weight gain, I'm an opportunistic hypochondriac: maybe it's not my fault! Could something else be going on? Is it my hormones, I wonder? I *have* been a little wacky lately . . .

Oh great, I think to myself as I wallow irrationally. *I'm thirty-four and premenopausal.*

That's it. It's *over.*

The next time I see Greg, walking around all tight and toned and shirtless (with more than a little resentment for his firm physique and manly muscles, *and* his ability to keep eating as much as I'm eating and still look like that), I agonize, how can he *stand* me?

One of the many rich ironies surrounding my mother concerns her teaching career. In three decades she's taught several subjects, including home economics and child development (aka sex education), and according to her devoted students, discussing the birds and the bees in the classroom she can be explicit to the point of making the hottest and loosest of hot and loose cheerleaders blush. However, for her actual children, for reasons of her own, to describe the vagaries of sex and love she primly resorted to a Shirelles lyric: *Will you still love me . . . to-mo-o-row.*

Denied further guidance on the subject except for that which I could glean from the almighty Catholic Church—not big on sex—I always figured that it was best to err on the side of caution: *no,* they wouldn't. And even married, maybe even *especially* married—especially during those inevitable periods when marital relations feel more like a chore than anything else—I still am not sure: Where does desire come from?

But I do feel sure about one thing: it can't *possibly* come from my old, fat ass. Can it?

 ~ ∘ ⌣

GREG PULLS ME FROM THE KITCHEN out into the yard.

"Look," he says, so I look, blinking in the bright sunlight, but I have not the vaguest idea what he's talking about. "Look!" he insists.

"What?!"

He stands mum. The sun's rays warm my cheeks. I have moved on to an obsession about my skin: I am wrinkled. Therefore, if it's going to be so damn bright outside, should I contemplate sunblock? . . . And then . . .

"Oh, my God! The sun! The sun's out!"

"And not just that," he jubilates. He drags me out the front gate and onto the road, pointing to the hedges growing thickly up and over the top of our stone wall. We get close. All over, the wood has swelled, the barest beginning of tiny green buds dimpling the branches. He grabs my hand and pulls me back into the yard, shows me the forsythia bush next to the gate by Marc and Sophie's house and its single darling yellow blossom. We pass through the gate and into their yard and along the hedges of the fields and everywhere we look there are the pulsing beginnings of new, green life.

"When did it happen?" I marvel. I realize that I have never, really *ever* before, in my entire long life as a Californian, seen the emergence of spring. Not really in Paris, even, where spring was constrained to trees budding in the parks or along the Seine, leaves unfurling too far up off the ground to be noticed until the day you finally realized with a shock that the trees were all green again. Granted, it's still early. It's still only the tail end of February (in San Diego, this is the time of year when we buy swimsuits), but spring's onset is evident and undeniable. I have never seen whole fields coming to life like this! Hedges, bushes, brush and undergrowth, pastures! I squeeze Greg's hand tightly. "It's *amazing*!" I yelp.

"I know," he says, stealing a kiss.

And then suddenly, just like that, there we are in the middle of the fields, making out like a couple of teenagers.

CHAPTER
17

A FEW DAYS LATER, we're up the road in Chablis, and I can't stop thinking about sex.

And from the looks of the other patrons sitting around us in the Laroche Wine Bar, neither can anyone else in the swanky little joint, either. It's like the budding vernal forces that have brought forth the forsythia blooms have given everyone in the room a bad case of the randies. Two banquettes over, for example, a buxom young blonde has shoe-horned herself into a tight-fitting purple sweater, her platinum hair tightly coiled in an elaborate naughty-librarian updo straight out of an '80s rock video. Her two male lunch companions, otherwise prim-looking young men, leer over their wineglasses, all but drooling. And at the table next to ours, the diners—a Russian with a Ron Jeremy mustache and his statuesque brunette companion—make smoochie faces at one another and openly play footsie under the table while downing a pricey bottle of Laroche *grand cru* Chablis.

Of course, maybe it's just me.

And if it is, it might be the influence of the weather, but it might also be the fault of the full-frontal pheromonal attack being waged upon me by my lunch, because I'm flushed. With every nibble I take of my chubby andouillette sausages—and a tiny mouthful at a time is all I can manage— the room around me shimmers feverishly. And Greg, reclining against the banquette's soft, pale blue pebbled leather, looks *awfully* cute . . .

"Open your mouth." He leans across the table with a forkful of his dish, a sliver of trout on top of a bed of briney black rice and olive risotto.

I nearly collapse on the table in a fit of nervous giggles, hearing innuendo where surely none was intended.

Bemused, he wags the proffered forkful. "What's your deal?"

I fan myself furiously with my napkin. "Nothing. Whew! Is it hot in here?" I decline the bite, not wanting to mix flavors. My investigation of the mysterious olfactory properties of the andouillette is consumptive.

"You don't like the andouillette, do you? I didn't think you would," he says, popping it into his own mouth. "My grandmother used to make them all the time, but I've always thought they were the kind of thing you only ate if you had to." He licks his lips, flicking a lingering bit of tapenade away with the tip of his tongue, and I blush hot pink. Really, this is embarrassing. *Especially* in front of the kids.

But they're oblivious. Before we hit the restaurant we'd gone shopping at one of Chablis's little posh gourmet stores and I bought a box of Burgundian snail shells. Scarlett has named two Julien and Lulu, and is busy feeding them rosemary leaves stripped from a sprig on Greg's plate. Indy has another and is studiously filling it with salt.

"Actually, quite the contrary." I spear another nugget and lick away its robe of rich Chablis sauce, then bite delicately through the crisp skin. Inside, the andouillette has a chewy, springy texture that resists like something alive against my gnashing teeth. It is a dish that goes down swinging. "Actually, I really like andouillette."

"Seriously?" He looks simultaneously surprised, intrigued, and a little repulsed, and turns away from the sight to coerce Indy into another bite of hamburger. "I can never get past the smell," he confesses. "Too . . . you know . . ."

Oh, yes. I know.

You can veil andouillettes in a savory sauce. You can caramelize their wrinkled exteriors until they are crispy and appealingly dark, innocuous as any other pork product. You can even put them on a menu and label them "a taste of terroir," as they have done here at the chichi wine bar. But there is, ultimately, no escaping from the incredibly nonpoetic, unlovely reality of andouillette: that they are made from the parts of the pig designed biologically for the elimination of that animal's feces. Or, as Greg so eloquently described them to Indiana when he innocently asked his dad if what I had ordered were hot dogs . . . they are pig butt. (It will be a long, long time before Indiana ever forgets that his mother once ate pig butt.)

Andouillette's characteristic smell and taste is wild and feral, risky and unsafe in the manner of a hundred other practices that temptingly skirt the line between exciting and repulsive, which for their enthusiasts is surely a part of their appeal. They are a food for the brash and the bold, for the brave, or for the very, very old school. For . . . me?

"Be right back."

Even the wine bar's bathrooms are chichi. I give myself a once-over in the mirror. Maybe it's good lighting, maybe it's the Chablis (probably it's the Chablis), maybe it's the andouillette, but *hot damn,* I think to myself. I look kind of . . . cool. I haven't colored my hair in months and my curls are streaked with thick bands of pure white. (A fun family trait: we go silver at, like, eighteen.) I've lined my eyes with smudgy kohl and my cheeks are blushed. My black leather jacket, though, is *stifling,* so I take it off and splash a little cool water on my wrists before heading back to the sausages, vowing not to be entirely debauched in front of the children but still excited, because this attitude—well, this attitude is rather newish.

While andouillette's detractors are abundant and vocal, their fans are equally ardent. Back in the swinging 1970s the most passionate among them—a prestigious group of French food writers and critics, today augmented by restaurateurs, charcutiers, and a handful of others deemed in the know—banded together and created the Association Amicale des Amateurs d'Andouillette Authentique. For short they call themselves the Five A, or *Cinq A,* declaring suggestively that the acronym—which they bestow selectively upon those they deem the most delicious and artisanal of all andouillette—stands not only for their organization and its mission, but also for the explosive(!) and involuntary response they have to the flavor of their favorite food: *Ah! Ah! Ah! Ah! Ah!*

I'm not even making that up.

It's a lot of hoopla for a coiled rope of poached colon, however copiously perfumed with herbs and spices.

"Here's what I wonder," I say on return to the table. "And I think this is a pretty interesting question: Would I love the andouillette as much if I were eating them anywhere else?"

"Kind of like a rose by any other name?" Greg questions.

"Kind of like *Green Eggs and Ham,* Dad," Indy clarifies.

"Exactly. Thanks, Indy. Because you have to say, this place *is* amazing."

Greg reaches across the table, cuts a bite from my andouillette, which releases a fresh waft of its telltale scent, and chews it reflectively. He scans the room, eyeing the blonde appreciatively and giving the brunette a lingering once-over that makes my gray roots suddenly feel less chic. Then he places his fork carefully back on the table and takes a sip of Chablis.

"Nope," he pronounces definitively. "It still tastes like ass."

THE TERM *RESTAURANT* IS ITSELF FRENCH, derived from *restaurer,* to restore or revitalize. Even way back in the eighteenth century when the first restaurants appeared in the streets of Paris—like the cafés that preceded them, haunts for writers and prerevolutionaries—there was an acknowledgment that the restaurant must seduce its customers in order to win their hard-earned francs. Thus, the name, and its implied promise of rejuvenation. After all, who would pay for just *food?* Then in the nineteenth century, the entrepreneurial French pioneered the risqué cancan—a dance designed to expose a titillating flash of the dancers' nether regions—setting the bar pretty damned high for dinner entertainment.

Today, restaurants have modern issues to overcome, including the fact that as of the dawn of 2008, hard as it is to imagine given the mythos of the smoky French food lair, there's no puffing away in a French restaurant, even post-andouillette.

And membership in the European Union has come with costs that have meant death to many restaurants, bars, and cafés, which have recently been closing at the shocking clip of a couple *thousand* per year: a value-added tax of a whopping 19.6 percent as opposed to the 5.5 percent tax levied on kebab shops, pizzerias, and McDonald's. (The discriminatory tax was finally readjusted in 2009.) The National Federation of Cafés, Brasseries, and Discothéques says that in 1960 there were some 200,000 cafés in France, but that their numbers have now dwindled to a mere 38,600.

At the wine bar, with help from a slew of designers, his well-heeled wife, and a high-profile Paris expert on *le branding*, owner Michel Laroche—who, Greg observes, stands at the bar reading documents and checking plates as they emerge from the kitchen—has harnessed the age-old-but-brand-spankin'-new-to-staid-Chablis formula to help you forget that nearly one-fifth of the price of your thirty-six-euro *menu terroir* (wine, of course, not included) is going to the government: He has made it very, very sexy. One might even say *contagiously* sexy.

Before the wine bar opened, the typical Chablis restaurant had white tablecloths and a dour, if veteran, waitstaff. Around town, there are still several of these older establishments and now, in contrast, they look archaic. Even though I really like the wine bar, these relics make me a little sad: I wonder how much longer they'll last, because just as with those Marseilles fishermen, one man's fresh start is often the end of another man's way of life. A change has come to town. The wine bar successfully pushes all of a worldly connoisseur's buttons. There are exotic flourishes, designed to evoke luxurious, moneyed travel: Moroccan rugs on the stone floor, Japanese dishes of coarse salt on the golden-hued wood tables, tiny horn salt spoons from Africa. And, if you so desire, there are

five well-appointed, chic, boutique hotel rooms upstairs. Guess where
the Russian is staying.

The sandblasted stone walls of the converted mustard mill glow like
nacre and beyond its immense plateglass-windowed bar the Serein River
rushes theatrically toward you before cascading in a torrent of white
water through ancient archways under the building. The river's viril-
ity suffuses the restaurant and reminds me of Carla Bruni—the nude-
posing-supermodel-*cum*-rockstar-girlfriend-*cum*-singer-*cum*-newly-
minted First Lady of France—who reportedly told the Paris daily *Le
Figaro* on the eve of her February 2008 marriage to French president
Nicolas Sarkozy: "I want a man with nuclear power."

After all, the biggest sex organ in the body is the brain.

But that's something my brain has known little about these many,
many, *many* months. It's been intensely preoccupied. Which is why this
has been the typical transcript of a night *chez* Amy and Greg:

GREG: (winking) So . . . are you coming to bed?

ME: (looking for dishes to wash, a newspaper to read, laundry to
fold) Sure! Just as soon as I finish this one last thing . . .

GREG: (resigned and not a little dejected) Ummm . . . Okay . . .
Good night, then.

But as I throw down the credit card for the heftiest check we've seen
since the bouillabaisse in Marseilles—not even *caring* how many euros
I've just blown on pig intestines—I suggest to Greg that we stop back by
the gourmet shop before heading home and buy a bottle of Chablis and a
little andouillette for later.

So, you never know . . .

Hope springs eternal, indeed.

THE NEXT DAY WE ARE ON THE ROAD SOUTH TO BRESSE, home of the most famous chickens in the whole world.

Here's what I can tell you about chickens.

When my parents got divorced, we were all living in a house that Dad had just built for us in the San Diego backcountry, isolated, surrounded by fields and horse farms. Kind of like how we are now in Brianny, back then it was just me and my mom and Casey out there all on our own for years before Mom married my stepdad, Jerry, and then they had all the rest of the family. I became a reader during those anxious interim years. And when I found Laura Ingalls Wilder, discovered a kindred spirit: a poor country girl. Lying on my bed or out on the grass, I read and reread certain passages of her books obsessively: Ma churning butter and boiling maple syrup to make hard, crunchy cakes of sugar. Pa butchering a pig and setting the strips of meat to smoke while the girls fought over a roasted pig's tail. In my child's heart I just *knew* that Ma and Pa's methodical stockpiling was their love made manifest: their family would make it through the darkest, hardest of winters intact and merry.

One of the happiest events I can remember of my own childhood was the discovery of a blackberry bush one summer, growing thick and wild off in a field behind our house. It was loaded with finger-staining berries that Casey and I picked and brought home to Mom and my grandparents, just like Laura would have done. In those days, Grandma and Grandpa were around a lot. Or else we were over at their house. They had stepped neatly into the void left by my father and helped pull my mother out, or at least helped take care of us, whenever she was going down her rabbit hole of fear and blame and loneliness, only thirty-one years old, financially wrecked by the divorce, with two scared little girls to take care of.

Ironic (again), considering how she taught home ec, Mom wasn't actually much of a cook, and she was flummoxed by my berries. Here's how Mom made macaroni and cheese: boil the noodles, drain them, pour cold milk over them, sprinkle them with the powdered cheese. She proposed a similar treatment of the berries. I went running for Grandma.

And Grandma—mercifully, considering the fragility of a budding food romantic—knew *exactly* what to do with such bounty: she'd grown up in the bayou country of northern Louisiana, offspring of a shopkeeper and a woman who'd cooked for all their neighbors during the Depression. "We'll make a pie, honey," she soothed me. Sugar coaxed forth the blackberries' juices. We made a crust, and braided the top. That pie remains, to this day, one of the most wonderful pies I have ever eaten.

And thankfully, Grandma also had mastery of the eight most beautiful words in the entire English language, used in salutation whenever we arrived at her front door: "Hello, dear. Can I make you a chicken?"

GRANDMA'S RESTAURANT FORAYS were largely limited to outings with her bridge group to homespun establishments with senior discounts. Since she mistrusted fussy restaurants, I'm pretty sure that she would have loved this one.

For every sex kitten there was at the wine bar, the Châlet de Brou counterpoints an octogenarian in support hose, which makes Greg and me the youngest people in the restaurant by a good many decades. Our children, with their American manners (or lack thereof), are conspicuous here. Running wild on the terrace earns them a rapid-fire scolding from an older waitress, like a mother hen with a couple of unruly chicks.

She reminds me of your stereotypical no-nonsense Midwesterner, which seems appropriate given that the flat plain of Bresse is like the

Midwest in miniature, with the Jura mountains looming as blue-gray chiaroscuro shadows on its eastern border. I wonder: Do cornfields breed uprightness of character? The region's timbered houses, built of packed earth, are even painted pale gold, the color of corn kernels, and in summer they'll be half-hidden by cornfields. Come fall, ropes of drying corn will hang from their eaves.

Children properly seated, the waitress goes to the kitchen and returns to our table with a groaning tray loaded with the plates of our lunch. An entire Bresse chicken—white-plumed, red-combed, and blue-footed in life, like the French flag made manifest in poultry—has given its life for our pleasure. The kids have the plump breasts and soft, steaming mounds of white rice with melting pats of butter. Greg and I have the legs and thighs, swaddled in crisp, golden skin and surrounded by a caramel slick of pan juices thickened with butter. But the waitress—who probably raised a handful of corn-fed children herself—looks like the type who would sooner swat your hand than smile, so we restrain ourselves from digging in while she sets down piping-hot terra-cotta dishes of *pommes dauphinoise* and vegetables stewed in wine and stock, then gives us all a stern once-over and finally wags a finger at Indy and Scarlett and admonishes them to *mangez bien!*

As soon as her back is turned, though, we fall on our food like the famished. For several long minutes the only sounds are the soft whoosh of traffic on the street, the call of songbirds rejoicing in the sunshine, the clicking of our cutlery on plates, and an occasional sigh as we devour the tender flesh of the regal, pampered chickens.

Even Scarlett is silent. Bite after bite disappears between her tiny, pearly teeth and I'm reminded of so many similar meals eaten around my grandmother's table, the same sense of security and contentment, the flavor of a perfectly roasted chicken the exact flavor of the best parts of my childhood.

AT THE DAWN OF THE SIXTEENTH CENTURY, right around the time that corn first arrived in this corner of France, Margaret of Austria came to Bourg-en-Bresse, and her enduring legacy to the region is the monastery of Brou right across the street from where we are sitting—the restaurant's namesake, and its visitors a big source of the Châlet's revenue and survival.

Her monastery is a frilly, pristine, white confection, the most feminine church I've ever seen in France. The village churches of Burgundy—most of which were constructed in a Romanesque style, Burgundy being Romanesque's northern limit before that reserved architectural influence gives way to lacey Gothic—all bear a similar stamp: they are uniformly stony and severe—masculine, in other words. Brianny actually has no church, since a prime church function is to anchor the village cemetery, and the soil around Brianny, according to Marc, is too soft and too wet for burials. (The pious of Brianny attend services in Montigny, where we hear the chapel bells peeling each evening.)

Brianny's village dead molder in its ossary, a sanctified repository for bones. The building has brought small-scale fame to Brianny among art historians. Inside, its walls are frescoed with a *danse macabre*: the dance of the dead. Popular in the late Middle Ages, the allegorical frescoes—popes and kings, peasants and merchants waltzing hand in hand with skeletons—recall the universality of death and incite the living to live virtuous, happy lives. In Brianny's celebrated fresco, though, unique in all of France, in place of mortal men, the dancers are all women.

Margaret, I think, would have approved. She has her own message for any woman who has ever complained about her lot in life, me definitely included.

I can no sooner imagine Scarlett a bride than I can imagine her taking wing and flying off the terrace, but when Margaret—a Hapsburg princess and the granddaughter of one of Burgundy's most rapscallious dukes, Charles the Bold—was just three years old, just a short year after losing her mother, she was *given* in marriage to the dauphin of France as part of a tremulous and short-lived peace treaty.

Ten years later, peace broken, she was returned to her father like an unwanted puppy, and four years after that, he married her off again to Juan, the infante of Spain, son of Ferdinand and Isabella, sealing yet another political alliance. (For good measure, he married her brother Philip off to the king and queen's daughter, the Infanta Joanna. Years later, Philip died, Joanna went stark-raving mad, and it was Margaret who ended up raising their three children, including Charles V, the future Holy Roman emperor.)

Margaret's new husband, Juan, died just six months into their marriage, leaving seventeen-year-old Margaret pregnant with a child who was delivered stillborn.

Already, that's a lot of heartache for a teenager.

So imagine the meeting of Margaret and her eventual third husband, Philibert, Duke of Savoy. They were both twenty-one. They had both survived other political marriages as children: when Philibert was sixteen, he'd been married to a nine-year-old child bride who made him king of Cyprus, Jerusalem, and Armenia before she died at the tender age of twelve.

With every rational reason to be jaded, instead Margaret and Philibert defied the odds and fell deeply in love. They were kindred spirits, intellectuals, lovers of music and art. Philibert had, for much of his life, been unintended for glory, the son of a man pointedly nicknamed Philip the Landless. And Margaret was pious and kind-hearted despite the intrigue and turmoil that had always surrounded her.

Of *course,* Philibert died just three years after they married.

I imagine Margaret howling in her grief.

I hope someone had the good sense and the good heart to cook her a chicken.

But even after all that, here is what Margaret emblazoned all over the

walls and the stained glass and the glorious, gleaming white marble stat-
uary of the church she raised in her beloved Philibert's memory:

Fortune and misfortune *both* make a woman stronger.

THE INDISPUTABLE FACT THAT ROASTED CHICKEN tasted better at my
grandma's house than anywhere else in the world is how I first came to
understand the mysterious concept of *terroir*. Grandma's chicken tasted
like her house: comfortable, comforting. That's a bit of a bastardization,
in that the real definition of *terroir* is that everything tastes uniquely *of*
its place, but it got me there conceptually.

Grandma's exquisite roasted chicken began as just an ordinary bird
from the Piggly Wiggly, not the pampered and praised Bresse chicken,
the flavor of which—a little gamy, a little sweet—is a factor of its fat, the
marbled fat a factor of its life. During a Bresse chicken's short life it grows
muscled and hearty on a heartland diet of milk, corn, and wheat sup-
plemented by the insects, seeds, and other tasty tidbits it scratches up
roaming in grassy pastures. Satiated, Bresse chickens end their lives loll-
ing about in a cozy wooden cage, unwinding after months of forage and
plumping up on extra rations.

Grandma's roasting method, designed to get maximum flavor from
an otherwise unremarkable bird, is the one I still use today. You take
the chicken and remove its giblets, neck, and gizzards, then blot it all
over with a paper towel to remove the watery, red-running juices. Then
you take softened butter and massage it all over the skin, caressing the
chicken like a newborn after a bath. You sprinkle the skin liberally with
salt and pepper. Then the chicken goes onto a roasting rack set inside of
a large pan, and then the large pan goes into a searing-hot oven. You play
approximately two hands of Old Maid before turning down the heat, and
then you cook the chicken until the thighs wobble in their joints and a

knife tip, thrust into the thick flesh just above the thigh bone, produces a gush of clear juices.

But to make Grandma's chicken taste so comforting and comfortable, you also had to serve it up in a particular way: on colorful plastic plates accompanied by crisp-fried slivers of shoestring potatoes. And to allow the eaters to gorge themselves while watching *The Muppet Show,* or *The Lawrence Welk Show,* or an old Doris Day comedy. And finally, to lavish so much attention on them that they didn't even for a minute think about any of the sorrows or anxieties in their young lives.

The Bresse birds, gifted from the start, need much less coercion to become the tender morsels on our plates. En route to the bathroom, I peek into the kitchen, standing just out of the way of the waitresses who move in and out in a constant, kinetic stream, bustling through the dining room with their tremendous trays loaded with heavy china plates of chicken and the terra-cotta dishes of sides, setting them down gracefully on the doily-topped tables as if they didn't each weigh probably fifty pounds.

In the kitchen, the chickens had all been skillfully broken down, legs and thighs arranged carefully on one set of high-sided baking sheets, breasts on another. A cook slid sheet after sheet in and out of a wall of massive ovens, and they emerged with perfectly golden, crisped skin and flesh tinged the palest blushing pink.

"Madame?" says a waitress, stepping between me and the kitchen door. "Can I help you?"

"No. Er . . . *désolée,*" I mutter. "I'm fine. Sorry." I slink back outside to the terrace.

So I can't see what happened next in the kitchen, but I can guess: the pan juices poured into a container and left to separate, then the yellow fat ladled off and the brown juices poured into a pot, reduced with a little white wine and then swirled with a bit of butter.

"Here's the only thing I wish," Greg says, sitting back at the table. He has literally licked his, Scarlett's, and Indiana's plates clean of any last traces of saucy chicken, so I zealously guard my own, mopping up the juices with a chunk of bread. "I just wish this place weren't so dowdy. Why couldn't it look more like the wine bar? I loved that place."

Like he's besmirched my own home, I flush angrily. "Well, it's like, why don't I look like the girl in the purple sweater anymore?"

"I am . . . totally not following you."

"In the wine bar. Remember? There was a girl in a purple sweater: blond hair, big boobs, sexy. I know you remember her. Well, she's just one stage of life, right? Or she *should* be one stage of life. And then maybe there should be another stage where you're less obvious, but no less sexy, and you've got battle scars and knowledge. And eventually, a stage of life where you're just really not sexy but you *don't even care* because you've got perspective!"

Greg appears fearful I'm laying a trap. What stage am I in? Am I calling myself not sexy? Are we still talking about food? "O-kaaaaay."

"It's just, now, everyone wants to be, or to have, the sex kitten all the time! Everyone wants the wine bar because it makes you *feel* good. And here, the food just *is* good. But if everyone's always chasing the sex kitten—Botox, lipo, crazy yoga after you've had two kids so your ass doesn't hit the floor—how are we ever going to be able to appreciate *this* stage? How will anyone ever be able to stop and taste the chicken if all they're thinking about is, '*Dang*, this place is frumpy'?"

Dear Lord, I think to myself. *I AM losing it.* I slump in my seat, staring at my hands, prepared for Greg's ridicule. *Go ahead. Tell your frumpy wife that she's crazy.*

But there's no detectable trace of scorn at all in his voice when he says, "I see what you mean." So I look up and I swear, he's looking at me like he's just seen me for the very first time ever and now he likes what he sees. "But baby," he says fondly, "*no* Paris stylist could ever dream you up. And I mean that in a good way."

Somebody . . . *please* . . . give that man a chicken.

CHAPTER
~ 19 ~

J UST BEFORE OUR CHABLIS/BRESSE WEEKEND, something interesting happened. And it's something that would have been interesting in its own right, and would have garnered a lot of press in its own right, but because of what else happened at the same time, it got caught up in something of a hullabaloo and I didn't even hear about it until after we got back.

Every year in early spring Paris hosts the Salon International d'Agriculture, and every year the current French president attends. Jacques Chirac in particular *loved* the agricultural fair. He might have been made for these kinds of events and always made a big deal of appearing—usually wearing a tweed cap and a rustic jacket, making a big show of mixing it up with the farmers populating the floor of the exhibition hall, slapping cows on their rumps and whatnot. He considered the rituals of the fair to be an important display of solidarity with the French countryside, symbolically reaffirming his country's deep agrarian roots.

But Sarkozy, who was born and raised in Paris (and though politially of Chirac's same party, is far more pro-business and -globalization), appeared at the fair in a bespoke suit and immediately started a controversy that was splashed all over the nightly news and then dominated the television talk-show circuit for days. Walking through the crowded hall, pressing the flesh, he offered his hand to a disgruntled farmer who said something rude like, "Don't touch me with your filthy hands." To which the distinguished French head of state responded, "Fine, then. Fuck off, you little prick."

Buried in all of this was the announcement that a more dignified (or scripted) Sarkozy made from the Salon podium: France would officially petition the United Nations Educational, Scientific, and Cultural Organization—UNESCO—for World Heritage status for French cuisine. "We have the best gastronomy in the world—at least from our point of view," he said, no doubt a veiled jab at the chorus of (largely American) critics who have volubly declared French cuisine *démodée* and Spanish cuisine—*la nueva cocina*—ascendant. "We want it to be recognized among world heritage."

Over a cup of coffee Marc gives me the article in *Le Monde* and I read it and then, leaving the kids behind to have lunch with his children, bring it home to Greg, who reads it sitting at the kitchen table while I work on a garlicky vinaigrette that may just end up in the refrigerator. We leave for a weekend in Lyon in a few days, and one of the city's most famous dishes is the *salade Lyonnaise*—crunchy greens tossed with croutons and lardons and big wedges of boiled egg and lavished with said garlicky vinaigrette. Betwen pantry and fridge I have lardons and old bread for the croutons and eggs and just about everything else required—a replication of the celebrated *salade* is within our reach—except for the greens. Fortuitously, though, walking to Marc's house I noticed tender dandelions sprouted all over the yard, some of the bunches as big around as dinner plates. (There is—or should be—something Palladianly perfect about food growing wild in one's very own yard.) I entered Marc and Sophie's library with a spring in my step and a menu on my lips, but Sophie quickly brought me down. This is how she greeted my suggestion that we pick and eat the dandelions for lunch: *"Mais non, Eh-mee!* Don't ever eat anything that doesn't grow above waist-high here. The foxes have a terrible parasite in their urine. It *kills* your liver! It's a terrible death!"

Stupid country. I am now terribly broody and I feel cheated. Why, oh *why*, does there always have to be such a gaping chasm between what you hope for and what you get?

"So, what does this mean?" Greg asks, finishing the article.

"Well, at the very least it means that Bocuse and Guy Savoy and Ducasse are hoping to feel relevant again," I say stingily, tapping the newspaper where it says that the three-star chefs (plus Michel Guérard of the Michelin three-star Les Prés d'Eugénie) are backing the president's motion. "Kind of ironic, though. Did you know that both Bocuse and Ducasse have their own fast-food chains? Bocuse does burgers and Ducasse peddles sandwiches."

"So?"

"So, are they trying to save French food or kill it?" I grouse. "Do you know what Root says? 'Every country possesses, it seems, the sort of cuisine it deserves, which is to say the sort of cuisine it is appreciative enough to want.'"

(Here is a grim statistic: In 1975, the average French meal lasted ninety long, languid minutes. But today, according to the Union des Métiers et des Industries de l'Hôtellerie, the average meal takes only thirty. Thierry Marx, a two-starred chef with restaurants and a culinary academy near Bordeaux, justified this trend to the *Wall Street Journal*, saying, "Takeaway food is very useful. We have fifteen to twenty minutes for lunch, and often we eat in front of the computer.")

Greg discards the double-dealing chefs along with the newspaper, balling it up and throwing it in our kindling bin, the Brianny version of recycling. "Well, anyway, if their goal is to be relevant, it seems like a stupid way to go about it. Who builds a monument to something alive and well?"

"*Touché.*"

I'm still lamenting the dandelions. Greg follows me outside through the gate and over to a freshly tilled patch of ground under the branches of Marc and Sophie's big oak tree; backlit against the sky it looks like a drawing of a lung's lacy capillaries. All over Brianny, several days in a row of fine weather have lured the Briannites out of their dark and damp houses, blinking in the unaccustomed sunlight like cave dwellers, and they've all fallen dutifully to work on their gardens. The air smells of earth. Every house in the village has a patch ready, bare but for a few rows of leeks still wintering in the ground, waiting, Sophie included. "Here's what I don't get," I say, pointing to where she has laid sheets of black plastic next to the leeks to warm the soil in preparation for planting. Not even Sophie will be spared *my* pissy mood. "Sophie says, 'Don't eat anything that doesn't grow above waist-high, *Eh-mee*,' but what about her garden? What is the point of a garden if you can't *eat* any of it? Just for once, I wouldn't mind a little consistency!"

"So, she told you the fox piss story."

I weigh my fear of a slow and excruciating death against my ardent desire for the dandelions and my *salade*. Greg turns and surveys the distance between the patch and the wooden deck with the kids' basketball hoop that juts off the big kitchen, maybe fifty feet away. "Maybe the foxes don't dare come too close to the house?" he theorizes.

I trudge home, disgruntled, no more certain whether or not to risk the dandelions.

"I have a question," Greg says, following me to the gate. "What's with the leeks?"

"Spring hasn't really arrived until the leeks come out of the ground," I harrumph, quoting Sophie. We see each other more frequently now that the weather's changed. (We're friendly enough now that I can even be mad at her.) She's much more inclined to stay home and putter when the sun is shining, she tells me. (*"Profitez-en,"* she says. "Take advantage of it.") "She says it means we're still in for bad weather."

Mud pools on our side of the fence. I fight a daily battle against muddy footprints. "So they stay good in the ground. Interesting. It seems like *that's* what needs to be protected," he muses. "You can't protect cuisine. What's going to happen? Bureaucrats showing up in your kitchen to see if you made your cassoulet properly?" He chuckles, because in France, well, maybe. "But people could know more about actual food. I, for example, never knew that about the leeks. I mean, not that I ever gave it a lot of thought before, but if I had, I probably would have said that if you left something in the ground too long, it would rot. Food's cool." Greg enters the kitchen but I halt in the doorway and survey a carpet of dandelions. One thick thatch grows near the rock pile in the middle of the yard. Another sprouts along the edge of the gravel drive. "So?" he asks. "Are we doing this?"

To hell with it. "Live dangerously?"

"Split the difference," he reasons. "Pick the ones right there by the door."

Back in the kitchen I throw the greens in the sink to soak, start a couple of eggs boiling, and peel more garlic. It takes a lot of garlic to make proper Lyonnais food: it is one of its telltale flavors, a fact that Root richly pilloried. For all his regional boosting (and tolerance, even admiration, for the Provençal fondness for garlic), Root was an unabashed—if eloquent—hater when it came to Lyon, which I can't understand. "The cooking of Lyon fits the character of the city," he wrote snobbishly. "It is hearty rather than graceful, and is apt to leave you with an overstuffed feeling." I rub a split clove all over the inside of my big salad bowl, the better to distribute its sharp bite all over the greens. I, for one, love garlic. Greg sits down at the table and kicks off his muddy boots.

Soon, I've placed a giant bowl of artfully messy salad before him: the greens torn into pieces, tossed with my garlicky vinaigrette and golden croutons crisped in the rendered fat of seared lardons. I heap the salad onto our two plates and place a peeled, quivering soft-boiled egg on top of each so that when we run our forks through them the warm yolks will run and mingle with the dressing. Greg uncorks a bottle of wine and pours us two glasses. I don't expect the kids back for an hour or so still. We can relax.

Greg spears a bite of salad. The yolk drips down, a swath of bright yellow against the emerald greens. I take a bite and close my eyes, chewing thoughtfully, the better to savor the crunch of the croutons and the bitterness of the dandelions, the garlic's bite, the sweet velvet sensation of the yolk on my tongue, and above all, the pleasure of sharing this hand-made meal with a husband I've fought hard for, regardless of whether the damned fox gets us in the end.

～ ⌒ ⌒ ～

. "ARE YOU AWAKE?" I nudge him gently but he only snorts and rolls onto his side, sound asleep, unaware of me in the bed lying awake like I should have known I'd be at three in the morning, fretting about the fox regardless of the spunk I'd exhibited earlier. I make Mom the shepherd to lead me back to sleep. She arrives in just three short weeks, my youngest sister, Yvette, and Jerry in tow. We're e-mailing just about daily: I write about the kids and our trips and I rant about the weather (well, not so much lately). Her e-mails back used to be reliably full of schemes for changing our tickets and coming home early ("You have nothing to prove, Amy"), but as our Easter trip draws closer, curiously— thankfully—now she seems happy to rhapsodize about Provence and the road trip I've planned as an elaborate Act of Contrition, an apology for not heeding her warning that all of the problems that Greg and I had in San Diego, we'd still have in France.

Her opposition had been formidable. Once, trying to make her understand the urgency I felt to get here and eat some of these dishes in situ before they disappeared or lost their bearings, I'd tried that same Root quote out on her: "Every country possesses, it seems, the sort of cuisine it deserves, which is to say the sort of cuisine that it is appreciative enough to want." Mom is erudite and scholarly, a lover of culture. Between Root and my case for how quickly conditions around food and eating were changing, surely she would be swayed, right? We weren't running away: we were food anthropologists.

Instead she'd taken a different tack entirely, but one that I still grasped as grudging blessing. She cocked her head like she does, birdlike, squinting a little, mulling it over, and then said, "Well, that's true of everything, isn't it." We sat side by side on her couch, but Mom doesn't sit still for long. She began gathering vases around her living room, tossing dead roses into the trash, preparing to clip new ones in her garden. "You know what kind of a family you want, Amy, and what you're willing to endure to get it, and that, my dear, is why, eventually, you will triumph." Mom squanders no resources on success. She thinks only in terms of outright victory.

"Stupid fox," I mutter to the darkness. "I'm going to sleep now." My eyes close and I imagine my mother kissing my forehead, wishing me good night and continued good work. And like that, without any further fox worries, released to drift on the memory of that afternoon's lovely meal, I fall asleep.

CHAPTER
~❧ 20 ❧~

I F ONLY OUR FIRST MEAL IN ACTUAL LYON WERE AS GOOD.
Lyon antagonized Root with graceless garlic. For me, it's the roads.
The city is split by two rivers, but an old joke goes that it's actually wet by
the waters of three: the Saône, the Rhône, and the freely flowing Beaujolais that gives it its reputation for lustiness. It was once the silk capital of
the world, and the way the *périphérique* encircling the old city twists and
winds, it does feel like the Kid is threading a giant loom as plied by the
deft fingers of one of Lyon's ancient *canuts*. "Oh God, *where's* the hotel?"
I plead as narrow, unmarked one-way streets fly by, but the map just flutters uselessly in Greg's hands: Lyon defies even his navigation. My knees
are wobbling when we finally squeal into a parking lot, but having successfully piloted my family *myself* through the most Byzantine of roadways, I'm also feeling, just like my mother promised, rather triumphant.

"Right," Greg says, sweating. He grabs Scarlett's arm to prevent her
staggering into traffic. "Beaujolais?"

Which is how we end up at the Restaurant Vieux Lyon. Sort of.

Easy question, hard answer: Where does French food come from?
The rigors of my culinary school training would suggest that it was
born under Escoffier's codification. The words of critics lately, lambast-
ing French restaurants, suggests that it lives and dies through France's
chefs. But the grandest tradition of Lyon, the *bouchon,* offers evidence
that some of the country's best cooking started out in the home kitchen.

Though today venerated and collectively and affectionately known as
les Mères—the Mothers—the *bouchon* progenitors were just eighteenth-

century housewives, not sophisticated restaurateurs, feeding the people who needed feeding the most, beginning with the poor *canuts,* the silk workers who lived in the hilly Croix-Rousse section near the heart of Lyon. The *bouchons* grew out of their private kitchens, and though they flourished in Lyon's early twentieth century, the meals remained scrupulously artless. For me the whole point of being in Lyon is to eat one. I too have a husband and a family, I too am a cook; *les Mères* and I share heritage. Which, of course, just front-loads my mission with portent. Gads, have I really learned nothing?

Cobblestones demand attention. But so does my *Guide Vert.* And how I'm supposed to read, walk, and scan the restaurant windows at the same time, anxiously stalking the elusive perfect lunch spot, I couldn't tell you. It is a testimony both to Greg's patience and to his resolve to butt out that he continues to indulge these long, indecisive walks of mine.

We are in the heart of the old town, the part of Lyon built during the Renaissance when the city was an importing center for Italian silks, and it looks surprisingly Florentine, the buildings tall and narrow with peaked archways and graceful covered passageways fronting their upper stories. (In the Croix-Rousse, the architecture bears the stamp of Lyon's lucrative transition from silk importer to silk manufacturer, the doorways and windows tall and wide enough to accommodate the passage of the *canuts'* bulky looms.) We tromp up and down the rue de Boeuf and the rue Saint-Jean, the two arteries of Vieux Lyon. There is no shortage of restaurants, but just about every awning shading the street is emblazoned BOUCHON SUCH AND SUCH or BOUCHON SO AND SO, and I'm wary. Some of them at least look the part, with sidewalk chalkboards trimmed cleverly into the shapes of pigs and roosters, and red-and-white-checkered tablecloths, and tripe and quenelles on the menu, but others are just blatantly exploiting the term in the hopes of snaring an unwary tourist or two. Across from our hotel, for instance, there is even a pizzeria masquerading as a *bouchon.* It's called, like, Bouchon Vito or something. There are more than a dozen entries for *bouchons* in the *Guide Vert,* but the more

I see, the more distrustful of guide books in general I grow. Nearly every window, after all, even those of the most obviously inauthentic, boasts a collage of stickers trumpeting the guides in which that restaurant has been mentioned. It's supposed to make you feel *more* confident, not less.

(A waiter outside one potential restaurant could use customer service training: he sneers mockingly the third, fourth, and fifth time we pass. *"Pour manger, Madame?"* he calls, voice dripping with sarcasm. *"Aujourd-hui?"*)

Finally, Indy's had it. He's made no such promise to let me lead. Ghandi-like, he roots himself to convey that he'll suffer the tyranny of my skepticism no more. "Pick one," he commands.

A final nervous scan of the guide. "Le Vieux Lyon, then," I sigh. "That one back there by the church? It looked okay." We schlep back down the street toward the restaurant's cheery red-painted storefront.

Inside, we seat ourselves around a table near the front door. The restaurant is long and narrow, every inch of its walls covered in an eclectic collage of French political advertisements and memorabilia. Our waiter, a young guy, zips around working the lunch shift solo. Before my chair is under the table I have a menu in my hand. Indiana, though, gets a gruff admonishment: *"Installez-vous, jeune homme."* It's not yet two o'clock, but we are practically alone. There's just one other group, a family of six sitting in preternatural silence.

Greg snaps open a menu. I open my purse and find a couple of pens for Indy and Scarlett to draw on the butcher paper covering the table's rust-colored ultrasuede tablecloth. "Here you go. Draw me a picture." Scarlett grips her pen inexpertly and begins drawing in loopy, energetic squiggles, her tongue jutting out between her teeth in concentration. She hums while she works, utterly content, and then jabs the paper with great finality and sits back to admire her work.

"It's a bunny," she tells Greg proudly.

The waiter materializes at my side, shaking his head vigorously as if I've just handed Scarlett a match and instructed her to torch the place.

"No, no, no," he says sternly. "*C'est intérdit.* The pens will rip the paper and mark the tablecloth." He stands there . . . *waiting* . . . while I confiscate the pens.

"Give it to Mama, baby." Scarlett's eyes rim with tears that don't move the black-hearted waiter. Her sniffle threatens to turn into a wail when I finally pry the pen from her hand. Alarm bells are going off in my head now. *Retreat! Retreat!* A look from the muted father at the adjoining table clearly says, *Save yourselves!* With a dozen quick steps we could be out the door, but the waiter leans against the front counter, posture loose but gaze stern, as cold and intimidating as a prison warden, like he's daring me to try to escape, and I freeze. Greg is equally transfixed. Such, by association, is a waiter's spell over us.

"Well, the food had better be good," Greg mutters.

A quick word about *métiers.*

In Paris we frequented a corner café where the waiter had salt-and-pepper hair and the most remarkable tableside manners: in a year of almost weekly visits, I swear he never, ever even once looked at me. Instead he'd approach our table with his eyes focused, I can only say, in our general direction, but at the critical moment . . . the menu extended . . . he'd avert his gaze toward another table and I'd wind up saying *merci* to his striking Gallic profile. And then ditto with our plates. And then ditto with the check. And because his attention was so theatrically elusive, of course I craved it. Over the course of that year I studied him furiously, noting jealously that he had the exact same manner at all of his other tables. (In fact, the closest we ever came to eye contact was the one time when he was waiting on the table next to ours.) There was no discourteousness or superciliousness in his demeanor, however rude it sounds. It might have started out as some kind of subversive deferential lampoon, back when he was young and cocky, and had only ended up as a mannerism so long practiced as to have become ingrained, but I'd have to say that his quiet, subtle theatrics, far from detracting from the meal, only enhanced it. He was a presence, even off duty, lounging against the bar and drinking from a thimble-sized glass of red wine. I was sad the few meals that we ate at the café when he wasn't there, and thus the omelets on those occasions, though oozing Emmental, were never as good. Unlike this Lyonnais waiter, *he* was a true practitioner of his *métier*, proof that waiting tables could be a noble calling. His attitude had actual *flavor*. He was as piquant as the cracked-black-pepper crust of Greg's favored *steak au poivre*. As tangy as the ketchup inside the battered bottle he'd grudgingly, and with averted eyes, bring to the table for my French fries.

A bell clangs in the *bouchon* kitchen. Our first plates arrive: *charcuterie* for Greg, the *salade Lyonnaise* for me, and a *steak frites* to split between the kids.

Like Alsace, Lyon is known for its way with the pig. A whole slew of famed sausages hail from here. There's the fat and jolly dried *jésus*, or its smaller doppelgänger the *petit jésus*. And there's *cervelas*, an uncooked sausage perfumed with truffles or studded with pistachios, often enrobed in brioche and served in hot, toasty, yeasty slices, the best of the bread and the pork world happily married. The *sabodet* is thick and meaty, composed of bits of fat and skin called *couennes*, along with chunks of tender head meat and tongue and bits of lean meat, the whole thing doused with potent eau-de-vie and red wine, then cooked and served lukewarm when the flavors are at their most pronounced. And above all there's the bawdy *rosette*, witness to Lyon's who-*gives*-a-damn side, poetically named for a pig's puckering, rose-shaped asshole, terminus of the intestines from which the saucisson's casing is made. (Perhaps it was such bawdiness that earned Lyon Root's scorn?) With such a bounty, Greg's *charcuterie* plate should have been nothing short of miraculous.

The waiter sets it down in front of him and backs away with a cocky shuffle: two thin slices of rosette, a single piece of pale, bloodless ham, and a miserly sprinkling of *grattons*, deep-fried pork skins that, when done right, are ethereal, that put the finest of fine pork rinds to shame. (As they should be if one is going to go to all the trouble of eating deep-fried pig skin in the first place, shaking a metaphorical fist in the face of nutritional wisdom.) I sneak a *gratton* from his plate and chew it thoughtfully, ready—hoping—to be transported, but it just leaves a fatty film inside my mouth that requires a giant swig of Beaujolais to wash away, as if I've swallowed a mouthful of Crisco. My salad is barely worth the energy required to chew. The waiter whisks our plates away and they are replaced by more travesties: pike dumplings called *quenelles* that are light and fluffy but as flavorless as actual pillows, a side of *gratin dauphinois* that has the unnatural orange hue of made-from-a-box scalloped potatoes. Greg's duck in Beaujolais sauce is overcooked, tough and chewy. I discover Indiana's been dropping meat bites on the floor, but I find I can't even summon a reprimand. It is the first truly *awful* meal we've had. Heretical. Matricidal. With each bite I feel like I'm going faster over the cliff edge of disappointment into the gaping abyss of outright disillusion but still I eat, robotically bringing fork to mouth, joylessly swallowing.

But then comes the ultimate affront.

It is nearing three o'clock when the waiter brings dessert to the table: slices of *tarte aux pralines roses,* a Lyon specialty, syrupy sweet as pecan pie but hot pink from the tinted sugar-coated almonds that make up its confectionary topping. Scarlett will eat just about anything but in particular she loves sweets. *Especially* if they are pink. Her eyes bulge in ecstasy when she sees the rosy dessert and she starts cramming bites into her mouth as quickly as she can manage. Her gamine cheeks grow pink and sticky. This restaurant has thoroughly defiled the legacy of *les Mères* but you can still see a mother's hand at work in a dessert like this: intended for unequivocal delight, nearly impossible to muck up, almost capable of salvaging an otherwise horrific meal. I very nearly soften.

But then the waiter, who'd disappeared down a winding staircase near the front door after dropping the tart slices at our table, reappears.

My first impulse is to shield Scarlett's eyes as if a flasher had just walked into the room. Honestly, it would have been preferable had he come back in stark naked, because what he has done is actually much, much worse.

Gone are his ill-fitting black waiter pants.

Gone is his thin, long-sleeved, white-collared waiter shirt.

Gone are his shining black waiter shoes.

Imagine taking your kid to Disneyland. Imagine Mickey Mouse suddenly whipping off his Mickey Mouse headdress, revealing the truth that there's nothing but a sweaty frat boy inside. Imagine the shopping-mall Santa yanking off his beard after giving your kid a candy cane. For me, it's like that.

The waiter is wearing . . . *his street clothes.*

After everything else the affront is more than I can bear, the shocking sight of him still in the restaurant but out of the uniform I so strongly associate with everything good about eating in France, just standing there . . . stupid . . . ordinary . . . in his tight-fitting long-sleeved black T-shirt and acid-washed jeans. I fumble for my purse under my seat and hastily spoon the last bite of tart into Scarlett's mouth. The tears are going to beat me to the door. "I've got to get out of here," I mumble, heartbroken, and hustle the children out in front of me.

"What's the matter, Mama?" Scarlett pleads. Sticky fingers paw the front of my long coat, making ropes of lapels, as she tries to climb up into my arms. I lift her and snuggle her blond hair.

"He just didn't care," I explain sadly. A condoling pat on my cheek with her sticky fingers leaves a pink mark like a spot of rouge.

"Who didn't?" Indy asks.

"The waiter. He didn't want to be there, and he didn't want us to be there, either, and that just makes me sad," I tell him simply. There is no reason to explain to a kid how it feels like something cherished and beloved and believed in is being murdered; though the waiter isn't *it,* he's just the last straw, turning a way of life into something mundane—a living. If stalwart, dependable French food succumbs and goes the way of the big bad world, overcome by marketing and money, faddishness, indifference, greed, hoopla, and self-interest, what chance do the rest of us possibly stand against their awesome diminishing power?

"If he wasn't a good waiter, then we shouldn't give him any money!"

"It's never quite that easy, kiddo," I tell him.

Greg holds the door for the waiter, who exits with a backpack slung over his shoulder. "*Au revoir,*" the waiter says perfunctorily, probably unaware of the depth of the psychic wound he's just inflicted, and, whipping out a cell phone, he disappears down the street into the mass of milling students. The Renaissance quarter seems to be where every person under twenty-five has congregated. It looks like a band of jesters has been set free on the town, their dreadlocks and loose, gypsy-bright clothing harmonizing with the richly ornamented stone buildings, painted in hues of ochre and gold, yellows and pinks and rich greens and reds, housing pubs and Indian restaurants and take-out Chinese and souvenir shops. We are out of place. And it doesn't feel good at all.

*

IN THE EARLY MORNING HOURS OF SATURDAY, gray mist off the rivers enshrouds the Presque-Isle. Indiana clutches my hand tightly and together we navigate the streets.

"And you promise I can have a treat when we get there, right?" he asks. Again.

"I promise," I tell him. Again.

"Okay," he says, momentarily mollified. "Promise?"

This modern section of the city sandwiched between the Saône and the Rhône must be the one that caters to the students who kept us all awake the night before, coming and going from the pubs around our hotel, music booming, bottles crashing onto the cobblestones, their voices loud and energetic and utterly destroying of sleep. Despite two coffees at breakfast, I'm still a little groggy and Indy is red-eyed. We pass tattoo parlors and shoe stores with Converse in every color and clothing stores with mannequins dressed in baggy sweatshirts and cargo pants. Indy makes me stop in front of a neon-lit display of skateboards. His eyes widen and he nods his head appreciatively. "Cool," he says.

On the banks of the Rhône where the morning *marché* is set up and stirring, I pull him to a stop in front of a stand dripping with sausages. "Cool," I say.

Nearby are several tables of booksellers. Indy stops in front of one heaped with old Astérix and Tintin comic books. He smirks. "Cool," he says.

I lead him to a table piled high with cookbooks and we both start grinning. "Cool," I say.

At the midpoint of the almost-island we tromp across the pavilion-lined Place Bellecour, one of the largest pedestrian strolling vistas in all of Europe, loose gravel crunching under our feet and a wind stirring the leaves in the trees. At its far end is a fenced-in playground, a few boys running wild and loud around the slides and spinning dizzily on fast-whirling carousels. "Cool," Indy says.

I pause in front of a bronze statue of Saint-Exupéry and the Little Prince. "Cool," I say.

On the other side of the Rhône, the tall, pointed tower of the Crédit Lyonnais offices looks like a silver crayon, dwarfing the other concrete-and-steel buildings of the sterile commercial sector. Near its foot is the gleaming glass box of Les Halles de Lyon Paul Bocuse, the modern market, replete with a parking garage, office space, and its very own signature bistro. Just opened in 2006, it replaced the far-funkier 1970s-era *halles* because, according to its Web site, "Les Halles de Lyon had to adapt to the market and meet the standards of hygiene and safety regulations."

Inside, under bright fluorescent lights the well-heeled crowd is several deep in front of Charcuterie Sibilia, the air peppery with the fragrance of its famed *saucisson*. A litter of lifeless eyes stares back at customers from the shop's glass cases, filled with the heads and ears and tails and trotters and other parts of the porkers, destined for the *bouchon* stew pots.

Another crowd gathers outside Renée Richard, who ripens the best Saint-Marcellin cheeses in Lyon; creamy and strong and rather like a Burgundian Époisses, but local and, I've read, the *bouchon* cheese of choice.

On the far side of the market, Indy presses his nose against a case of macaroons tinted every Technicolor hue of the rainbow and in every flavor combination imaginable. The glass reflects our twin images: me standing behind him in my long camel coat and turquoise scarf, curly hair damp and poofy from the morning fog; he with big, wide eyes, long hair hanging, gray puffer jacket zipped up tight under his chin.

I love him so I could stay here forever. And here's something I know to be true: there's not one damn thing that's simple or uncomplicated about womanhood or motherhood—the decisions and choices—except for this feeling.

"Cool?" I ask him.

"Cool." He smiles, and together we pick out a dozen of the ganache-, jam-, and crème-filled almond cookies, some for our walk home, some to share when we get there.

CHAPTER
22

O UR CONCIERGE PRESSES A CARD INTO MY HAND when we cross the lobby with our bag of cookies. "Madame," he defers, "I hope it is all right: I took the liberty of making your family a reservation here for lunch this afternoon." I examine the white-and-green oversize card. The previous afternoon, he'd seen me skulk back into the hotel from our disastrous lunch and, being kind, intercepted Greg that evening to inquire, What troubles Madame? CHEZ BRUNET, the card reads: BOUCHON-COMPTOIR. It is decorated with a cartoon of Guignol and Gnafron, witty slapstick marionettes from the puppet shows first performed in Lyon just after the Revolution. (There's a Guignol museum just around the corner.) "Your husband told me about your travels. Please, enjoy it with my compliments." He retreats back behind his desk as we mount the stairs. "Oh, and Madame!" he calls after us. "It's very easy to find; it's just around the corner from the Starbucks."

THERE IS EATING AND THEN THERE IS *EATING,* and the critical difference is that one sustains the body but the other sustains the soul. To sustain the body with food is relatively easy because it wants to be sustained. The biological instinct to survive ensures that calories of any type—whether from a perfect peach, or a pampered chicken, or a tortured cow, or a bag of Cheetos—will be converted to energy to fuel the mechanisms of life. Calorie-wise, basically all meals are created equal. There are whole industries, whole empires, founded on the certainty of this premise.

But the soul? The soul isn't just delicate; it is discriminating and discerning and unyielding in its judgment, and it accommodates no abuse. Witness the degree of my funk post–Vieux Lyon: the soul is so easily sickened and so difficult to resuscitate that one should be very careful of how many soul-depleting episodes one exposes oneself to. There should be safeguards and warning systems: *Halt! Do not enter this restaurant!*

But almost immediately, I love Chez Brunet. I would even swear that it beckoned me from the street.

"Let's get all the good stuff," I goad Greg, greedily pointing out the dish I intend to order, the *ragoût de Beatiles,* a red-wine–fortified stew of cock's combs and chicken gizzards, hearts, and kidneys, organs like altar sacrifices to the spirit of *les Mères.* Sleeping Scarlett tolerates the noise of the bustling restaurant, the popping of Champagne corks, and the sonorous *da-da-da-da-da* ring of an old Philips telephone pealing behind the brass and wood bar, as if they were the lilting notes of a lullaby, which warrants a toast. We clink our glasses of Beaujolais and watch Indy thread the dining room, as at ease here as the chef's own son, who plys the tables, delivering complimentary dishes of *rosette.* Chef Gilles Maysonnave, Chez Brunet's chef and owner, keeps his personal collection of vintage marionettes in a side room to amuse young visitors. Indy dodges Chef greeting guests at the door with twin *bisoux,* and slides past the chef's petite wife, Yvette, rearranging platters of pencil-thin asparagus and pedestals of pound cake on the center table to better accommodate newly arrived diners as the room fills up. He resumes our table in unison with the *saucisson.*

"Can't do innards. I'll take the Brunet cassoulet. Is that sufficiently gory?" Greg asks, and reads aloud from the menu. Indy apes at his narration. "Pig tails, *lard*—relax, that's just pork belly, dude." Indy's tongue is out in a show of distaste. "Bacon. You *like* bacon." Indy shrugs, as if *maybe* he could stomach the idea of a little bacon, and takes a timid nibble from a slice of *rosette,* something at least he's accustomed to, *saucisson* being a fixture of our table at home thanks to Saulieu's gaggle of old ladies. "Sausages and white flageolet beans," Greg finishes and closes his menu. "Sounds perfect."

"You mean sounds like all the *gross* stuff," Indy gags.

"What's so gross about it?" I ask, though it's hardly like I'm a dyed-in-the-wool offal eater myself, nor that Indy is the first person ever to have rejected out of hand the notion of eating all of an animal's grisly miscellaneous bits, sacrificial offerings or otherwise. But where or when, I wonder, does the attitude that we are better than our food start?

"When I was little," I tell Indy, immediately aware that in pursuit of some kind of moral I've just started one of *those* kinds of stories: *When I was your age.* "I used to bug Mamie to buy me four things every time we'd go to the grocery store. I wanted tripe—that's the inside of the cow's stomach; tongue; salt pork; and lard." With each word, Indy looks a little more likely to retch, at least in jest. "But not lard like French lard," I press on. "I wanted Mamie to buy me a box of the kind of lard that was just grease."

"Blech. You *wanted* to eat all that?"

"Well, honestly, no. Mainly it was because of Laura, this girl in these books that I was reading at the time—she ate those kinds of things. And mostly, I just wanted Mamie to buy it so I could *look* at it: I never even considered eating it then. But I would now. Tripe looks like pure white honeycomb and it's got these big circles on it that look like octopus suckers. I used to poke the suckers through the plastic wrapper, wondering if they would stick to my finger. And the tongues were soooooo big! As big as your arm!"

"How come I've never seen those things at the store?" Sickened or not, he sounds genuinely disappointed.

"Well, they're hard to find now. Not so many people want to eat them."

Indiana brightens. "Oh, I get it. Because they think it's gross and they'd rather eat hamburger, right? So, you can't find all the cool gross stuff anymore, but there's a lot of hamburger instead."

"Exactly."

He nibbles *rosette* while we wait for our dishes. "But, actually Mom, *I* think people don't like all that stuff because it's just all the *parts,* instead of the *meat.*"

This is true: most adults I know won't eat offal, either, unless it's on a dare or something. (Although periodically offal comes back into fashion and when it does, there's usually a crew of chefs getting press and macho street-cred for cooking it.) These days, true offal enthusiasts are a rather cultish bunch, like the andouillette fanatics of the Cinq A. But offal has always featured prominently at the *bouchons* because *les Mères* were great proponents of it, an attitude born of their intolerance for waste, their insistence on simplicity, and their instinctual certainty that these attributes were important not just in the kitchen, but in life. And that their maternal duty was to inculcate their patrons likewise through their cooking, as if they were serving life lessons disguised as kidneys. They may have been on to something. By embracing the unlovely bits of your external life I bet you *can* eventually learn acceptance before the unlovely bits of your own inner life. Or at least, with my grisly stew, I intend to try. No guts . . . no glory.

It's like an antidote. Chef Maysonnave is a hunter. At various times of the year his freshly bagged game features on his menu. He understands sacrifice. The stew is a study in textures: chewy gumball-size chicken hearts, slippery, gelatinous cock's combs. With every robust bite I can feel my Vieux Lyon malaise weakening until at last it is vanquished, digested with the last toothsome gizzard. Greg is as delighted as a prairie child by his sizzling pig tail.

Scarlett wakes up just in time for dessert, placed on the table by a young woman sporting a dainty polka-dotted silk shirt and a lip ring, surrounded by a nest of spoons. It is a cake moist and pudding-like in texture, probably baked in a ramekin and then inverted, because its pralines—deep red this time instead of hot pink—are caramelized and they spill over the edges of the soft apple-and-pear-studded dessert like the topping of a pineapple upside cake. And when we finish it, we linger, and then we linger a little more, and then a little more, like guests at a party who don't want to leave. Wallflowers we might be—content just to sit and observe the merriment of regulars and friends, and diners who aren't regulars or friends but who are treated exactly like they are—but no one ever insinuates that we should go although now the restaurant fairly bursts at the seams. This is the magic I'd hoped for. The check doesn't even arrive until we finally ask for it, and then it's delivered with two rose-colored macaroons, one each for Indy and Scarlett, by the chef himself. They gobble them up with sugary grins. When we finally exit, the sun is waning and Chef escorts us out into the crisp, open air of the street. *"A très bientôt!"* he says, waving good-bye. *See you very soon!*

I beam my gratitude, but normally taciturn Greg pumps Chef's hand energetically. *"Merci,* Chef," he says. "Thank you so much. That meal . . . wow. *Merci."*

"De rien." Chef Maysonnave smiles modestly. "Really, it was *my* pleasure."

CHAPTER
23

BUTTRESSING THE PROPHECY OF THE GROUND-WINTERING LEEKS, the weather turns frosty right as school lets out for three weeks of spring break. "I told you it would happen," Sophie laughs when I show up on her doorstep, shivering in the optimistically thin sweater I'd adopted as my uniform during our brief thaw.

For the first part of the vacation, Sophie takes Joseph to visit friends in Paris, leaving Marc behind to watch Lulu and Julien. With friends around, it is high times for Indy and Scarlett. Like clockwork, Julien and Lulu appear in our kitchen each afternoon promptly at two o'clock, and I'm not entirely sure whether or not Marc, alternately puttering in his barn or devouring architectural plans in his library, even notices, accustomed to their meandering rural liberty. By 2:05, the boys have colonized my living room.

The girls congregate in the kitchen. Scarlett is in awe of Lulu. This is Lulu's favorite new English phrase: "I want . . ." Having so commandeered a snack, with a graceful, nonchalant, very *ooh-la-la* shrug, she'll finally consent to play with baby Scarlett, who trails her like an obedient puppy while the boys hunch over Indy's Game Boy, cozy by the roaring fire.

These spring storms exhaust themselves like warring lovers, onslaughts of fury and bluster interrupted by periods of fragile tranquillity. During lulls we pull on our muddy boots and I lead the four children to Greg's makeshift rope swing, hung from a branch of the giant oak tree. I push them higher and higher and higher, their toes skimming the sky, until they beg for me to stop. Or we race twigs down the rising creek, creating obstacles of leaves and branches and making bets on whose will survive the swirling eddies and float away first under the fence line. One day, I look around me and think, *How very lovely the country is, even under its gray blanket,* and realize with astonishment that I've grown smitten.

I've safeguarded a *cervelas au pistache* in the refrigerator, and a few days before my mother is due, bake it in a casing of sweet, tender brioche. At dinnertime, I deliver Marc's children and a great chunk of the golden-crusted *saucisson* to the big house. Marc plunders it with his hands, exclaiming over nutty morsels of pistachio and licking buttery brioche crumbs, well-saturated with garlicky pork juices, from his pudgy fingers.

To my question, the one I've been pondering quite a bit—What does he consider the most old-fashioned dish in all French cooking?—he responds without hesitation. "Boom boom *boom!* Well, Amy, that's an easy one. *Tête de veau.* Of course," he says.

<hr />

I CAN BARELY SEE THE ROAD.

"Just to keep things interesting," I say to defuse the palpable tension in the van, "I'm taking bets. My money's on Scarlett awake on Jeanne's lap when we get home."

"Jeanne is a very good babysitter, Amy," Sophie carps, but the edge in her voice reflects, I'm pretty sure, not irritation with me, but with Marc, who is driving. "Marky . . . wait! . . . I said to turn left. *Left! À gauche,* Marky! *Merde . . .*"

Snow flutters in the beam of the van's headlights, a surprise flurry, the lover's grown frigid. In the narrow field of illumination the thick-growing trees of the Morvan press up against the road like solid walls. Street signs, already sparse and difficult to interpret, pop out of them suddenly and then just as suddenly disappear back into the darkness. I know Marc and Sophie have been to the Auberge Ensoleillée many times before for *tête de veau,* but we've been en route for almost an hour now. No one is saying that we're lost, but then, for the last fifteen minutes or so, no one has said much of anything, either. Marc wears a look of grim-faced determination.

Greg wears a leer. Sophie peeks at us, wedged snugly in between booster seats in the backseat, and I hope I don't look as uncomfortable as I feel. Greg is using the vantage to run fingers up the back of my thigh and the groping has me vacillating somewhere between excitement and really, really wishing that he would just keep his damn hands to himself since he's drawing my attention to how snugly my corduroy pants are starting to fit. But with characteristic first date jitters—our quartet's never gone out before—I'm more concerned with Sophie: Will she misinterpret the face of prudishness as a look of reproach? I could actually care less if we're lost.

"I'm so sorry," she says. "You know, I think this happened to us last time, too?" Marc grunts his blamelessness and earns a slap. "It's too bad you can't really see it; the forest here is very beautiful. It is so dense, the Resistance was using it for a base during the war. There's a museum."

"It is absolutely no big deal, Sophie," Greg reassures her, a hand sliding up the inside of my leg. "There are no kids in this car, and that makes this the most pleasurable drive I've had in two months."

I grab his wrist as Sophie and Marc quibble over directions. "Stop it," I murmur.

"Why?" he whispers, tickling my ear with his lips.

"Because," I pout. "I'm fat."

"You're delicious."

"Boom boom *BOOM!*" Marc suddenly swerves around a corner and the van grinds to a halt in front of a hedge. Beyond the hedge is a driveway and a low wooden building that looks like a hunting lodge. There are curlicued shutters around the windows and what, in summer, is probably a gorgeous twining vine of wisteria wrapping the front porch. *"Voilà!"* he trumpets.

The restaurant is dark. Sophie stops a woman in the driveway. A few words and the woman shakes her head, climbs into an older car parked in front of ours, and drives away. "*Alors!* Is it closed?" Marc barks.

"Today is Friday, *non*?" Sophie looks troubled. "Of course it is. I made a reservation. It's usually crowded with people driving down from Paris for the weekend."

"Well, we'll just go see." Marc places a hand on the small of her back and they briskly climb the front porch, leaving us behind on the driveway.

"I'm not sure if I'm upset or relieved," I confide as we follow.

Marc had described the Auberge décor as *rusticus maximus,* and lamented the likelihood of television sets blaring in the far corners of the dining room. But it's silent and entirely empty. Sophie and Marc interrogate the proprietress, a dowager who scrutinizes her calendar thoughtfully, though closing rituals are obviously under way. "I see Verlez . . ." She runs her finger down and across the page. "But, for Saturday." She measures her mistake, gathering a stack of red vinyl-bound menus. "But I remember: I thought to myself, it hasn't been so busy. You probably didn't even need a reservation for Friday night. But then, it's in my hand . . . on *Saturday. Alors* . . ." She sticks her head in the kitchen. "We have guests!" In the dining room she turns on a single lamp near a round corner table directly under one of the silent televisions. Pans clatter as the kitchen comes back to life.

"We don't want to be a burden," Marc apologizes and explains, "These are our friends from America. We've promised them a *tête de veau*." Greg blanches as the order is set in motion, but the proprietress heartens and bustles from the dining room. We can hear her muffled conversation as we habitually peruse our menus. "And for you, Sophie?" Marc asks knowingly, moving on to the wine list.

"*Canard,*" she answers, setting hers aside. "I'm sorry to . . . how do you say it? Abandon ship? But I don't like the *tête de veau* at all."

"That's okay," Greg mutters dutifully. "I'm sure it'll be delicious . . ."

"My only complaint here is the wine," Marc intones. "Too expensive. But . . . ah . . . how do you like Irancy, Greg?" It's a light red wine, produced just east of Chablis, one of the area's rare reds, and Greg nods approval. "Perfect," Marc says. "It's also the cheapest. *Voilà.*"

The proprietress reappears tableside. "A bottle of your finest Irancy," he orders, our self-elected spokesman, and hands over the menus. "And the wife will have the *canard au poivre vert.* And some *crudités* and the *terrine maison,* please, to start."

Jitters return. In the absolute, complete silence that follows her departure, with no food or wine yet at hand for distraction, I fear we'll never start talking. It's bizarre. Without other diners to ogle—or kids to quiet or entertain—it's like waiting in the fussy dining room of a distant relative; too personal for levity, too impersonal for silence. I consider confessing to all assembled about my ill-fitting pants, or outing Greg's fear of the *tête,* but that doesn't seem quite right, so instead I fumble with my napkin and Marc feigns interest in a fork. Greg turns to Sophie.

"So, you don't like *tête de veau?*"

"*Non. Pas du tout,*" she says, voice flooded with relief. "I think it's revolting."

"About once a year we bring friends here," Marc says, relinquishing the fork. "They come for the weekend and after a few bottles of wine, you know, it always sounds like a good idea."

"That's not much in the way of recommendation," I note.

"No, no! Actually, it is. It's that *this* is that kind of place," he sputters. His look caresses the dining room, taking in the worn tablecloths and the bookcases under the windows, the leaflets overflowing from a plastic holder, the dowdy lamps, even the unholy televisions. "It's comfortable, familiar, just like *tête de veau.* You call it that, right? Comfort food?"

The proprietress places a platter in the center of the table and Marc digs in hungrily, full of appetite as always. Inside the earthenware crocks are cold salads: one of lentils, another of cubed garnet beets flecked with emerald parsley that he mounds on his plate. Sophie delicately spoons from the third crock, filled with nuggets of shellfish and plump mussels swimming in vinaigrette. And then there is Greg's favorite, *carottes râpées,* grated carrot mixed with a sweet, honey-laced dressing. He piles some onto his plate and makes a little mound on mine. The last crock reminds me of cooking school: tiny, precisely cubed, blanched carrots and turnips with peas and inch-long trimmed green beans suspended in mayonnaise. We made it all the time in Chef's class: all those exacting vegetables were good practice for our knife cuts.

"You Americans have the most wonderful comfort food," Marc opines. He used to live in the States. Fresh out of school with his degree in architecture, he moved to Chicago and got his first job—through a series of odd, serendipitous events—as a boy Friday to a billionaire. One of his favorite memories from his Chicago days is of a night he was throwing a dinner party. Quite the cook, he wanted to serve brains, so he ran through his local supermarket shouting, "Do you have any brains here?" and was accosted by the manager. "I'm the store manager," the man said. "And that's a loaded question!"

"When Sophie's away the children get Daddy's cooking," he continues. "So I do very American things for them. Comfort food: like tuna fish sandwiches on white bread with very finely chopped onion and pickle relish." He smacks his lips. "Marvelous." With the *terrine* the proprietress has brought a basket of sliced baguette and a gigantic bowl of cornichons. Marc fishes for one of the tiny pickles and chews the coarse pâté thoughtfully. "Actually, it's funny, isn't it? How alike the flavors are? I never thought about that before. Pâté and the tuna fish, both soft and a little salty, and mixed with something sweet. Is that a comfort-food criteria perhaps, cook?"

"My grandmother always cooked roasted chicken," I reply. "And homemade French fries. So those are my comfort foods."

"No, Marky, comfort is just a matter of ass-o-ci-a-tion." Sophie tiptoes over the English word but nails the definition. "My grandmother was Basque, and so she was cooking dishes like *brandade,* which is *my* comfort food."

I wince and Greg laughs, recalling my disastrous first experience with *brandade* at Uncle DD's house.

"She thought it was just mashed potatoes," he explains, which draws a chortle from Sophie. *Brandade* is a dish of dried, pure white salt cod, reconstituted, mashed, and mixed with a potato purée, and it is one of the few dishes to which I have a pure, unadulterated, uncompromising aversion. At first taste I took its artifice—its masquerading in the guise of innocuous mashed potatoes—*personally.*

"*Ugh.* It was horrible! I took a giant bite, you know, expecting mashed potatoes—and of course, Greg's uncle was there and I didn't want to be rude—and then it tasted like *fish!*"

"And not just any fish!" Sophie cackles. "It's so strong! That must have been a shock!"

"Wait until you try your first *tête de veau,*" Marc needles.

As if on cue, in walks the proprietress with the platter.

Our butcher in Saulieu no longer keeps *tête de veau* in his case, though he will special-order it for you. ("I don't sell enough," he lamented when I inquired as to why he didn't stock any.) But there were two or three in the butcher's case at Intermarché in Semur one day, and they were as mesmerizing to behold as the tripes and tongues of my childhood.

Not actually a head—*tête*—the dish consists instead of the full face of the baby cow, peeled Hannibal Lecter–style from its skull, painstakingly deboned, epilated, and skinned, and then rolled around the calf's tongue, its ears, and morsels of its brain, and generally precooked slowly and gently in flavorful stock with plenty of onion and herbs, clove and peppercorns, and a little flour and vinegar, rather like corned beef. It is an absolutely iconic dish, in one fell swoop symbolizing both the country's modern republican origins—the calf's visage substituting for the guillotined head of Louis XVI—and its traditional, rural heart. Tellingly, perhaps, "Bling-Bling" Sarkozy is not a fan.

The tight little twine-tied rolls in the Intermarché case were white and gray in color and leathery in appearance, with a discernible eyelid to one side and an unmistakable patch of nose on another: a Picasso-like rendering of the face, *prêt à manger.*

I summoned the butcher to ask about the *tête de veau's* preparation. He met my inquiry dubiously. *"C'est pour vous?"*

Yes, I assured him: *and* I knew what it was.

"Okay, then. You make a nice, rich bouillon," he then confided, "and boil some potatoes. Cut it in pieces and simmer the *tête* until it's just warmed through and serve it with the potatoes. You know *ravigote?*" I nodded—it's a sauce like a vinaigrette, enriched with chopped capers and shallots and minced parsley, chives, chervil, and tarragon. "It is *obligatoire,*" he added pointedly.

The meat heaped on our platter falls into two categories: there are pinkish-red, stringy slices (mostly the tongue, Marc instructs), and chunks that are largely composed of a thick white layer of what resembles gelled cream.

"And that is . . . ?" I question, poking at the morsels. They quiver like Jell-O.

"That is best left to the imagination." Marc spears a bite and slathers it with *ravigote.* "The artistry of *tête de veau* is in its deconstruction. Come on now, woman, eat! *On attaque!"*

Having been so ordered to attack the meal, I plate a few slices of the red meat and a quantity of *ravigote.* Greg begins, bravely, with a quivering white bit and Sophie watches in abject horror, chewing her duck, which she pronounces excellent. Greg gamely spreads the white piece with *ravigote,* pops the whole thing into his mouth, sinks into it with his teeth, chews—and promptly gags. His shoulders heave, and though I'm terrified he's going to hurl onto the table—and let me tell you, *that* would have made for an interesting first date experience—he brings his napkin to his lips, pauses, swallows . . . slowly, and contains the reflex. I know *exactly* how he feels—I think I had the same startled reaction to the *brandade*—so in solidarity I squeeze his knee under the table. He washes the bite down with a swig of wine and grimaces gracefully.

But now I am absolutely *terrified* of the menacing white chunks. Marc eats bite after bite, and he and Sophie and Greg—now fully recovered—chatter on all about the Morvan during the war, but I can barely follow their conversation. Marc has delicately noted Greg's revulsion, but even in his gusto, still politely leaves a quantity of the white morsels for me, and they loom, wobbly, on the platter, as intimidating as cubes of hemlock.

Are you afraid that you'll embarrass yourself?

Well, yes. Of course I am.

But what would be so embarrassing about not liking it? Or even gagging? Greg did it.

Yeah, well, but Greg's not the food expert. I am.

So, it's a competition?

No. Who said that? I never said it was a competition.

(*Silence.*)

Okay. So it's a little bit of a competition.

(*Continued silence.*)

Well, *come on,* for once it would be nice to be better at something than Greg.

How's that attitude working out for you?

"*On attaque,*" I mumble, and bite into a gelatinous mass.

The rectangle of mysterious flesh is much more savory than I'd expected: it's like a delicious beef broth, but richer. And creamy, but not at all greasy or flabby as I'd feared. It doesn't melt in the mouth like I'd expected, either; it is firm and requires chewing. I like it, and as the awareness of my liking of it blooms and threatens to overseason the experience, I try to block out the self-congratulatory glow and focus on texture and flavor, which continue to morph and change until I swallow. I finish with a sip of Irancy, which is fruity and crisp, made from Pinot Noir grapes. All together—salty, soft, rich, and mellow. Harmonious. I spear another chunk. Greg, I notice, can't watch. I swallow my rising pride.

He's just finished telling Marc and Sophie about his grandparents who worked for the Resistance.

"And you, Amy?" Sophie asks. "What is your family like?"

"Catholic."

"Boom *BOOM!*" Marc raises his full glass in salute, a fellow survivor. "I wouldn't have it any other way. We Catholics always have the best stories. Lots of tragedy and guilt."

"Exactly," I agree. Like a drunken king to a bard at the banquet, he urges me on with his sloshing glass. "Okay. In ours, it's my mother, who you'll meet this weekend." The king indicates that he wants details. "When she was very young, before me, she had a baby—"

"In secret?" he interrupts. I nod affirmative. It was a remarkable skeleton, concealed for twenty-four years, until my last day of college, when she sprung the news of my older brother Bob on us like he was my graduation present. "And it was a very big deal, right?" I nod again: Mom nearly collapsed after delivering the news. ("I think I'm having a heart attack," she'd wailed.) "Of course," Marc says, sipping happily. "Go on."

"And . . . to this day, even though they're reunited and even though he's part of the family now, I think her guilt makes her *terrified* that she'll lose one of us someday. Penance."

"So she holds the reins very tightly, correct?"

"VERY tightly," Greg blurts.

"Well, let's be fair," I defend her. "But, yes, Marc, we're very close, if that's what you mean. Remember, we live in her backyard." I'd described the bungalow during a pre-trip exploratory get-to-know-each-other phone conversation. He'd raised the notion of a house swap—in lieu of rent, maybe they'd visit San Diego. So we compared notes and when he casually mentioned that their house was more than ten thousand square feet, I'd quickly calculated that fifteen or so of ours would fit inside the one of theirs and squashed the idea, silently cursing Greg, who'd been the biggest bungalow booster. "But building in her backyard was our idea."

"Real estate market went insane." Greg provides his boilerplate backstory. "And actually, we asked my parents first and they turned us down flat. Which should tell you a lot about our two families."

"*Totally* different," I agree.

"Yes, that's family," says Marc. "You know, Amy, there's actually a name for a family like yours."

"What?" I snort. "Repressed? Dysfunctional?"

"No, no." Full of wine and good food—French—he'll chase down the more interesting intellectual answer if it takes him all night. He rubs his hands in spirited anticipation, warming to his enterprise. "But first, a question: When you left home for the very first time, how did it feel?"

"You mean the freedom?"

"Yes!" Silverware clatters to the floor when he smacks the table, drawing the hostess, peering around the corner to make sure the party crashers aren't trashing the place. "The very fact that you would *call* it freedom!" he continues, quieter, but no less animated. "Yes. The freedom: Was it pleasurable?" He studies my reaction across our empty plates. Just a few bites of the *tête* remain, but there's still a bowl of *fromage blanc* with salt and pepper left to be eaten, and an apple tart on the way. These are proud memories: the drive to UCLA to begin freshman year, chasing Greg to Paris in 2000, moving to Burgundy.

"Well, *yes* . . ." But always, also, there was Mom: her tears and sticky regrets, and within me this waging war between hope and fear, independence and something that still feels distinctly like disloyalty. "But . . ."

"It feels awful, doesn't it. Like committing treason."

"I've never heard a better word for it."

"That's because you are a *souche*."

"A what?" Greg asks. He refills our dwindling wineglasses from our third bottle of Irancy.

"*Souche*. Literally, in French it means stump, but I think that our friend who got quite famous for this work translates it as stem: a stem family, right, Sophie?" She nods in confirmation. "Here's the basic idea." From his pocket he pulls a pen and a scrap of paper and begins making a chart.

"Basically, there are seven types of families, and if you examine the relationships between parents and adult children, and then between siblings, you get a model for attitudes toward two essential human values: authority and equality," he places them on his grid, "that ultimately predict most of the world's political ideologies." My, how the French *love* their theories. "So," he points to his chart, "you can have liberty or authority, and you can have equality or inequality, and then you combine those in various manners." Expounding amid the wreckage of our meal, he leaves his chart splattered with traces of *ravigote*. He flicks away an errant caper and continues. "For example, there is the nuclear family, which is by far the most common type in America." He draws a line connecting liberty and equality. "In the nuclear family, parental authority over adult children is lax: you are expected to grow up and leave the nest and make your own family."

"That's mine," Greg says.

"Voilà," Marc agrees. "You get it from your American side, of course, but also from your French side, because these were the prevailing family types in most of northern France, especially around Paris, where you're from. The Revolution just imposed these family values on the rest of the country, with greater or less success, which is why we have such widely different political parties all around the country. Good Lord, we have Communists! Could you imagine an American Communist Party? Ho-ho! And Socialists aren't particularly popular in America, either, are they? Now, siblings." He studiously returns to his chart. "Commonly, in the nuclear family, siblings are equals. Unless there is a mitigating circumstance, inheritance is equally divided and the parents treat the children with equal attention and affection. So, nuclear corresponds neatly with your American democracy—do your own thing, make your own way, go west young man, all men are created equal—and also with the French, *liberté, égalité, fraternité.*"

I'm a little confused. "So, what you're saying is my family doesn't believe in equality?"

"Well, not precisely," Marc explains. "But we're not vilifying anyone here, my dear. The *souche* family is very impressive: dynastic. I consider myself a *souche*. Most Catholics are. When my parents were alive, I felt it very important to be continually connected to them. It's just that in the *souche* family, parental authority is of supreme importance. Think of the Church! And it is *never* surrendered to adult children until the reigning family member dies or is incapacitated. Now, question: Did your mother ever push you out of the nest, Amy? Or did she let you build a nice, cozy little perch for yourself right there in her very own backyard?" I flush at the insinuation. "You see, you're a *souche*. In a nuclear family, the idea of adult children living with their parents would be unthinkable! A total failure!"

"We say *slackers* in English," Greg tells him.

"Well, I'm *not* a slacker, Greg," I retort hotly. "And living with my mother was *your* idea. I *always* said it would cause problems."

"Aha!" Marc interjects. "Now, *this* is interesting. Can I ask you both a few impertinent and probably presumptuous questions?" I glare at Greg. Why not, if he's going to go ahead and rewrite history. "Amy: Was one of the things that you first loved about Greg the fact that he had such total freedom to live anywhere in the world that he wanted? Freedom that you lacked?" Was it? I deliberate uncomfortably under Greg's and Marc's watchful eyes. It's . . . odd to scrutinize the romantic spark. Marc has put it so bluntly: Did I want what Greg had? It almost sounds like he, too, suspects me of golddigging, though he knows nothing of our ancient histories, so how could he? He's speaking emotionally, of course. And emotionally, yes, Greg's freedom *was* breathtaking. "Yes," I finally confess. "That was attractive."

"And you." Marc turns his attention on Greg. "Since apparently it was your idea, why did you want to live in Amy's mother's backyard?"

"We were broke!" he hoots. "Housing market went insane: What else were we going to do?"

"Come now," Marc goads him.

"Okay," he concedes. "*And* I thought it would be good for the kids. My dad was always working and I missed my grandparents when we moved to America."

"*Voilà.*" Marc gloats. "Cross-pollination. One craves freedom, the other connection. You see before, a nuclear marrying a *souche,* a *souche* marrying a nuclear, it would never have happened. The children of the *souche* family require parental approval for just about everything, and *especially* for choosing a spouse since that person is incorporated into the family, and the family is paramount. A nuclear would be a threatening, potentially disruptive force, bringing an alien set of expectations and values into the family. Weakening it."

"But, Marc, in this time everything is different," Sophie dissents. "There are different stresses and different influences. Families break apart because of jobs and money, and other families live together *avec plusieurs générations* . . . How do you say this?"

"Multigenerationally."

"Multigenerationally because it is cheaper, not because they were destined to do so."

"Precisely," he concludes. "And our friend, I think, in his most recent book, argues that the tumult of our current times arises from that social convergence, the forced mixing and morphing of values and expectations. But, Capulets and Montagues: there have always been attractive aspects of each family type that have drawn rivals toward each other, even if their unions were probably destined to be fraught. And ultimately, the only thing that really matters is the deployment of power. My dear," his wineglass is his scepter, "indulge me one last rude, prying question, and then I will ply you with alcohol and make you feel all better. And try not to think about your mother: How do you feel living in the backyard?"

Without considering my mother, the answer is easy. "Trapped." Across the table, Greg looks stricken. Not that he hasn't known it.

I'm spent, but Marc has promised to be done with me and hails our hostess. "Your bottle of eau-de-vie, *s'il vous plaît*," he orders. "And four glasses." Sophie shakes her head no: she's driving. "No? *Alors.* Three, then." The strong, clear, potent drink burns my throat but quiets my nerves. Quite a first date it's turned out to be! Henceforth I'll tred lightly through theories, especially those that ring of truth.

But Marc, after all, can't resist a closing thought. "I think the pertinent question for *you,* Amy, is: Do you, product of a certain type of family, preprogrammed to submit to authority—and with a husband like Greg who's naturally comfortable wielding it—do you ever give yourself permission to make a decision? Because if not, what does the future hold?"

Kaboom! Dynamite to the heart of the mountain.

"Well, I'm no shrinking violet, Marc. But how does the saying go? Damned if you do, damned if you don't?" I reach for the bottle with shaky hands.

"Oh God! I know, I *know,*" he stammers, mortified. "I forgot. That was insensitive. I'm drunk. I apologize. *Profusely.*"

Sophie clucks, "Marky . . ."

"No, it's okay. We're working on it." I pat Greg's hand to show, *See? No hard feelings,* then throw back the shot and fill another, in need of rapid fortification and a way out of the path of the landslide. "Besides, I think I'm proud to be a *souche.* Dynasties keep traditions alive, don't they? I liked the *tête,* but I still think it's the kind of dish that would die out if people's grandmothers didn't make them try it."

"Hmm . . ." Marc reflects, gratefully following me out of dangerous territory. "Good point. It's like Brillat-Savarin."

" 'Tell me what you eat, and I'll tell you who you are.' "

"Very good," he guffaws proudly. Sophie and Greg chuckle at our geeky expense. "Wife!" Marc playfully punches her arm. "Let us have our fun!"

Greg slurps a final shot and bangs his glass on the table, ready to call it a night. "Well, I, for one, could still do without *tête de veau.*"

"And me, too," Sophie titters.

"Fine, then, selfish beasts!" Marc slams his last shot and rises unsteadily to his feet. "Then we *souches* will be the ones that save French cooking, and you two will thank us for it! *Tête de veau* for everyone! Let's come back again this weekend. We'll make the children eat it!"

"Nope, *this* weekend my *souche* mother arrives and I must flee to her side and do her bidding and take her to Provence."

"Then I shall carry on without you," Marc crows, making for the door. "It's late and I'm drunk. Wife! Take me home!"

Outside, it's icy and slick and I'm buzzed and clumsy, slipping and sliding on the driveway, graceless and emotionally exhausted. Wordlessly, Greg helps me to the van. Marc dozes in the front seat and Sophie drives us cautiously through the drifting snow back home to Brianny. Where Scarlett is, indeed, and just as I predicted, still wide awake.

I NEVITABLY, couples' therapy eventually devolves into individual therapy, I guess because there's no point in trying to coach a couple out
of their accumulated bad, marriage-toxifying habits without first deter-
mining which of them—by dint of troubled childhood or psychological
repression or trauma or whatever—is responsible for introducing the
various parts of all that bad mojo in the first place. It's as if, to make
progress, the therapist would like you to stop talking about why you hate
each other, and *start* talking about why you hate *yourselves*.

I think it was at right about that transitional moment that Greg and
I mutually agreed to quit therapy. I know for me, the trigger was when
the therapist said, "What we really have to figure out, Amy, is why your
mother wields such a . . . *supernatural* influence over you." That was in
August. Soon after was when I looked at Greg across the dinner table and
said, "You know what? I think we should move back to France."

But if I *had* to give an explanation to that therapist right now, I would
have to say that it's because of this: because stuff just always seems to
happen to me around my mother.

For example, for weeks I haven't worried at all about driving the car.
It's never even really crossed my mind again, Zelda finally vanquished as
Greg and I have grown closer and I've surrendered the past, reaching a
kind of peace with it even if I'm not yet quite ready to think hard about
the future. And, since Strasbourg, I have taken both Indiana and Scarlett
out on solo ventures and *nothing* has ever happened.

But on the very day that Mom and Jerry and Yvette are due to arrive in France, Greg and the kids and I make the hour's drive to Montbard so that he can catch the train to Paris. The plan is this: he will meet them at Charles de Gaulle, pick up the Mercedes van that we've rented for Provence, and then drive everyone in it back to Brianny. All I have to do is drive the Kid home from Montbard. So I slide into the driver's seat, start up the engine, pull out of the parking lot . . .

And then everything goes kablooey.

Another wild spring storm is passing through. It is pouring blinding, pelting, sideways rain, through which the kids and I dash in and out of the grocery store in Montbard to pick up a few last things. Soaking wet, we get back into the car and I back out of our parking spot. The parking lot is a total scrum: cars are honking and swerving and there's a crush of traffic trying to get out of the driveway and lights are flashing, but we finally make it back out onto the road. The windshield wipers whip at full speed and in the backseat there's the usual cacophony, a medley of laughter and music requests and loud, indignant tattling.

And then suddenly I can't see.

I blink, but there remains a big, fat hole in my vision right where the car in front of me should be. I rub my eyes and blink again and try squinting but it still won't reappear, even though I know that it's there. My breathing gets a little ragged. My fingers are tingling and my palms start to sweat and to calm myself, I decide I'll try reading the car's license plate number instead. And it's the weirdest thing . . . I can still see the plate's outline, but every time I try to focus on an individual letter, the letter goes all wobbly and wavy and though I know the letters are there, I even know, somehow, what the letters are, I can't actually *see* them. It's as though my eyesight has been reduced to nothing more than peripheral vision.

"Are you okay, Mama?" Indy asks, as well he should: I'm clutching the steering wheel like a life preserver and shaking my head wildly, trying to clear the gauzy veil. My heart beats so fast, I'm sure I am going to die right there in the front seat and that the car is going to crash and burn with my beautiful, loud, demanding children inside of it. But I don't want to scare them.

"I'm fine!" I chirp. "Boy! It sure is raining hard!"

Do I pull over? I'm too afraid to stop the car. What if I can't get back on the road again? Oh God, I don't even have a cell phone, I realize. I can't call for help. Am I having a stroke? A seizure? This has never happened to me before! *Keep going,* instinct says. *Just get the kids home safely.* I want my mother so badly, I could cry.

If I cock my head sideways I discover that I can drive looking out of the corner of just one eye, letting my peripheral vision dominate. *Okay, so let's just do that.* I turn off the Montbard street and onto the shoulder of the rural road toward home. *You're doing fine. This is the way,* I coach myself gently, speaking soothingly as if I were my own child. *Good girl. Now, don't overthink it, and don't scare the kids. Just keep going.*

Slowly, slowly, the Kid and me both shaking like a leaf whenever a truck zooms past, I drive from Montbard to Semur. It's an hour's drive that takes us nearly two. And then somehow, muttering prayers and invocations and promises under my breath, I find all the right roads back to Brianny. And thankfully, by the time we pull into the driveway, my vision has returned.

But I'm still quivering and shaken from the experience. In the house, I can't even light a match to get the fireplace going. One after another they just sputter and snap and fizzle and refuse to burn until I'm not sure if it's *me* or if it's the matches that are the problem. And Indy stands behind me the whole time, rubbing my back and whispering words of encouragement, so that I am so ashamed of myself for acting like an absolute infant and making him be the adult, that I finally just throw the matches back into the tinder box and call it quits. "Let's go see Marc and Sophie."

So by late, late that night—by the time I've put the kids to bed and finally fallen asleep myself in front of the fireplace, and woken abruptly to the sound of gravel crunching on the drive, and walked into the kitchen to see my mother standing on my threshold draped in her full-length fur coat, as natural as if she's always been there—by that time, and after all that, I am totally prepared to receive her as if I'm receiving a miraculous vision.

And things just sort of went on from there.

A CARDINAL FACT ABOUT MY FAMILY: WHEREVER WE GO, we are the loudest. It is a defining characteristic of our tribe. (A corollary applies to Indy and Scarlett: that they will be the loudest *and dirtiest* in any assembled group of children.)

No one will claim responsibility for originating the practice, but if, for example, in a large crowd of people we can't find each other, we just simply shout as if we are the only players in an exclusive Marco Polo game. We become primitive, like loud jungle animals, even in France, where behaving in public like loud jungle animals is way, way beyond *gauche*.

For the vacation I've rented us a peach-colored stucco house with pale-turquoise-painted shutters and a yard filled with olive trees, lavender bushes, rosemary, and waist-high weeds, and a pool that when we arrive is a far cry from the one that we were expecting, half-drained and filled with a nasty layer of thick green algae. I walk around it several times, miffed, cursing the Internet and its broken promises. After we've lugged the suitcases inside, Jerry stands in the doorway and whistles through his teeth. "It sure looked prettier in the pictures," he says.

The house is in the suburbs of the village of Isle-sur-la-Sorgue, the Venice of Provence, a town of watery byways, ponds, and paddle wheels spinning slowly, the remnants of the town's days as a silk- and paper-making center. In a few days, the town will commence its annual Antiques Fair, and it is for this that I have chosen Isle-sur-la-Sorgue as our hub. Mom and Jerry are consummate bargain hunters. (Although, acknowledgment: Peter Mayle wrote of Isle-sur-la-Sorgue and its antiques, "The only thing that can't be had . . . is a bargain.") The festival draws dealers, collectors, and designers from every corner of the globe and Mom is so excited about it—and so pleased with me—she can barely contain herself. It promises to be a gigantic, if expensive, garage sale, the likes of which she and Jerry have only ever dreamed about. And the antiques shops we've perused along the village waterfront have only whetted her appetite, filled as they are to the rafters with quilts and ironwork, crystal and faience pottery. Mom brought an extra suitcase. She is not leaving until it is filled.

But the first order of business, once we've unpacked, is groceries.

And in the grocery store, the game begins.

"Jerome!" my mother yells from the front of the store, where she is helping Indy and Scarlett select easily a year's worth of Kinder chocolates.

"Kate!" Jerry booms from the cheese counter. I have attached myself to Jerry, the most vulnerable and conspicuous member of our group: the anti-French, necessitating a translator *and* an interpreter, his tall, robust frame, Hawaiian shirt, and long white ponytail eliciting stares from our fellow French shoppers. He wants *Swiss* cheese to make sandwiches: I'm trying to explain to him about Gruyère. It is getting lost in translation.

"Mom!" Yvette hollers from near the alcohol aisle, and I scurry to her side, bearing a handful of euros from Jerry, to help her pick out her very first bottle of cheap wine. She's just turned eighteen, France's legal drinking age, so she chooses the rosé with the prancing deer on the label. "It's cute!" she says.

"Amy!" Mom cries, and I leave Yvette and scamper over to the produce section, where I find Indiana standing smack in the middle of a mess of spilled cherries and my mother, baffled by the store's electronic scale, aimlessly pushing buttons trying to produce a price sticker for the gargantuan bag of carrots that Scarlett has just filled. Scarlett clutches her brown Easter bunny, a gift from Mamie. "My rabbit is hungry," she whines.

And then it begins all over again.

Provence is fabled for its produce and I intend to shop in earnest at the *marché,* so like good basket shoppers, Greg and I grab just the essentials—butter, milk, pasta—but Mom and Jerry and Yvette cartwheel through the store, astounded by the novelty of French packaging and launching things into their cart with abandon as if we might never see a supermarket again. Microwaveable Coquilles Saint-Jacques! Croque Monsieur for the toaster! Choco-Crack! (It's a cereal.)

In search of some deli ham for Jerry's sandwiches, I take him and Yvette to the meat counter, and after showing them the skinned rabbits with their eyes bugging out like alien creatures, and the Bresse chickens with skinny necks dangling limp white plumage and with heads and feet intact so that the discerning shopper can verify, by the red comb and the blue feet, that it is, indeed, a Bresse chicken they are about to pay premium for, Jerry and Yvette collectively thank me for the tour of, in their words, gross food.

We leave the supermarket with enough provisions for an army, *plus* a scanty yellow negligee for Yvette. She climbs back into the van clutching her rosé in one hand, her lacy nightgown in the other, and settles in between Indy and Scarlett in the very backseat.

"I love this country already," she declares, and promptly falls asleep.

CHAPTER 26

IN THE MIDDLE OF THE NIGHT I SIT BOLT UPRIGHT IN BED and almost whack my head on the ceiling, startled awake by the sound of shattering glass.

"Did you hear that?" I peer over the side of the top bunk at Greg's silent figure, curled up on his side in a ball of blankets. "Greg!" I hiss, but he doesn't stir. The kids and Yvette share the room next door. My parents have the master suite down the hall. The ladder's metal rungs are icy cold under my bare feet, the hallway tile freezing, but I tiptoe, pause to listen at each doorway. The kids are silent but Yvette mumbles in her sleep. Doobie comes sleepily down the hallway, toenails clicking. "It's okay, Doobs," I soothe. "Go back to Daddy." But he loyally follows me down the stairs anyway and I'm glad for his company.

The living room is silent and still.

No sounds at all from the dark kitchen.

And then BANG! It's right outside, just by the front door, so loud I nearly jump out of my skin. Doobie growls. I halt, petrified, useless if it's an intruder. It BANGS again, followed by a rattling and a clattering that I recognize with relief as the front door's wooden shutters come loose. My breath makes frosty circles on the living room window. By the streetlight's glow I can see our olive tree being whipped into a frenzy, and the tall cypresses bent over nearly sideways, their tips pointing at a precarious ninety-degree angle to the gravel driveway. And then it begins—a long, low whistling, the sound of the wind gusting through the thousands of tiny cracks in the stucco all around the windows.

"Well, now it's just like home," I sigh to Doobie, and we wearily climb the stairs back to bed.

By morning, it's worse. The cypresses are festooned with bits of blowing trash. They look like gaudy papier-mâché Christmas trees caught in a cyclone. There's broken glass everywhere, too, shards of the neighbor's recycling bottles blown right off of his low wall and smashed to smithereens on our driveway. While the rest of us eat breakfast, Greg sweeps behind the van so that we can leave, but I have no idea where we'll go. I have a thick notebook crammed with notes, reservations, plans, and itineraries, but none took into consideration freezing gale-force winds.

"Is it raining, too, Jerome?" Mom wants to know. She feeds baby bird Scarlett tiny bites of toast.

"No, it's the damndest thing, Kate," he answers, staring out the window. "Bright, beautiful, sunny blue skies. Gorgeous day. Just windy as all hell."

"It must be the mistral," I fret. "It blows in the winter."

"Well, how long does it last?" he asks, peeved.

As it turns out, we are all about to find out.

For three long days and three long nights the freezing-cold northerly wind blows mercilessly, and though I've seen weather in Brianny, I have never seen *anything* like the mistral. It never stops. It blows and blows and blows and blows, at once so stirring and so monotonous it's enough to make you crazy. My Zelda sensors go on high alert and my carefully crafted itinerary, made for calm, warm, blissful weather, is obliterated. But we have to do something: we're on vacation. *The* vacation. So we visit the storied hilltop villages anyway—Gordes and Ménerbes and Roussillon, Lacroix and Bonnieux. From their heights, the floor of the Luberon valley is a dusty green-gold mosaic of stone and pines and fig trees and scrub. The lavender fields are checkerboarded, earthy brown tufted with the pale blue-green first growth of the young bushes. In the almond and apricot orchards, the trees are bare and the ground concealed by a snowfall of blossoms.

But the villages are ghostly places. The shopkeepers' solicitude is gone with the wind. Mom's charming banter (which, of course, they don't understand) elicits little more than brief, halfhearted smiles from them though she buys lavender sachets and burled olive wood bowls and richly hued Provençal tablecloths and pottery and postcards and would just keep right on buying if I didn't keep sending Yvette, my minion, into the stores after her, pleading for her to *please* come out and move on, because my children are crazy in the streets, as berserk and kinetic as if they were a couple of tiny turbines being fed by the wind itself. Sometimes Greg helps me, but he's perpetually scowly and grumpy about it, and keeps wandering off with Doobie, solo. Jerry paces, surly, with his cold hands thrust deep into his pockets and his ponytail whipping wildly. Only Mom is snug in her fur. The clear, crisp air crackles and shimmers and from time to time I think I'm seeing halos and starbursts again, so that I draw close to her, as certain as I've ever been that nothing bad can possibly happen to me so long as she is nearby.

She has always had this draw, this magnetism, for all of us kids, as if she were the sun around which we orbit. But me, closest to her celestial star, I'm sure I've always felt her tug the strongest. And just as I have often at home, here I wonder if her magnet isn't polarizing. Because the closer I draw to her, the farther away from me it seems Greg is propelled.

SURPRISED YELPING FROM THE ARCTIC KITCHEN. Jerry flies backward out the doorway. It's an inauspicious beginning to day four.

"Oh, Greg," he summons.

Sharing a property at home, the men have developed a curious relationship. Even after a mostly loving quarter century, Mom still savages Jerry for his ineptness with tools, either not realizing or willfully misinterpreting the fact that he actually doesn't give a damn about wiring or plumbing or fixing things up around their house. Like Mom, he's a gardener. Greg, on the other hand, is incapable of seeing things go undone. So he's become their handyman, a service that's mostly helped stand him in Mom's good graces. I wonder if sometimes Jerry, too, feels usurped by Greg's proficiency, but if he does, he does a damn good job of hiding it.

The cold has crept under the eaves and blown down our chimney and settled into the tiled floor. Jerry rubs numb hands and waits for Greg's help. Greg lurches past him into the kitchen on limbs stiff with cold.

"Holy shit!" The garage door opens and closes.

Jerry cackles in the doorway. "You guys really should come see this."

The wind has even driven nature indoors. Greg has a spatula, trying to goad a refugee family of scuttling, inky black scorpions into a shoe box. Mom screams in terror, dragging Indy and Scarlett behind her back to the sofa. "Oh, Jerry! How could you! Why didn't you warn me?!"

Doobie will save us! He squeezes through my legs, barking menacingly, and the scorpions scatter in four directions, flaring their pointed stingers. "*No.* Back off, Doobs!" Greg swats him across the nose with his free hand. "God *damn it,* Amy! He'll get stung! Get him out of here!"

"I want to go home," Yvette moans, following Mom.

The children are crying, the adults are pissed, the dog is cowering, and the mistral doesn't give a shit that we're on vacation. There is only one thing to be done.

"That's it!" I announce firmly, and with far more authority than I actually feel given the way Greg has just pounced on me. "Everybody into the van!"

THE WIND BLOWS FROM THE NORTH, so we put it at our backs. It's the opening day of *la corrida,* the bullfights in old Arles, a painterly Roman city that once wooed Van Gogh with women in colorful lace dresses, its atmospheric soot-stained stone buildings, and filtered amber light. But when we get there, the streets are mobbed with people, and although the wind blows more gently down here, the crowd looks testy. On the sidewalks, vendors stir giant steaming cauldrons of paella, as native here as it is in Spain. Its spicy aroma wafts enticingly through the van's open windows, rumbling bellies. "Park?" Greg calls from the driver's seat.

But I can hear a swelling, intensifying chant from the arena, can sense the building bloodlust in a gang of young men on the sidewalk, loud and obnoxious in pursuit of a group of girls who turn around and shout them down in the street as we drive past. Do we need *more* testosterone today?

"Keep going," I yell from the backseat and scratch Arles off the agenda.

We drive and we drive and we drive, more distance between us and the wind, more distance between me and my husband. He shares navigation with Jerry. I share snacks with Scarlett.

Where the single-lane road south ends in the Mediterranean, the violent spectacle of *la corrida* is replaced by the most gentle of bullfights, as though the nearness of the sea or the overhead flight of hot pink flamingos has mellowed everyone out. Thank God. The wind is a mere whisper. The air smells of salt.

Here in the Camargue—a silted, marshy delta mottled with lagoons and brine ponds, wrapped by two arms of the Rhône river—the local boys run the *course Camarguaise*: vaulting and twirling, spinning, leaping, dodging, and racing the charging bull before at last delicately plucking a pair of ribbons from its horns and dancing out of the stadium to wild applause and catcalls from their lascivious female fans. In exchange for its emasculation, the bull lives. The marshes cut the Camargue off from civilization. Here at the end of the world, yin and yang have had to learn to coexist.

Music and cheering pour from the tiny, rickety stadium next to Saintes-Maries-de-la-Mer's beach. Off the kids go, skipping ahead and doubling back, begging for ice cream, merry-go-round rides, some fried beignets or a sugary *sirop*. Greg says no to everything, so I say yes, backed by Mamie and her open wallet. After the almost aggressive prettiness of Provence, it's as if we've traveled back in time here. Saintes-Maries is run down, but in the way of a funky old beach town, with hand-painted signs at the snack bars, and curio shops selling wind chimes made of seashells and macramé. Black-dressed men on white horses ride out of the marshes toward the arena, bells on their bridles jangling. There's even an old rusted-out Citroën driving slowly through the streets around the church with a bullhorn strapped to its roof. "Today only," a man's voice drones, "come to see the beautiful boys."

"I like-a the beautiful boys," Yvette drawls when I translate.

The sun is warm. The sea is sparkling. It's a lazy day, tailor-made for teenage couples, rolling and laughing on the white sand. I want my own baby back. But he's off again, clowning with Yvette and the kids. Jerry hovers near Mom. "Kate? Care to come dip your toes with me?"

"Oh, no, you go, Jerome." Instead she plops beside me on the blanket. Jerry kicks off his shoes, rolls up his pants legs, and goes wading in the Mediterranean for the first time ever in his life. It's sweet to have helped him get here. This part of this vacation at least, I will consider a success. At the water's edge he gives Mom a thumbs-up. She sighs contentedly. "I'm taking pictures with my heart, Amy."

"I'm sorry about the wind."

"Remember, *you* don't control the weather."

We'll put volumes in e-mail, but when we're together, Mom and I barely speak. Communication is largely wordless: through long habit, we read each other almost perfectly. Watchfulness means *I'm lonely.* A knee tucked under my chin says, *I miss him.*

"How are things with Greg?"

"Mostly fine."

I stretch out, lest I imply more. Mom the stem: how fitting she's a gardener. But her specialty is roses, which must be pruned ruthlessly to keep them from getting unruly. One stem to one flower.

"Well, that's good. Everything's fixed. So, are you going to come home, then?"

Clip, clip, clip.

"Not until the Fourth of July, Mom."

"Perfect."

What?

"Because Erin wants to come and stay with you for a while. What do you think? You could use the help, right?"

"Is this your idea or Erin's?"

If I'm Mercury, Erin's Mars, the fourth of the sisters, with a commensurate ability to float free. The idea of her staying with us is both intriguing and a little terrifying.

"It's her idea. Of course." Mom huffs. "She's *not* the lost sister, Amy. She just finished her last quarter at Santa Barbara. And you said that you could use the help. She'll be the nanny."

Never mind that a nanny was actually *her* idea. "Well, yeah. Okay. I'm sure it'll be great. I can't imagine Greg will mind. He seems to appreciate the company."

"You're sure? He won't consider it an invasion of your privacy or anything?" she asks with deliberate delicacy.

Her New York scar: Greg, in the middle of a breakdown, shouting that he found living in her backyard stifling. (I'd been glad *someone* had said it—someone who wasn't me—but you can imagine the fences he's had to mend since.)

"Our coming here had nothing to do with you guys, Mom." What else can the bloom say? "We'd love to have Erin."

"Well, I'm just glad everything's okay now. And in exchange for doing this for me, I am going to do something for you: I want to buy you a ticket to New York. Go get your show back, Amy. Erin will help Greg with the kids while you're gone."

The suggestion is so incongruous, so entirely out of the blue, I can only stare, astonished. I'd swear she was joking but she never jokes. Levity isn't in her DNA.

"Jesus, Mom, why would you even suggest that?"

"So. I take it you two still don't talk about it?"

"No, we still don't talk about it. Because there's *nothing* to talk about."

"So then, everything between you two is fine, so long as you never talk about anything that isn't fine. Is that right?"

I return her level stare, but my drawn knees say, *Leave me the hell alone.* "Personally, Mom, I fail to see what you think there is left to talk about."

"Oh, no? Well, how about this, then: *What* are you going to do when you get back home, Amy? Hm? When this *fantasy*," her sweeping gesture includes the beach, Provence, France, "is all *over*, and you have *nothing* to show for it?"

I stop rocking, stung, or clipped, as she'd intended. "Thanks, Mom."

"Well, *somebody* has to say it, Amy. Am I the only one who remembers why you did the show in the first place? You were miserable, and let me tell you, a miserable mother is not a good mother, even if you are there twenty-four hours a day, seven days a week. You *deserve* to work. And you had a very good point back then, one that even Greg should acknowledge: you're a cook. And you haven't worked in, what, six, nearly seven years? How *employable* are you? And do you really want to start *all over again* with two little kids at home? Is that really what Greg wants? Or are you just *done* now. You're never going to work again because this last thing didn't work out. What happens next, Amy?"

Marc, Mom . . . Why does everyone want to talk about our goddamned future?

"I thought you came here to make me feel better! Why did you come?"

"Running away is not a coping mechanism, Amy."

"And leaving home isn't always running away! *None* of this has been easy, Mom, but this was *my* choice: *I* gave up the show!"

"Well, what other option did he leave you?" she snaps as the kids race toward us; she's never been one to relinquish the last word. "If everything was really fine, you could have made it work. It was a dream job, Amy, a golden opportunity. And I've seen you get scared and walk away from so many other jobs before, it's heartbreaking."

"Mama!" Scarlett throws herself into my arms, her twenty-five pounds all it takes to knock me flat on my back. Then Indy pounces in a wild jumble of flying sand and flailing arms and legs. They laugh and holler that Greg says it's time for lunch, and beneath their hot, sweaty bodies, I allow myself just one tiny, furtive, defeated sigh.

CHAPTER
27

A ND I WISH I COULD SAY THAT THAT WAS THE END OF IT, because
lunch should have been lovely: A sun-warmed terrace splashed by
the town fountain. A platter of grilled sardines drizzled in fruity olive oil.
A rich and savory *estouffade de taureau* made of the meat of the hulking
black bulls that graze in the saline marshes, braised slowly with red wine
and black olives until the meat falls to tender shreds.

A trio of guitarists playing gypsy-flamenco surrounded us, Jerry and
Yvette and Greg grooving in their seats to the music, but me, I just sat
there, avoiding Mom's baleful stare and helping the kids with their fish.
In between bites, I picked at my own plate of *tellines,* tiny shellfish from
the beach, each no bigger than my thumbnail, so minuscule, though,
that to eat them required more effort than I could muster. If I could have,
I would have just left the table and roamed. Freedom . . . connection . . .
Why couldn't I have both? Eric, our waiter, brought me the smallest of
forks, a diminutive instrument to pry open the *telline* shells and dig out
their sweet morsel of flesh, an absorbing task that ended up well suited
to my brooding.

This is the source of my mother's supernatural power: she is my biggest fan, my fiercest champion, and in most ways the role model for the
kind of mother I want to be. She praises her children to high heaven,
she is interested, and passionate, and involved, and she keeps a running
commentary going on all of our lives, her monologue a mixture of ob-
servation and intuition, of instinct, interpolation, opinion, projection,
speculation, and sometimes just flat-out conjecture. And for me, that has

always been the hardest part of it: just because she speaks *some* truth, does it mean she speaks all of it?

A run-in with my mother can leave me adrift in a riptide of self-doubt, and even after thirty-four years, I'm still no good at turning myself parallel to the shore and paddling until I eventually find my way out of it.

Was it really *my* dream job? Or was it just *a* dream job? For somebody else, just not for me. Had I given up the show, or had I conveniently given in? And, dear God, what *does* come next? *Anything?*

"I just don't want to think about it."

Absorbed in my thoughts, a million miles away from the table, I accidentally mutter the words right out loud.

Greg can just barely hear me over the flamenco. "Think about what?"

I offer him a bite of my *tellines*. "Nothing."

———

THE NEXT DAY IS OUR LAST IN PROVENCE. We'll be traveling homeward on Easter morning.

"And, dear cook, Yvette wonders if you could make her some vegetarian soup."

Jerry backs out of the kitchen feigning deference. He's learned this living with Mom: drop the bomb, then retreat. Issues regarding the Easter eve dinner I'm cooking: not too much garlic, no onions, Mom doesn't particularly care for olives, and am I totally sure about the goat?

She and I are still barely speaking, scrupulously avoiding each other ever since the beach. Yvette is too busy lounging on the couch, I suppose, drinking her parting glass of rosé to come speak to me directly. Jerry's been appointed their emissary.

"Since when is Yvette a vegetarian!" I shout at his back. "Greg!"

He comes in scowling. "Dude. You don't have to yell."

"Well, this whole damn dinner is going to hell," I gripe, setting the baby kid racks on the counter to rest. Method: douse with olive oil, rub with herbes de Provence, roast in the oven. Done. They smell amazing. Too bad no one but Greg and I will eat them. "What's the big deal, it's just goat."

I hand him a spatula. "Here. Scoop up all the stuff around it. Apparently, no one wants it." The racks are surrounded by olives and peeled cloves of pickled garlic, onions, quarters of baby artichokes, and small, juicy tomatoes bursting through their split skins. "*Now* I've got to make Yvette soup."

"You don't *have* to do anything."

Greg puts an equal portion of steaming vegetables on each person's plate, Mom's, Jerry's, and Yvette's included. He points the spatula at a colander of boiled new potatoes draining in the sink. "Everyone gets some of those, too, right? What do I do to them? Butter? Salt? Pepper?"

"Here." I shove the dish of softened butter into his hands and dig through the pantry. There's spaghetti sauce: perfect. I dump it into a pot and top it off with water. Add a bag of frozen mixed vegetables. Throw it all on a high flame.

"There. Soup."

Greg snorts. "Fine. Your decision." He butters the potatoes.

"Right. Like I *ever* get to make a decision."

"What's your problem? Ever since the beach you've been acting real pissy, you know that?"

"I'm surprised you even noticed. You're the one who's been on self-imposed exile from me ever since we got down here."

"What's that supposed to mean?"

"It means, this whole trip you've been *gone*. I don't think you've even said three words to me. You're always off with Yvette, or off with Jerry, or off with Doobie, or off with the kids . . ."

"Dude, well, maybe that's because *you're* always *off* with your mother."

"Well, at least my mother cares about me." I grab a knife and slice the racks into meaty chops.

"Stop acting how you feel," he jeers. "Grow up."

"*You* grow up!" I fling chops onto plates. One slides across the dish on a slick of its own rosy juices. It flies through the air and lands on the kitchen floor with a wet smack. Perfect.

"Dude." Greg shakes his head in disgust.

"AND STOP CALLING ME DUDE!" I brandish the last chop overhead like a weapon. "I'M YOUR WIFE, NOT YOUR BUDDY!"

Suddenly it strikes me for what it is: incredibly, incredibly funny in a totally, totally pathetic way.

What, because Mom can't accept what I *know* is the truth—that I actually walked away from television of my own volition and for good, real reasons—now I'm going to beat him down with a goat chop?

I start laughing uncontrollably.

"I . . . was going to hit you . . . in the face!" I howl. I drop the menacing chop on the cutting board.

Greg watches, shocked. "Dude, did you just get a sense of humor?"

"Okay . . . seriously . . ." I struggle for breath. "You have *got* . . . to stop calling me dude."

Jerry peeks in the kitchen. "Everything okay in here?" he asks timidly.

Greg nods. I cover my face with a dishtowel and the spasms shake all the last uncertainty she'd sown right out of me. Silly Mama. I *love* Greg. I would give up a thousand jobs for Greg. But he didn't *make* me give up this one.

"Yeah. Uh, did Indy set the table yet?" Greg asks.

"I'll go see." Jerry retreats to supervise the final preparations.

"Jerome, ask Amy if she wants us to light the candles." I can hear Mom using her tight, wounded, I-haven't-yet-won-the-argument voice.

"Light the damn candles, Mom!"

I want my baby back. Three steps across the kitchen are not so many to have to take to wrap him in my arms myself. I'll keep fighting for him.

"Look, Greg. I have no idea what we're going to do when we get back home. We'll still be broke, I'll be fat, I need a job, we're going back to the bungalow . . . I am not even ready to think about it all yet. But if *that's* the real world, then *this,*" I squeeze him tight, "is just as real: They just don't know us there anymore. They haven't been here, Greg. But they're not going to believe in us if we don't believe in each other."

Are we . . . dancing? We sway a moment.

Then he kisses the top of my head, retrieves the errant chop from the floor, puts it back on its plate, and heads for the table. "Goat chops!" he cries. "Yummy!"

CHAPTER
28

TWO NIGHTS LATER, pale moonlight sparkles on the last patches of freshly fallen snow in Brianny, and Mom, Jerry, and Yvette are safely on a plane to San Diego.

It began falling the previous day, on Easter, as we sped homeward on the A7, the storm still beating us to Brianny. Yvette tried catching flakes on her tongue, yelling, "Good-bye, France!"

It's baffling how something that drifts so silently can be so loud underfoot in the predawn dark. Jerry and I loaded suitcases to a crunching like a twenty-one-gun salute. A fitting send-off to my family.

"You ready for this? You've never driven in snow before, have you, Amy?"

"I'll be fine."

"You always were the mouse that roared, kid."

Our achingly slow way to Charles de Gaulle was red-lit by a snowplow threatening to make us miss their flight. By the time we were curbside, there was barely time for them to grab their bags and race for the check-in. I only had seconds to make amends.

As she wheeled away her suitcase, I grabbed Mom by her fur coat. "'Every person possesses the family they deserve; that is to say, the family that they are appreciative enough to want.' Apologies to Root. I love you, Mama."

"Me, too," she said generously and kissed me good-bye. "We'll see you soon. Take good care of your sister."

But this morning's snow, like Provence, is now mostly a memory,

With *swooshes* and *thuds,* more slides off the roof. Wet piles will linger longest in the farmhouse's cold shadows.

Muffled through his T-shirt, my head on his chest, Greg's heartbeat sounds like the snow. "You know what I've been thinking? We haven't celebrated even once since we've been here, and we've been here almost eighty days. Why don't we do something?"

"You mean like a party?" He closes his book.

"Actually, I was thinking more like a sacrifice."

<hr />

BUT IN THE END, I couldn't kill the rabbit.

It fell to Greg to wield the paddle, and to me to cook the feast.

And later that night, full of *lapin à la moutarde* as we lugged Erin's mattress up the ladder into the loft above the office, I was still wondering *why* at the last minute I couldn't do it. Nerves? Cowardice? A lack of commitment to my declared principles?

"Seriously, babe, don't sweat it," he grunts, using his one free hand to try to shove the fifty-pound mattress off his head into the loft. I have the clean bedding at my feet, hands over my head, ready to bolt if the mattress starts to fall on me. "I figure it's like this. If we keep playing our cards right, you'll always have me around to do your dirty work for you."

CHAPTER
29

*T*HIS IS AN APPROPRIATE WAY TO RESPOND TO YOUR SISTER-IN-LAW going missing at four o'clock in the morning: panic.

This is *not*: laugh.

"She's *fine*." Greg stays in bed. On the cold floor, ear pressed to the baby monitor, mostly all I hear are static crackles from the kids' hotel room next door anyway. Periodically, Indy exhaling loudly and flopping over in bed, or Scarlett's *suck suck suck* on her pacifier. But no sound of Erin arriving home.

Greg starts to speak but I shush him emphatically—I thought I'd heard something.

Footfalls? Drunken belching? *Anything?* Please!

First I'd woken at two, and then again at three, each time in hyper-awareness of the near silence. How could Greg sleep? I elbowed him awake at four. "She's still out," I hissed, crawling from between the warm covers, and started this vigil, imagining all sorts of sordid fates befalling my temporary ward.

A little more about Erin: She is the only one in the family ever to have been arrested. Twice. For things like skateboarding. For all her pluck, though, over the weeks she's been with us she's proven that she is likely the most mild-mannered and easygoing of all our family. She is laid-back with the kids, a willing playmate, Greg's drinking buddy, a confidante for me. The farmhouse is 100 percent less lonely with her in it. Our lives in Brianny have been transformed.

But what Erin also has is this: an uncanny knack for being in the wrong place at the wrong time, which seems to make her a magnet for a disproportionate share of the world's hassles. Like getting arrested. Twice. For skateboarding. And who knows *what* is happening out there on the . . . well . . . not-so-mean streets of Le Puy-en-Velay.

Greg, of course, has kept watch with me cracking jokes about all the precarious situations she is probably getting into: robbed by a band of gypsies, captive in one of the New Age brookside yurts you can rent outside of town, hypothermic from skinny-dipping in the icy waters of the crystalline gorge. Le Puy could be Portland. Not a lot of hijinks going down in Portland.

I cling to Erin's promise that she was just going out to a bar.

Silence still; I guess I didn't hear anything. "She only had five euros! How do you stay out drinking until four in the morning on five euros?"

"Maybe she isn't drinking."

"*Not* funny."

Forlorn, I sit back on my heels and the monitor falls in my lap. I'm bone tired and unamused.

"You're going to have to go look for her, Greg. She doesn't even speak French. What if she needs help?"

"What? You're afraid she's going to get kumbaya'd to death by the hippies?"

We'd all noticed the scruffy pilgrims immediately when we drove into tree-fringed, bucolic Le Puy, arriving through lentil fields. Le Puy sits atop a dormant cinder cone high in the volcanic range that blasted the Massif Central into being a couple of million years ago. The lentils, *lentilles vertes du Puy,* have earned the town a culinary reputation. But the pilgrims make it famous.

I sigh wistfully. "Don't you kind of wish we could do it, too?"

Le Puy is a starting point for the Chemin de Saint-Jacques-de-Compostelle, the ancient meditative route to the spot in northern Spain where legend holds that the bones of Saint James—apostle, brother of

John—are buried. Looming over Le Puy, at the top of a steep path lined with rusty volcanic rock, like a red carpet to its stone porticos, is a fresco-adorned cathedral from whence pilgrims depart each morning after a ritual blessing. It takes them weeks or even months of walking to travel the distance to Galicia. Along the way, friendships are made, lovers are united, prayers are actualized. I want to walk to Spain! Specifically, at this moment, I want to do anything but brood in a hotel room over the fate of my sister. Truthfully, I'm not entirely certain whether I am actually worried about her, or just jealous. The pilgrims are merry-makers. No doubt she and the pilgrims are all merrymaking away into these wee starlit hours.

"I wouldn't mind being that young again," he says, though, actually, there were many grizzled walkers among them, with lighter and newer backpacks, sensible shoes, and slender aluminum hiking poles in place of purloined tree branches. The couples among them tenderly smeared sunscreen on each other, but on the whole they kept to themselves, as if aware that in contrast they looked old enough to have been among the original road walkers millennia before, though they emanated steely determination.

"It's *good* that your sister is out there! Remember when you were in Europe for the first time all by yourself?"

"She's *not* all by herself. She's with us."

"I know, poor thing." He smiles lasciviously. Pats the mattress beside him. "Come back to bed. We can keep each other awake."

But when I don't move away from the monitor—I'm frozen—he rises dutifully and pulls on his sweater, then sits for his shoes. Knees creaking as if I were about a hundred, I push myself up off the cold floor and rest my head on his shoulder. We stay like this for what feels like an eternity.

Finally the monitor lights start flashing along with the sounds of creaking stairs. "Oh, thank God," I breathe when we hear her stumble over her bags and swear colorfully under her breath.

"I'm home," she slurs in a loud whisper, for my benefit, obviously.

We crawl back under the covers and curl up tightly. I dream of pilgrims and a long and winding road.

⌒　○　⌒

IN THE MORNING, the cool air still holds the promise of bright, brilliant sunshine. Before we head out for the Saturday market, I tiptoe across the floor of the kids' room where Erin lies, still sleeping in a tangle of sheets and blankets, and scribble her a note.

Meet us at l'Écu d'Or for lunch, 1:00pm, I write. *The place next to the butcher.*

Then I creep back out and join Greg and the kids downstairs for buttery brioche and coffee.

⌒　○　⌒

THE PILGRIMS OUT ON THE STREET are outfitted with sleeping-bag-strung backpacks, thick boots, bota bags, and walking sticks. They look like modern minstrels, medieval creatures teleported into the future.

Their earnestness is almost palpable. It has texture like the nubby tweed coats and bright yarn hats and woolen scarves that a group of girls wears, dancing spontaneously, footloose on the black-stone-cobbled street. Flavor like the *saucisson,* bread, cheese, and wine another group shares for breakfast around the feet of a fellow guitar-strumming traveler.

Okay. The chances of this actually happening? Nil.

But if *ever* there were a market where a spontaneous song-and-dance number was likely to break out, the one sprawling all over the streets of Le Puy would definitely be it.

I can picture it clearly: the gargantuan, pink, hilltop Mary overlooking the town would give a finger-snapping *five, six, seven, eight!* and away the market would swing.

That guy in the red-and-black windbreaker, with the dark, tousled hair, selling floury hearth-baked bread and fat cylinders of blue-veined *fourme d'Ambert*? That's the guy. He'd slap out a rhythm on his hard-rinded cheeses, summon a deep bass note from the bread's hollows, and that guy next to him with the thick rounds of creamy Saint-Nectaire, you can just tell, he would join right in. *Thunka thunka thunka thunka thunk thunk thunk thunk.* Lordy! Just walking through the market I can *feel* their rhythm. It's better than a drum circle.

Coins in my pocket jangle like castanets and my feet are *moving*, shuffling around the market with minds of their own, dragging Greg and the kids with me from table to table. It's Django Reinhardt meets Manu Chao with a little funk thrown in on the chorus, irresistible even to the head-scarved, robe-wearing women gathered around a table of peppers and pumpkins. They keep glancing at me over their shoulders as if they're daring me to notice their toe-tapping.

But I see you, ladies.

Home-brewed bottles of beer would become wind instruments in the hands of a bearded young guy in a chunky hand-knit blue sweater. And wouldn't you know it? The old guys on the corner, the foragers with the dirt under their fingernails and a few precious baskets of morels and others of leafy greens, they would go all diggity James Brown when the mood overtook them, shaking and popping as if the mountain wind were blowing right through their bones.

The pilgrims would break out their accordions. It's a groove fest.

Scarlett grabs my hand urgently and we skip away from Indy and Greg, over the stones, past baskets of knobby carrots and potatoes and parsnips still dusted with dirt, past a veritable dredded dude in a fisherman sweater selling honey as silky and sweet as his lothario gaze, to where a bunch of cardboard boxes sit by the fountain, housing gray-pelted rabbits and cages of cooing doves and pigeons. Their heads bob in perfect rhythm with the cadence in my head.

Scarlett's peals of delight are more musical than the ringing church bells, brighter than the golden sunshine.

This is the best town *ever*.

ERIN MEETS US AT THE RESTAURANT WEARING SUNGLASSES, looking pale and a little rough, and she doesn't take off the glasses until we're inside and seated.

"Good night?" Greg teases.

She has a sleepy smile. "This place is *crazy*."

For lunch, Greg takes local lamb roasted in hay from the mountains, we order the kids two plates of chicken stewed in wine, and Erin and I have fresh trout, farmed, according to the menu, nearby, in the cold rushing waters of the *eaux du Vourzac*.

We've been led to l'Écu d'Or, and by extension to those fish, by something I will forever after think of as the Miracle of the Red Lollipop.

It goes something like this. Right before Erin arrived in France, and commencing on the exact day that my mother departed the country, a series of seemingly random events began to occur.

First, there was the snow, the fraught drive to Charles de Gaulle, and my emotional good-bye with Mom, so that by the time I returned to Brianny on the afternoon train, I was in desperate need of hot, gooey comfort food.

Which led me to Madame's cheese shop. Where I asked myself the following question: Considering that we were expected at Marc and Sophie's for dinner that night, what were the odds, if I made fondue for lunch, that they'd make fondue again for dinner?

Ask not *ever* this question. Not even Marc's antics could make that second fondue entirely pleasurable.

And then, a few days later, there was my Snail Party, an event with the Verlezes that I organized at the beseeching of Indy and Scarlett, the highlight of which was to be the eating of several dozen snails, using the tantalizing shells I'd bought in Chablis. I didn't kid myself: for the children, I made *bons bons escargots,* green-tinted marzipan stuffed into their shells for dessert. Scarlett helped me prepare the adults' dinner: morsels of canned snail from ATAC topped with copious amounts of my homemade snail butter.

And they were *awful.*

Well, not awful. According to Marc—odd. They were odd. A function of too much parsley and not enough garlic in the snail butter, which gave the snails a fresh, grassy flavor. They tasted not unpleasantly of a spring garden, but that association, rather than masking the somewhat intimidating thought of eating a garden snail, instead rather reinforced the idea that one was doing so. Greg choked down two and then called it quits. Sophie had five. I swallowed a half dozen and Marc—thank heavens for Marc—Marc gamely stomached the rest along with two full bottles of Irancy and then chided the rest of us for our temerity. "Now, let's go dig up the worms from the garden and eat those!"

Then, finally, the day before Erin arrived, the bunny.

So . . .

Am I to be forgiven for serving her naught but the meager bunny leftovers as her very first dinner in France? Or for requesting take-out Turkish from Semur for her very first lunch? How about for the series of pasta dinners and sandwich lunches that then ensued while for a couple of weeks I went to great lengths to avoid the kitchen, finally so tired of cooking and eating that the mere mention of another road trip had me marinating in food-phobic anxiety?

This was, I tell you, a troubled time. There I was, repudiating every principle I'd been arguing for. What was wrong with me?! Big, small, or whatever, whichever way I looked at France, there was *so much* left to eat!

Things could have gone on like that for quite some time, if not for

Erin. I wouldn't—I couldn't—let her down. The rural transition is a rough one, even in good weather. Quickly, I could see the same boredom that had once settled on me, settling in on her. A slow country day has about a thousand hours in it. Hop on a bike, as she did, borrowing Sophie's, and pedal as far as your legs can take you and still the scenery, if beautiful, remains . . . unvaried. Equally lovely. There are cows; where's an abbator when you need one?

The odd-looking alien plants pushing up through the soil were at least interesting. "Broccoli?" she guessed, returning home. "Colza," I told her, having just learned myself. "Rapeseed: for canola oil." "Never would have guessed," she replied.

She quit smoking and went through nicotine withdrawal but still summoned the humor to play circus in the yard. *And* earned a hundred euros' traveling money from Marc and Sophie by suffering through her dread of worms and planting a hundred baby trees along their property line in ground alive, as Marc had mentioned, with fat, wiggling earthworms.

The least I could do was head back to the office.

I brushed the dust off Root, opened the map, traced highways, and made reservations—and here we are. We're making a loop: from Le Puy down to Carcassonne, through Toulouse and the redbrick town of Albi (where Toulouse-Lautrec painted), and then back up again through the Auvergne village of Saint-Flour. It'll take us more than a week, our longest trip yet.

But about the Miracle.

Is this a shock? Every major French town has a major church or cathedral. It's a smart policy to visit them first. One, because they are usually splendid. Two, because then you can do other things and not feel bad about not visiting the splendid church. We climbed the hill to Le Puy's, unwittingly following in the footsteps of a Druidic woman who, nearly two thousand years before, burning with fever, had heeded a vision of the Virgin Mary and stumbled blindly but faithfully along the same path. At the top of the hill, where the cathedral now stands, just as she'd been promised, the Druid found a dolmen: an altar stone, black as night, the same miraculous stone that now lies just off the cathedral altar in its own darkened chapel.

The trusting grip of Scarlett's small fingers makes my heart flutter: when she consents to walk at all, she insists on holding hands. She regarded me curiously when I knelt down in front of the healing stone. "What are you doing, Mama?"

"Come here." I unzipped her pink jacket and lay it beside my bag.

"Like this?" She hoisted her polka-dotted dress, smoothed her woolen tights, and, sensing the seriousness of the event, solemnly got down on her knees. You're to close your eyes and place your hands and one cheek on the smooth, cool stone, just as the woman had. When the Druid arose, her fever had broken. The local priests heard the story and they called it a miracle.

No otherworldly voices, just the echoes of Erin's and Indy's and a bland humming like the ocean in a seashell. I was startled by the closeness of Scarlett's face when I opened my eyes, suddenly mere centimeters from mine. "I want a red lollipop."

"Okay," I chuckled. A classic two-year-old non sequitur. "Later."

After the cathedral, exploring, we found a pastry shop selling celadon-hued cookies made from lentil flour.

"Would you like some cookies instead, Scarlett?"

Such a face! Indy circled her, teasing. "Ha-ha, cookies, all you can have are cookies!" Oh, but it's a menace to have an older brother. "Why are you such a baby, Scarlett," he jeered.

"Shut up, Indy! Mom, I want a red lollipop!"

"Shut up, Indy," Greg warned. "So. Where are we eating dinner?"

As many times as we've repeated this scene, is it any wonder that we're both *tired* of food?

"Do we have to?" I groaned.

Lured by a handsome pilgrim, Erin went off on her own leaving us to a grumpy meal of ham-and-cheese crêpes made with the region's tangy

Cantal, a dinner I thought would make Indy, the cheese lover, happy, but no, the stinker. "I hate it." He slumped under the table.

"Eat your crêpe, Indy," Greg growled.

"I'm not going to."

"Eat your crêpe."

"No!"

When you're too burnt out to threaten, instead, offer rewards to the good child: more of my mother's parenting wisdom.

"Scarlett, do you want some ice cream for dessert?"

"No, Mama! I want a red lollipop!"

"All right!" The groovy pilgrims were staring. "Jiminy, Scarlett."

"What's with the lollipop?" Greg asked.

"I have no idea. She asked for one when were back at the church and I thought she'd forget about it. But apparently not."

"Where do we get a red lollipop?"

"Hell if I know."

But the most likely lollipop, I did know, had known, was at the *supermarché* near our hotel. I'll do nearly anything for my kids, but I'll be damned if I was going to tramp to the outskirts of the old town just for a sucker. (Thus had checked pastry shops. Little groceries. Even a kids' boutique. No lollipop.)

They make gorgeous sausages in the Auvergne—that rich, volcanic soil spent on dairy cow pastures and lentil fields, leaving the part of the protein in the region's cuisine to the pig. After dinner, I stopped to admire a butcher's window. Scarlett went nearly apoplectic.

"I. WANT. A. RED. LOLLIPOP!" she screamed, stamping her boots, smack in the middle of the road.

This was too much. "Scarlett!" I scolded her harshly. "That's enough! I *heard* you about the lollipop, but Mama does not know where to get one! Now, be a big girl."

"That guy's got one," Indy said, pointing.

I looked. Next door to the butcher, a chef in whites, apron tied around his waist, lounged in his restaurant doorway, indeed sucking on a bright, cherry-red lollipop. The awning of his restaurant read L'ÉCU D'OR.

While I watched, slack-jawed in disbelief, a boy and a girl about Indy's age came running down the street carrying an armful of baguettes. The chef greeted them with *bisous* and shooed them inside the restaurant. "Go see Maman."

"Madame!" he called to me.

Abashed, I rescued Scarlett from the street and walked forward. He retrieved two more red lollipops from his apron pocket. *"Pour les enfants."* He gestured back toward the swinging kitchen door through which his own two children had just disappeared. "I have the small ones, too," he said kindly.

I kid you not. Indy and Scarlett held *hands* on the way back to the hotel that night, sucking contentedly on their lollipops.

Tucking them into bed, I grabbed Greg's arm across Scarlett's pillow. "Tomorrow, *that's* where we eat."

A COOK'S LIFE ENDS UP IN HER FOOD, which can be either a blessing or a curse, depending on the life. When we leave Le Puy, for example, we'll travel south from the Auvergne through the Aveyron, where the colors bleach from the dark greens of conifers to the lichen tones of wind-swept knobby sheep pastures pocked with granite boulders, where from yawning caves big enough to house cathedrals emanates the tangy perfume of the Roquefort cheeses ripening within.

In the stark, streamlined kitchen at his restaurant in a glass building cantilevered over the landscape in the town of Laguiole, Michel Bras— one of the most celebrated French chefs of recent memory—puts his hushed, intense personality on every plate. The artistic mélange of tiny spring vegetables that is his signature dish, the *gargouillou,* tastes of meticulous care and meditative stillness. It's the food of a reclusive aesthete with no greater wish, it seems, than to be noiselessly in the kitchen.

Chef Joël's food at l'Écu d'Or looks and tastes happy, like food made by a man sporting an apron full of red lollipops.

The restaurant is loud with conversation and the din of laughter at lunchtime. If you lived in Le Puy, l'Écu d'Or would be your neighborhood restaurant, not necessarily the one you ate at every night, but probably the one where you'd take friends from out of town. Not fancy, although the ceiling's vaulted and the walls are frescoed with scenes from medieval mountain life. They're charmingly homespun, like the mural of a Mexican village that's painted on the wall of the taco shop where Greg and I had our first date.

L'Ecu's menu is inexpensive, the ingredients local. Greg's lamb comes from the butcher shop next door, a native race called the *noir de Velay,* a true black sheep. Chef Joël wraps it in a gauzy veil of hay and slow roasts it in a sealed cocotte. Sizzling bistro-style steaks stream out of his kitchen, each topped with a creamy slice of *bleu d'Auvergne.* Lentils are his popular side dish.

Erin divulges the gory details of her big night out so Greg and I can vicariously make merry with the pilgrims.

A flash of silver! Indiana's fork darts across my plate and snags a nugget of trout.

With upturned eyebrows I signal Greg, *Don't say anything.* He continues to help Scarlett with her chicken leg.

The bite goes in. Is considered. And accepted. The fork sneaks back to the trout. It's a beautiful fish: whole, its skin sautéed crispy golden brown, flesh the palest pink, floating on a delicious puddle of buttery, garlicky sauce. Indy smuggles a third mouthful. Then a fourth. And then I quietly slide my plate across the table and he finishes the entire thing, mops up the remaining sauce with a piece of bread like a *vrai* Frenchman, and reclines with a blissful sigh.

Erin's only half-finished her fish in the same amount of time. "You ate the whole thing? I can't believe it!"

"I didn't even care about the bones," he says, beaming.

It occurs to me then that ever since having kids, everything I've ever loved in my life, I seem to love just a little bit *more,* because of the fact that one day, Indy and Scarlett will get to discover these things, too.

It seems that we're all in this together now, and that, my friends, is a miracle.

CHAPTER 31

I**N CARCASSONE**, I'm woken by light rapping on the door. Our hotel is weird, if cheap, seemingly run by workers who appear at night like elves to the shoemaker, generating bills and slipping them under doors, setting out the complementary continental breakfast buffet in the lobby, straightening the magazines on the coffee table, and then disappearing before dawn. I have yet to see one during daylight hours.

Erin is in the hallway with her backpack on. "Hey," she murmurs. "I checked yesterday, and I can catch the train to Barcelona this morning. Do you mind? I just *really* want to go to Spain." She looks pained, as if she's afraid she'll hurt my feelings. She should know that she's not cheating on France, or on me or anything, by leaving the country.

"Of course not," I whisper. I leave the door open just a crack behind me so I don't wake Greg and step into the hallway. "What time is it?"

"Five. I couldn't sleep. The kids are cool, though. I was quiet."

"Go. Of course, go. I've never been, but I hear it's beautiful. How are you going to get home?"

Her shamefaced smile speaks clearly of her total lack of a plan. "I've got Marc and Sophie's money, though," she says by way of mollifying me. "And I took Spanish in high school. I bet I can catch a bus or something back to Montbard, right?"

Mom's going to kill me, I think, but nod and try to look positive. *Sure* she can catch a bus back to Montbard or something. *Whatever.* "E-mail me. Let me know where you want me to come get you. And when."

I get a cheek kiss then she strolls down the badly lit hallway to the stairs, waving. "Kiss the kids for me. And Greg. I love you guys. Bye!"

"Be safe!" I can't stop myself.

In bed, Greg chuckles into his pillow. "Well, we'll see how that goes, sister hen."

CARCASSONNE, its neighbor Castelnaudary, and Toulouse all claim cassoulet as their own native dish, but only Castelnaudary seems to have a chip on its shoulder about it. It proclaims itself the World Capital of Cassoulet and exerts an awful lot of energy reminding people that *its* recipe for cassoulet is probably the oldest. But that's likely because Castelnaudary, compared to Toulouse and Carcassonne, would never be considered the pretty city. Age before beauty, right? Carcassonne is the pretty one. Redbrick Toulouse, a university town, is the cool one. So by default, Castelnaudary is the one where you can cassoulet yourself right into a heart attack.

But lest a tourist forget to go there, it has set up an embassy within the UNESCO-acknowledged, drop-dead-gorgeous, fortified medieval section of Carcassonne. Aptly, it is called simply the Maison du Cassoulet. And there, you are assured, you can sample the *vrai cassoulet de Castelnaudary.*

As with bouillabaisse and fringe political movements, cassoulet inspires partisan bickering about its real constituents, with minor variations noted among the three towns that claim it. Which led me to believe that, in renewed eating due diligence, having abandoned all dignity anyway with regard to my tight-fitting clothes, I should try each of them.

And let me tell you . . . somewhere right around that third cassoulet, I no longer even came close to caring whether or not they were the same, different, *vrai, faux,* or sent to Earth on the wings of angels. Three cassoulets in three days is very nearly three too many.

"You are a masochist, you know," Greg heckles. He and the kids have foregone my number three in Toulouse in favor of a feather-light *croustade,* something like a torte, native to the region: layers of flaky pastry enclosing a filling, theirs of potatoes and baby spinach.

The weather is, as luck would *not* have it, balmy. Only eating in Carcassonne (two dishes: the Maison's Castelnaudary version *and* an, I presume, native Carcassonnian one) had the weather cooperated with a sufficiently cool drizzle. Cassoulet is a heavy, hearty meal, at bare minimum a robust stew of white beans—*lingots* or *tarbais,* generally—and various bits of pork cooked in a cone-shaped earthenware *cassole* until a crackling crust forms over the top. (Tradition dictates that during the slow cooking of the dish, the crust should be broken and stirred into the cassoulet exactly seven times. Or, I think hell freezes over.)

It's a favorite dish of Uncle DD's. It is also one of those rare, exceptional dishes that preserves well, even growing better with time, true to its origins as a peasant dish that was kept cooking continuously on the back burner or in a pot hung over the fire, refreshed whenever it ran low and more ingredients became available. (The French poet Anatole France once swore that the cassoulet at his favorite Paris restaurant had been cooking for twenty years.) DD always has a couple of cans of cassoulet in his cupboard in Paris, purchased on his biannual trips to the southwest, where his late wife was born, literally saved for a rainy day. Which is not to imply that you can only get cassoulet in the southwest: you can get it anywhere in France. It has entered the pantheon of national dishes. There are gastro versions and cheap versions, handmade and industrialized. I'll admit: during culinary school, I actually used to buy cheap canned cassoulet, one that was studded with fatty bits of pork belly but that was suspiciously lean on duck, at our corner grocer. And it was awesome.

On a blustery day savored with a glass of red *vin de pays d'Oc,* cassoulet is like a glowing, smoldering ember that warms the belly and suffuses the soul with well-being.

On a warm day, however, eating cassoulet is like swallowing a lead ingot.

"Any difference this time?" Greg quizzes.

I shake my head miserably, *no*. I feel ill. If you were to cut me, I'm afraid I would bleed beans and duck confit.

"I'm calling it," I'm forced to concede wretchedly. "Cassoulet . . . is cassoulet . . . is cassoulet."

DUCK CONFIT—which, according to Root, was originally a distinguishing characteristic of only the Toulouse version—is now, along with garlicky Toulouse sausages, a ubiquitous cassoulet ingredient.

And it may also be becoming the signature dish of the entire southwest of France. As in, The Dish You Can't Escape.

Here's the first thing that's odd about that, if you think about it: the notion that there even *is* a super-region called Southwestern France. Anti-monolithic Root never acknowledged one. Like a trawl net, that title scoops up everything on the French west coast from Bordeaux on down to the Basque country, then heads east over Gascony and through Languedoc and over to the border of Provence, and then goes up through Périgord and even sometimes snags a little corner of Aveyron and the Auvergne. Geographically, it grabs salt marshes and forests, a long strip of coast, the mountains of the Pyrenees, and at its heart, some lush, fertile lowlands, native homes to an astonishingly different variety of foods and traditions, butter-, oil-, and lard-based dishes all among them.

And the southwest is a cultural hodgepodge, too. Not even language is homogenous in the super-region. Not with the Occitan language in revival in some parts of the south, but not on the west coast, and with Euskara once again in use as the colloquial language for many Basques.

But ask someone to name a dish *de la sud-ouest*, or look in a cookbook (especially American ones) dedicated to southwestern French cookery, and there's a single common refrain: *confit de canard*.

Now, the dish itself has serious merit: I'm sure as hell not going to disparage it. You start with at least one whole duck—one with lots of fat on it, like a moulard, the same duck from which they pluck the fattened liver to make foie gras—and with a sharp knife you cut off the duck's thighs, keeping the legs intact. You strip the rest of the duck clean of its fat and skin, and then you render this down in a big pot until there is nothing left but cracklings and liquid fat. The legs are cured with salt and spices overnight and then they're poached slowly and gently in the duck's fat until the meat is so tender it looks like shredded stockings clinging to a bony bare leg. To serve—like cassoulet, it only gets better and better with age—it gets sizzled in a pan until the skin is crisp and the meat is heated through.

See? *Amazing.*

It's just the ubiquity of confit in the south that gets me. I mean, I guess I do get it. I just don't like it. It all goes along with the modern obsession with branding, right? Mass consumption of any product, including Southwestestern French Cooking™, requires that that product be clearly understood, and clearly, cleanly, and easily differentiated from its competitors—branded. It must be reliable, and it must conform to expectations over and over and over again. Honestly, would you really want to be the only restaurateur in Southwestern France who failed to put confit on his menu, knowing full well that every visitor who stepped off of a tour bus was expecting it? And was ready and willing to pay for it? Of course not. You'd be an idiot. But there's a give and a take implied here. In exchange for the recognition and the profits associated with mass consumption, the product agrees to this constrained, branded version of itself.

On the plus side, you can always find tasty, tasty duck confit in the south.

But on the downside, in some places, you just might not find much else.

CHAPTER
32

I AM MORE THAN READY TO LEAVE THE LAND OF CASSOULET and duck confit behind and remount the Massif Central. Destination, Saint-Flour.

And the farther north we drive, the more extreme the view outside my window becomes. The gentle fields in the southwest were already bright yellow with blooming colza, mirroring the sun. In the parks, lush leaves cast translucent emerald shadows. But north of Rodez, there's a startling moment when the landscape becomes gray and desolate, cold and lunar. It's the moment when it feels as if we've left the south far, far behind.

Then suddenly, around a bend, the colors reawaken riotously, so pretty that I gasp, even though the air is cooling quickly and it looks like rain. The road pitches steeply. The Kid labors with the grade. We drive past gorges and a river that's almost black, reflecting the wet sky above. Greg stops for a picture, and then we continue through hillsides mottled purple, brown, and deep green, past waving bare branches shrouded in scaly, pale green lichen.

The kids have a jerry-rigged setup to watch movies: a portable DVD player lashed to the back of Greg's seat. But they're too quiet, even for movie watching. I see mischief in their posture, heads together conspiratorially. An old high school friend of mine sends out regular online photo updates of her two kids, a boy and a girl who are nearly the exact same ages as Indy and Scarlett. They could *be* Indy and Scarlett except that they're always so clean! Her daughter's hair is always brushed, silky, and shiny and adorned with bows that match her outfits. And her son gets kitted out in attire befitting the particular occasion: preppy sweater vests for lunch with his grandparents, rock-star T-shirts for playdates, a suit and tie for synagogue on the holidays. The fact that neither boy nor girl is smeared or filthy or grimy is astonishing enough. But even more amazing is the way they interact: They cuddle. They preen. They form a mutual admiration society of two. Never once has my friend sent out a photo in which one has the other in a headlock, or one is crying because the other has just taken a favorite toy and smashed it to smithereens just because, or in which they stick their tongues out at each other and blow raspberries in unmitigated fury.

In Saint-Flour the drizzle becomes an outright downpour that Doobie at least has the good sense to avoid, refusing to leave the hotel room. We grab umbrellas. Scarlett, however, will listen to no reason. She splashes until she's soaked to the skin and blue with cold, and then she begins to cry.

"Pick me up, Dada!"

"I told you not to, Scarlett," he scolds.

"Mama!" she screams. I pretend she must be someone else's urchin child when she plops down on her rump in the sloshing gutter and starts kicking

But what else am I going to do, really. Leave her there? My poor clean coat, now covered in mud.

And no matter how fast or slow we walk, Indy is always a hundred yards behind us, hands thrust deep into his jacket pockets, head down.

Hot chocolate doesn't help. Pastries for *goûter* don't help.

And they both *hate* the museum, although Greg and I go a little nutty, the repressed urge to scream at them bursting forth in the form of unadulterated goofiness and probably an honest desire to embarrass them, like, a lot. The Auvergnats are descended from the Celts and on one floor, loud, raucous bagpipe music pipes over the speakers. He whirls me into an impromptu jig. "You should love this!" I yell over the music, madly twirling around the floor. Other than us, the museum is completely empty, drafty and echoing. "You guys are Celts from me and French from Dad, just like these people were!"

Indiana looks as if he'd like to melt into the floor. Scarlett? Scarlett's trying out big-girl undies for the first time. (She's been pleading for them ever since Lulu let slip that only *babies* wear diapers.) *She* walks into the corner, squats, and pees.

So back at the hotel, while Greg flips on the laptop and works, I strip off the kids' wet clothes, toss the undies in the garbage, give them both a hot bath, put a movie on the DVD player, and then lock them in their room.

I clump back down the hallway and flop beside Greg on the afghan-covered bed. (This hotel takes the cake, each room done up in high-grandmother style.)

Do they miss Erin? What's *up*?

I wouldn't be surprised if they do miss their playmate: I'm an awful substitute. In Albi we blew off steam on the playground while Greg Skyped in to a conference call. By now I've been to hundreds of play-grounds and I could have kissed the genius who encircled the play equipment of this one with a chain-link fence, and positioned benches all around the *outside* of its perimeter for all the worn-out grandmothers, nannies, and exhausted mothers. Not one of us ladies broke ranks. It was too perfect an excuse: "No, I *can't* play with you. See the fence? The grownups have to stay *outside*."

"I hate Mama."

"Me, too. I hate Mama." The traitorous, flashing baby monitor lights are throwing a party in honor of my baby girl's first betrayal. Greg closes the laptop with a soft click. I feel like I've been punched. We've each heard Indy say he hates us before: his five-year-old sense of injustice is sharp. But from Scarlett? This is heartbreak!

"She hates me?"

"They're tired." The laptop goes on the doily-topped bedside table and he nudges me onto my side to spoon. "They just want to go home. I hate you, too, a little, when you don't do what I want."

"Why don't they hate you?"

"Well, they love you more, so they hate you more."

"That's ridiculous," I sigh. "They don't love me any more than they love you."

"Sure they do. It comes with the territory, Mom. What would make this better?"

"Well, I can't have my child's innocence back, so . . . I don't know. A vacation? Why were things so much nicer in Le Puy?"

"Actually, I was thinking about tonight. Like for food."

"Tonight, that's easy. Can we go to the place with the sheep's feet? I read about those."

"Done. Now . . ."

· "But we could all use a vacation." Rolling away from him, I stretch for Root and the map on my side table and flip the switch on my tasseled reading lamp. "I've got to say, I'm not sure who's going to fall apart first: us or the Kid. Look at this place! Bordeaux, that'll be another long one. Dordogne. Perigord. Basque country . . . These are all, like, ten-hour drives, Greg."

"Hey . . ."

"Corsica! That would be a good vacation. And then we wouldn't be blowing off France, either."

"I'm starting to hate you now."

"Why?" I tease, folding up the map. Root gets tossed to the floor with the kids' dirty clothes.

"I need attention."

"I should go check on them . . ."

"Forget it. They hate you, remember? The monitor's on."

"Oh, right." I grin. "Then, will you make them be nice to me at dinner?"

"I will if you stop talking."

CHAPTER
33

Back home, at the cheese shop, an older woman rolls her eyes when she hears I've just returned from the Auvergne. "Oh, it's beautiful," she says dismissively, "but they eat *nothing* but *aligot,* morning, noon, and night!"

I have something like a confit flashback. "Well, actually . . ."

But I know. It's pointless.

But, oh . . . such a meal I could describe! That night in Saint-Flour we restored our family peace over dinner at Chez Geneviève.

"Do they have trout?" Indy asked hopefully.

And Lord, I would have killed for trout—*anything* to make him happy. But, no.

"Duck, then?" Yes! Confit with peaches for him it was, and me never, ever happier to see a duck leg.

The way in which a meal is eaten can itself be a form of reconciliation. Greg placed his charcuterie plate in the middle of the table so that Scarlett and I could both nibble on the *saucisson, rillettes* and *pâté de campagne,* and slices of *jambon d'Auvergne,* cured like prosciutto and served with a bracing dish of dried apricots and figs soaked in vinegar served alongside. When his duck came, Indy offered me the first bite, and Scarlett the second.

Madame is diplomatic. "Did you like the *aligot?*"

She has the fresh water-logged Cantal cheese curds used to make it, called *tomme,* in her cold case. "You can make it yourself," Monsieur suggests. He loves to cook. He briefly describes how to whip the *tomme* violently into piping-hot mashed potatoes until if falls away in long, gooey strands. My mouth waters. My memories of *aligot* will be savored for years, especially of how delighted the kids were when the waitress showed them how to wind the cheesy strands around their forks like spaghetti.

But the older woman clucks, "Morning, noon, and night!"

Haranguing respectable elderly women is a definite no-no in France, especially about their own native dishes, so I bite my tongue. But a variety of snarky responses come to mind anyway.

Oh, so you've never tried pounti, *then?* To call it pork bread pudding does it no favors, but that's essentially the dish: pork, shallots, garlic, Swiss chard, and prunes, sweet and savory all at once.

Or, delectable sheep's feet! Called *tripoux,* they were nothing like I'd expected. They were marbled like pancetta: the sheep's feet actually braised and shredded, mixed with ham, and then stuffed into the sheep's stomach, tied, and slowly braised again. Then the cook cut them in slices and sautéed the slices until they were crunchy and caramelized. They were served to me in a gratin dish with Saint-Flour golden lentils cooked in cream. *And you've never tried* tripoux?

Ten days is a long time to spend on the road, crammed into a *petit* car, sleeping in strange beds. That meal in Saint-Flour, every bit of it, *aligot* included, was like a benediction, so that after dinner, we did something rare for us. We went back to the hotel and without even changing from our clothes, fell asleep all in the same bed, legs and arms and bodies akimbo, cozy and cramped, my very own tribe.

"I *like aligot,*" is what I do finally say to the woman. That seems to say enough.

CHAPTER

~❧34❧~

In Brianny, April is a month of indecision. It is said of the weather, *en Avril, ne te découvre pas d'un fil,* which basically means, "Don't get your hopes up." It is the month notorious for breaking your heart—warmth and light giving way to gloom and gray without warning—and the month when the different personalities of the village are most obvious. Neighbors to the east and west of us are at odds about the future: Madame still hasn't pulled up her leeks but Monsieur Rideau has loosed his spring lambs into their pasture. Optimists go crazy, high on brilliant sunshine.

Geography is announced in wildflowers. Thankfully, so far the days are fine, but at night it rains, and rains, and rains. Wherever water pools and bogs, tall purple spikes lord it over the dainty buttercups and celery-leafed crow's-foot that spread elsewhere like a sunshine carpet. Borders are pocked by the first currants, which no one will eat, thanks to the fox.

The morning hours are a tapestry of sound: the lambs' insistent bleating, the jangling of cowbells, the rumble of tractors on the road, and a chorus of birdsong. I pull out my flip-flops for the first time in what feels like a century and decide to join the optimists. I waggle my toes at Erin in the kitchen. "Those are some seriously white feet," she snickers. In Barcelona, her bank account forced a decision: cigarettes or a bus ticket. She's making up for nicotine with coffee and snark. "But have you seen Greg's?" She points with fingers curled as if she's holding an imaginary cigarette. "I swear, his are purple."

He's lying in the grass surrounded by dainty yellow-belled coucous flowers, pants hiked up around his knobby knees, an old copy of *The Economist* over his face, warming himself like a corduroy-clad, sweater-swathed lizard. Or a gecko: Erin's right, his skin is so pale, it looks translucent. We need Corsica. I'll be glad to see him with a little color. Right now his pallor reminds me uncomfortably of sickbeds and the time before Scarlett was born when he drove through a red light with his seat belt—you guessed it—unbuckled, distracted by the doughnut he was eating, and ended up with a totaled car and a broken collarbone. I charged into the emergency room ready to give him hell, but wearing a hospital gown and hooked up to an IV, he'd looked so surprisingly frail, those pale, skinny legs splayed over the thin sheets, that rather than berate him, I'd held my big belly with one hand, twisting a long toe with the other, and wished that I could gather him up inside of me to protect him, too, the big, dumb idiot.

"Let's get some sun on those feet." Erin helps me carry the kitchen table into the yard. She sips coffee and pretends to smoke, I page through the mushroom identification guide Thierry, one of Marc's oldest friends, has lent me.

Thierry is terrifying.

Two grandfathers who'd been going after cêpes *for decades ate some in a carpaccio late one night while the rest of the family slept.* Bam! *Dead.*

Morels build up toxins in the liver. One taste too many and bam! *Dead.*

He successfully sprinkled the spores of mycophobia. I show Erin the illustration of *tricholoma equestre,* bright yellow with white spores and a large, furled cap, sometimes known as *chevaliers* or "man on horseback." "It's a killer, now," Thierry had said of it menacingly, tapping the book page like a rap sheet. "But it used to be a delicacy, reserved only for the knights. In the Middle Ages, the peasants were forbidden from eating them, so that *les chevaliers* could take the whole harvest. You could buy them at the *marché.* And then, *poof,* a few years ago, something happens. No one is sure what. Did it mutate? Is there something in the soil?

Seven *dead* in France from the *chevaliers*. *Eighty* dead in Poland. It was gruesome: like the entire course of MS running through the body in just five days. No antidote. The mycologists are still baffled, they don't know what happened. But they've changed its classification: killer." Thierry has been battling cancer and is gaunt like a veteran; lank pitch-black hair against skin paler than Greg's, watery sky blue eyes. ("Is he dying?" I asked Marc after Thierry left. "Not today," he replied.) Already he's lost his stomach and part of his liver to the disease, and he blames environmental contamination. He sees mushrooms, which clean and filter the soil, as canaries in the coal mine warning of the disaster we court by dumping pollutants on the Earth.

"Do *you* still eat mushrooms?" I'd asked.

Gravely, he nodded. Yes. "But the more you know, the less you eat."

"Thierry actually said there's probably an edible one called the *tricholome de Saint-Georges* in Marc's field right now," I tell Erin. I've nearly kept this uneasy news to myself. Knowing she and Greg, I've spared them the horror stories about amateurs and misidentification; don't share my nagging circular dilemma, like the bunny all over again: *I want to eat the mushrooms. But I'm afraid of the mushrooms. But I want to eat the mushrooms.*

(I did tell Sophie right away, though—technically, they're her mushrooms. "*Tricholome? Non, c'est inconnue.* I don't know them." *Inconnue*—unknown. It sounded so ominous in French.)

She's halfway to the kitchen to put on her boots.

"We don't have to go right now!"

"I'm in." Greg creeps through the delicate flowers and hands over his magazine. "There's still an hour or so before I get the kids. I've actually been thinking that we should learn more about wild food sources like this. You know, we might need it someday. *The Economist* is even talking about resources."

"Oh, really?"

"Uh-huh. Look at Marc and all his friends with their places out here in the country. Their . . . what does he call them? Their bolt holes. *They* know what's up."

"What's *up*?"

"Food and water. Because of global warming, the next civil wars will all be over food and water." He follows Erin into the kitchen.

I kick a path through the maddening jumble of boots in the doorway and finger them both from among the kitchen's shadows. "Erin, *you* should be more careful. And Greg, sometimes you are *so* French! So, to be ready for this post-apocalyptic, bolt-hole society where we will revert to hunting and gathering, we should potentially poison our entire family?"

"They're *not* poisonous; Thierry said they were edible." My stiff-sided market basket was retired above the stove. He hands it to Erin. "Are you angry?" He lacks Mom's skill to read that from amid wary, joking, and deathly serious; I'm a little of each.

"That's not the point. The point is, why do you always have to be Mister Doom and Gloom?" My other point is that with him so confident it'll be all right, I feel 100 percent capable of going after the mushrooms, but I won't tell *him* how much stock I put in his certainty: like heck will I give Frenchie and his conspiracy theories the satisfaction.

"You're the one who's afraid of the mushrooms," he laughs.

"I'm not afraid," I sputter. "I'm *cautious*. Geez, Greg, there's a difference. But all this other stuff . . . bolt holes and food and water . . . that's just . . ." I look to Erin for support.

"Crazy talk?" she offers.

"Yeah. Crazy talk," I say. "Thanks, Erin."

"I'm not reckless, either, by the way, Amy," she sulks.

"You went to Spain with basically no money and no way to get home!"

"Aha, but I *did* get home. Maybe you should live a little."

"Lecture me about taking risks when you've got kids, Erin."

"You guys gambled when you moved here *with* your kids . . ."

"Why does this bother you so much?" Greg rummages through the silverware drawer in search of my pocketknife.

"*Because!* Move." I get the knife from its hiding spot away from the kids in the sideboard and put it in my pocket. "Everybody, myself included, gives you all the credit for being the sensible one. And meanwhile, you're actually much riskier than I'll ever be, because you're a lone wolf. Both of you: lone wolves." I point to them each in turn. "You both do what you like because *you* are male, and *you* are still young and single. And I get stuck worrying about the consequences!" I storm out the door with my book.

"Where are you going?" Greg calls.

"Where do you think?" I holler, halfway to the fence. "Sometimes, *marriage* is like mushrooms," I grumble to myself. "The more you know, the less you want to eat."

With no clear idea of what we're looking for—Thierry said the mushrooms grow in fairy rings . . . What's a fairy ring?—we split in three: Greg works the upper field. Erin scours the fence line. I head for the bog by the creek. How much wetter it is down here since we were last on the swing! Flip-flops are folly now, unless you like muck and stinging nettle welts. And, I'm harrassed by skittering spiders and fat, oozy, red slugs. I assumed mushrooms would require moist conditions. But it's more like primordial soup down here.

"Up here!" Greg calls.

If you're lucky enough ever to hunt the *tricholome,* here's how to spot the ring: look for the puffy raised doughnuts of thick-growing grass. As soon as your eyes are open to them, they pop out of the landscape. Once summoned by Greg, I see two and Erin spots a third near her baby trees. The mushrooms hide in crowded clusters down in the darkness along the ring's outer edge. They're fawn colored and smell, as Thierry said they *must,* precisely like flour. "What does flour smell like?" Erin asks, not a baker.

"Like this."

"But then what does *this* smell like?"

"Erin . . ."

Always, always, always get wild mushrooms verified! We drive our basket to Vitteaux, dozens and dozens of mushrooms and that leaves hundreds of full-size and baby ones still growing. The rings spread and sprout annually. Eight feet across, these are old. It's an embarrassment of riches.

"*Sans souci,*" the handsome pharmacist assures me: no worries.

"*Sans souci*? Because I've got a lot of *soucis.*"

"No. *Sans souci.* No doubt at all. *Mousseron.* You have *very* good luck." His two female colleagues pluck mushrooms from our basket and sniff them as if they were delicate perfume samples.

"I thought they were the *tricholome de Saint-Georges.*"

"Oui. *Mousseron: Tricholome de Saint-Georges.* The same thing." He compares the entry in my verification guide to his. "Floury scent: most important identifying characteristic. But also, there's not so many other mushrooms right now. *Very* good eating. Where did you find them?" His eyes glitter rapaciously.

The women laugh. "Don't tell!" one warns.

"They're very rare now," the pharmacist concedes. "When the fields are treated for weeds, *alors,* it kills everything else, too. But if you invite me to enjoy them, I'll bring a good bottle of wine!"

～ ◡ ～

AT HOME, the word spreads quickly: the ingenue fungi is a culinary celebrity! Sophie calls and chastises Thierry immediately: he's such a scientist! "I didn't know the *tricholome.* But *mousseron,* Thierry, I know very well!" He can only nibble, but Thierry, the self-sacrificing vanguard, will be guest of honor at dinner.

Marc knows the mushrooms from his old days in the Ritz dining room. "The Ritz!" he booms. "In my own field! We're kings again!"

Here is the regal meal: wild mushrooms, sautéed and sprinkled with a little Camargue sea salt dusted with ground pepper, served over buttered noodles. Three ingredients (without counting seasoning). Thirty minutes (the bulk of it spent slicing). And like many of life's best pleasures, essentially free.

"To the marriage of knowledge, property, and labor," Marc intones.

"To reckless abandon!" Erin cheers.

"To life," urges Thierry.

"To Marky," says Sophie.

"To the cook." Greg lifts his glass.

"To marriage," I conclude. "It's like mushrooms: when you find a good one, dig in."

S CARLETT TROTS DOWN THE STAIRS WEARING nothing but her pink
boots and brand-new big-girl panties and hands me her pacifier.
"Here, Mama," she says and runs out the door yelling, "Me! Me! Wait
for me!" She grabs Lulu's hand—she's only half her height but just as
quick—and together they run screaming across the yard, dodging the
spray from Indy's, Joseph's, and Julien's squirt guns.

I put her pacifier in a dish on the sideboard, ready for bedtime, but
she never actually asks me for it again.

It seems the longer the days grow, lilac twilight stretching later and
later into the evening, the faster they fly. There are only eighty days left
of the trip, and then seventy. Then sixty-five. There's a food festival in
Saulieu and a medieval fair in Semur, and all over the country there are
vide greniers—"empty the attic"—communal garage sales, whole villages' worth of knickknacks and treasures and junk, all put out on the
street and sold for a pittance.

And I would adore them if it weren't for the fact that every object Greg
sees is introduced in exactly the same manner: "What do you think?
Could we use this back home?"

Eventually, the *vide greniers* themselves become fodder for more
back-at-home talk. "What do you think? Maybe, *back at home,* we could
start a shop and you could come here every summer and shop the sales?"

Even Erin is eager for home. She has a summer job lined up. She'll
be living in a tent and cataloging plants in the desert (where there are no
worms), which is her idea of paradise, and she's itching to leave. I catch

her red circling the day of her departure on her calendar. She leaves right after we get back from Corsica, and we leave for Corsica in just three weeks . . . Then two weeks . . .

The schools are sending home materials about commencement at the end of June, even though it's only May.

Marc and Sophie have a regular stream of weekend visitors and dinner parties and the villagers have started the rumor mill back up again about their purported activities. "They think we have orgies!" Marc bellows. "Because of all the candles."

Trucks moving snowy cattle to summer pastures rattle by on the road. The colza is harvested and the wheat is growing quickly, the fields turning from celadon to turquoise to amber as the shafts thicken and multiply and wave and finally droop under their own weight and the influence of the long, warm days. Blood-red poppies spring up everywhere. Because they're her daddy's favorites, Scarlett gathers them and puts them in dishes and cups and vases and bowls. The farmhouse looks like it is bedecked for a wedding.

The lambs are loud, the chickens are boisterous, the cows are contented, the children are wild, the rabbits are multiplying, the mushrooms are eaten, the red currants are ripening, the grass grows higher and higher and higher . . .

It's enough to make me just want to go stand in the yard and yell, "STOP IT! JUST STOP IT RIGHT NOW!"

Because—the irony—I, who was once afraid to stay, am now actually afraid to leave.

S OON THERE IS JUST ONE LAST THING STANDING BETWEEN US and Corsica: Normandy.

And obviously I mean that in a figurative sense—time-wise, and not geographically—because Normandy is just right there on the other side of Paris. Normandy has always been within the comfortable radius of a weekend trip, but I have postponed visiting it for months and months, always wondering whether and when someone was going to call me on it. And I have put it off for the oddest of reasons:

Madame Bovary.

I knew her story before I ever read the book: a naïve young woman marries a provincial doctor, is tormented by the suffocating banalities of marriage and motherhood, has a torrid affair, and dies a slow and sordid death after swallowing a measure of arsenic. She lived in Normandy. The book is all fragrant landscapes and missed opportunities and the absolute, exquisite anguish of wanting *more* but being confined by the circumstances of one's life.

I finally read it for the first time in December, just before we left for France. Actually, first I picked it up, and then I put it down. And then I picked it up and put it back down again, and finally I just said *fine* and read the whole thing start to finish and when I was done, I put it high, high up at the top of our bookshelf where I wouldn't even be able to see it anymore. I gave Indy and Scarlett each a great big kiss, and then I told myself, "I do *not* want to go to Normandy."

Leave it to Marc to find the macabre reason that finally entices me to go.

"Surely, you've heard about the ducks?" he says.

I had heard about the ducks. Here is what Root wrote: "The usual method of killing poultry in France is to bleed it; but in the Rouen region, ducks are strangled."

Marc drops down into what looks like a three-point stance, and then quickly leaps back up, wrangling an imaginary duck that appears to struggle and fight valiantly as he suffocates it under his arm and, for some unknown reason, gives it what looks like a noogie.

The most famous restaurant in the world serving *canard à la rouennaise*, also known as *canard au sang*—or, duck in blood—is actually *not* in Normandy, but in Paris, where the Tour d'Argent has been serving serially-numbered ducks since 1890. Even though I've read how they were killed, it had never occurred to me before Marc's graphic demonstration to imagine the duck's actual death. The implication that the Tour d'Argent gives is that the death is very quick—in fact, that perhaps the ducks don't even die until the very minute you order one. (Which summons a vision of a waiter carrying the order *cum* death sentence into some shadowy back room where dozens of ducks await, quacking and quivering; dispassionately pulling on a pair of black gloves; picking his mark; and then squeezing the living daylights out of it.)

"You should definitely taste it now." Marc loosens his grip and lets the imaginary duck go. "Who knows how much longer before the activists say you can't strangle a duck."

There is a point to the suffocation: it isn't just wanton cruelty. And it comes with another legend.

Legend holds that a long time ago in the village of Duclair, north of Rouen, across the river from the waterfront town of Dieppe (which isn't famous for duck, but rather for seafood, especially dishes made with sole, ray, and mussels), a little girl was taking her ducks to market in a boat.

And, that during her crossing, one of her ducks was accidentally strangled. (This sounds suspiciously like a story Scarlett would tell: "What happened to the duck?" "I don't know, but it was an *accident*.") So that the duck wasn't wasted, the mother cooked it anyway, and low and behold discovered that the duck had a delicious, rich, gamey taste, almost like wild duck, because during its last moments of probable panic, as its life was being snuffed away, its heart beat very quickly, rushing blood deep into every last fiber of its muscles and infusing it with flavor.

By now, I'm not squeamish about methods of killing. The reality of meat is this: something dies. And I'm not convinced that waiting in a queue of quacking, flapping ducks to have your head cut off is any more terrifying than waiting in a queue of quacking, flapping ducks to have someone grab you and throw you into a headlock.

All the same, if it's going to die a rather violent death on my behalf, I would at least like to be able to enjoy it.

But in Rouen at La Couronne—the second most famous restaurant in the world serving *canard à la rouennaise*—I'm having a problem because, (a) it's date night (Erin is babysitting at the hotel), and (b) I feel like a sausage wrapped in a Rorschach test.

Oh, date night! Why do you have to introduce such pressure? And such longing? And such expectation? Why have you compelled me to squish myself into a dress I haven't even thought about since I packed it seventeen weeks and twenty pounds ago, back when I could still fit into all of my pants?

Julia Child recounts that she stood outside La Couronne and fretted that she didn't look chic enough to venture inside. I've got that, too. Especially since it's a fancy dining room, replete with hanging tapestries, heavy silverware, rose-hued tablecloths, waiters in the waiter versions of tuxedos, ducks spit-roasting over a roaring fire, and a couple of women in strapless cocktail dresses who are unnerving me, wandering the room smiling beatifically at really nothing in particular.

And our waiter isn't helping things any, either.

First there is the issue of wine.

He asks Greg for the order, of course, not me. "A demi bottle of Gewürztraminer," Greg responds, sliding the wine list across the table. I should mention that the demi bottle of Gewürztraminer is one of the cheapest bottles on the menu. I should also mention that the duck dish, served for a minimum of two people, is fifty euros apiece.

The waiter cocks his head and raises an eyebrow, as if maybe he hasn't heard Greg correctly. "The demi?"

"The demi. Of Gewürztraminer."

This isn't just the economical choice. *Canard à la rouennaise* is a very rich dish, a primary component of it being its sauce, which in general resembles a bordelaise sauce: shallots and a bottle or so of Bordeaux reduced, then blended with rich duck stock. The *rouennaise* sauce is then thickened, like a civet, with the duck's blood—pressed from its carcass midway through the roasting—and a purée of its liver. One philosophy of wine pairing is to drink a wine that is similar to the dish, especially when the dish is made with wine. And for that express purpose, no doubt, there are many fine bottles of Bordeaux on the restaurant's list, many in the range of a hundred euros. The waiter seems eager that we choose one of those fine vintages.

But another philosophy of wine pairing is that you should drink a wine that is *opposite* in character to the dish.

Gewürztraminer = sweet and acidic.

Duck = savory and rich.

So there, waiter.

Then there is the duck itself.

Its strangulation is a private affair, but the rest of the duck's preparation is billed as a peepshow, a showy dining-room spectacle that has even spawned its own organization: the Ordre des Canardiers. The *canardiers,* our waiter among their number, boast their own coat of arms— a duck, dancing across a field trailing a banner on which is emblazoned the instrument of its eventual dismemberment, the gleaming silver press.

By my own casual survey of the dining room—ourselves, two families out celebrating, and two other couples possibly also having date night—many if not most of us have taken the duck. It is, after all, the specialty of the house . . . and of the town . . . and of the region.

But the waiter, who has snootily ignored Greg and me since plunking our demi in a tableside ice bucket, re-enters the dining room from the kitchen carrying precisely *one* duck on a silver platter.

It is a very nicely roasted duck by all appearances, the skin already golden brown although the recipe requires that the duck be roasted for no more than twenty minutes before the breasts are removed and served as the first course. Greg and I and everyone else in the dining room watch in rapt attention as he places the platter on a white-draped table set next to the fire. With a flourish, he picks up a thin-bladed knife and flicks it along the wishbone, untethering the breasts. Then he runs the blade along both sides of the sternum and flips the knife so that the blade is flat and runs it, expertly, just under the skin, taking it off in two long, perfect ribbons. He removes the two blushing breasts and places them on a plate that is whisked away to the kitchen. The legs and the wings are sent away separately for finishing. He cracks the backbone and reaches within the carcass to retrieve the liver, which he places on a third plate.

And then comes the Big Dramatic Moment.

The whole room holds its breath.

The press looks like a nutcracker, or like a vise, cast in silver. The carcass goes inside the press and he slowly turns the screw.

At the table next to ours, a family is having dinner with their blind, elderly grandfather. "What's he doing now?!" he yells excitedly before his granddaughter can shush him.

When the carcass is pressed, a great gush of bright red blood comes flowing from the spigot onto the silver platter. And then, for extra flair (and flavor), the waiter douses it with a glass of Cognac and sets the whole thing on fire. There is an audible collective gasp.

"What's he doing now?!" the grandfather shouts again.

The waiter finishes the sauce by ladling it with stock and the wine reduction and then he and the dish disappear into the kitchen. *Uh, thank ya. Thank ya very much.*

Soon after, our plates with the breasts arrive and we tuck in. Greg chews thoughtfully and looks up, anxious for my reaction.

The sauce really is quite delicious. Blood in a sauce adds an undeniable level of thrill. The flavor is so dark, so like iron, that it tastes forbidden.

But *under* my sauce, rather than a rare, plump breast, what I have instead is a tangle of sinewy tenders. I pick at them with my fork. I have never understood why those strands of breast meat, the ones connected to the back of the breast by a tough, chewy bit of tendon, are even called tenders. (In French they are called *aiglets.*) I also don't understand why I have about five of them on my plate. There is no duck alive with breasts consisting of five tenders. Basically, I have no breast. I have the remnants of the breasts of about two and a half ducks.

"What's yours like?"

He digs through his sauce and comes up with a bit of actual breast meat and several more of the fibrous tenders. "But," he reconciles, "the sauce is outstanding."

I'm disappointed. And I *look* disappointed. The older and the blonder of the two women appears alongside our table. *"Ça va?"* she asks brightly. "It's very special, this sauce," she says in heavily accented English. She must think I don't like it. *Hah!* I want to tell her. *You're speaking to a woman who has eaten a baby calf's face, lady! Pig butt! Chicken hearts! I am entirely undaunted by a blood sauce.*

But unwilling to make a scene on date night, instead I grumble, *"Ça va."* She wanders elsewhere to spread more sunshine around the dining room.

"Do you want me to say something?"

"No. It's all right." I do my best to eat around the chewy bits.

Then the second course arrives.

La Courrone's duck recipe is younger than that of the Tour d'Argent, and it descends from an innovation of one Henri Denise, former head chef of the Hôtel de Dieppe. Back in the 1920s, Chef Denise began serving the duck's legs, thighs, and wings as a second course, grilled and coated with mustard and bread crumbs. And because his hotel was across the river from Duclair, home of that first strangled duck, the *canardiers* decided to recognize his recipe, and thus La Couronne's, as the official ancillary of *canard à la rouennaise*. (Which would probably cause the Tour d'Argent no end of grief it wasn't for the fact that they've sold, in just over a century, more than one million of their own ducks.)

This time, it's Greg turn to be miffed.

If there's a thigh on his plate, he can't find it. Instead, his plate boasts more wings than a choir of angels.

The waiter has never again appeared in the dining room to work his mojo with the press, giving lie to the conceit that each duck is made to order for a pair of diners, regardless of whether or not they force you to order—and pay for it—that way.

"You know what they're doing back there?" I kvetch. "There's just a big old jumble of duck parts on baking sheets and a big old vat of sauce."

Greg can't cut his wings, either. He tries with his knife but they scoot around the plate, sending lettuce leaves flying. (I wouldn't call it salad because there doesn't seem to be any dressing.) He picks up a wing with his fingers and nibbles on it as if he were at a tailgate party. I have a leg and possibly part of a thigh and a wing, and the bread crumbs on all three are greasy and limp.

"They're fucking with date night," Greg says ominously.

Grandpa starts wheezing and coughing. He also begins shouting for the waiter, who finally stands stiffly tableside while the granddaughter grimaces apologetically and looks embarrassed.

"The duck!" the grandfather shouts. He must be hard of hearing, too. "Where did it start? Here or the Tour d'Argent?"

The waiter turns on his heel and is walking away before the word is even out of his lips. It's spat over his shoulder: "Here."

We walk home through the market square where a cross towers at the spot where Joan of Arc was martyred in 1431. Greg remembers that I mentioned Julia Child ate her first ever French meal at La Couronne.

"Did Julia have the duck?" he asks.

"The minx. Nope. As always, Julia knew best. No duck; she had the fish."

From Rouen we drive north along the coast to Honfleur. And since things will end there rather abruptly, before I move on, I want to say a word in Rouen's defense, lest my impression of La Couronne imply that the whole town—monuments, restaurants, et cetera—was just one big tourist trap.

We found a remarkable street in Rouen far away from the tourist train and the cathedral and the museum and even the central *marché*. It was a pedestrian street with lots of strollers, and down its side, a shallow channel, crossed by footbridges, flowed with clear water. But most remarkably, there was a café there, Le Son du Cor, with a crowded outdoor terrace fronting a pétanque court. Indy and Scarlett stood timidly along its edge, watching the flying balls.

On two of the courts, the prototypical old men in the prototypical windbreakers wearing the prototypical woolen caps tossed the *boules*. But on the third court, there were two young guys with tattoos, eyebrow piercings, and beards braided and strung with silver beads . . . *and a woman*. A young one, in Converse, a black tank top, and skinny gray jeans.

We watched them all for a while. Periodically the old guys would insult the young ones' game and then the young ones would say that they hoped the old guys didn't die of a *crise de coeur* or anything and then, right in the middle of it all, the woman's toddler came toddling across the court and she picked him up and put him on her hip *and kept right on playing*.

And considering how afraid I am that when we go home I'll just revert right back into mind-numbing mommydom—except that suddenly my kids are growing up and growing independent and growing out of their pacifiers and diapers and food aversions and getting ready to lose first teeth and soon might not even *need* their stay-at-home mommy anymore, and *then* what am I supposed to do?—the sight of her made me shiver proudly, as if she were a sister, or a sign, or a saint.

"Maybe we could live here."

But Greg smiled, sat down at a table, and ordered a glass of cider. "Nah. This isn't real life, remember?"

~ ❡ ~

COULD ANY REAL LIFE EXIST IN HONFLEUR? Hard to tell.

Although I'll give you that my first impression may have been stilted, due to the fact that it arrived all in a rush in the middle of being almost sandwiched between two tourist buses. Like most other old French city centers, the heart of Honfleur is a mess of one-way streets. "Look out!" Erin shouted, and I yelled "Greg!" and Indy hollered "Dad!"—all of us at the same time—and then the brakes squealed and we braced for impact while the Kid slid to a screeching stop between two massive coaches with signs on their sides declaring VACANCES EN SOLEIL!

But conveniently, we had all stopped in front of our hotel.

My second impression was that these buses were spewing forth pasty people. My third was that these people were disproportionately British. And my fourth was that a disproportionate number of these people were women with the kind of quirky hairdos that I'm afraid I'll someday succumb to, too. The kinds that are the result of walking into your hairdresser's and saying, "I feel old. Can you give me something that's a little spunky?" And the next thing you know, you've got a magenta buzz cut.

Our hotel is a short walk from the Vieux Bassin and so my fifth impression confirms what Sophie had already told me about Honfleur: it is gorgeous. The *bassin,* which is the old port, looks much less like a port and much more like a Dorothy Draper–designed nautical scene, very overblown and cinematic, like an overly large, perfectly rectangular swimming pool surrounded by colorful, tall, narrow buildings strewn with flags, reflected on the glittering water's surface. Even Scarlett and Indy are obviously impressed by it, and usually all they notice is whether or not there's a merry-go-round. (There is.) The basin is ringed by bobbing boats with names like *Chérie* and *l'Amour* and at its far short end, wide stone steps descend into the water. That's where Indy and Scarlett plop themselves down with ice cream cones and simply stare, mesmerized. (Or, possibly, tired.)

All around the basin are waterfront terraces shaded by brightly colored awnings. "We'll meet you guys at the carousel, okay?" I take Erin to have a quick look around.

Menus mounted on sandwich board dot the sidewalk. They are unfailingly uniform: four side-by-side panels, one in French, one in English, one in German, and one in Italian, the national flags of each language group emblazoned across the top as visual aid. I stop and read the first one slowly. When I finish, Erin is four tents down, reading another. "What do they have?" I ask.

"Mussels," she answers. "What did they have there?"

"Mussels."

We move on to the next menu: mussels.

We circle the basin faster as we learn to speed-read: *Moules. Moules. Moules.*

Greg's and my British friends, Karen and Sebastian, lived in Paris when we did, but eventually moved home to London. They were always keen to buy a French summer house and eventually did in Brittany on the northwestern coast. I told Karen I thought Brittany was a surprising choice for them, considering that it's rather cold and damp and windy there all year round. So . . . like England. "Well, we considered Normandy." England and Normandy's tumultuous past stems from cross-channel proximity. "But you can only eat so many *moules frites*."

Mussels are one of my very favorite dishes, and I'm not indisposed to cooking them in creative ways. The basic *moules* recipe is to take the shellfish (and Normandy has an excellent native species called the Trouville), scrub them well, and just before cooking, relieve them of their stringy beards. Then add them to a pot of sautéed shallots and garlic in good butter. (Normandy boasts *beurre d'Isigny*, which is naturally sweet-salty from the cows' salt marsh pasturage.) You pour over white wine, add herbs, and close the lid, and let the mussels cook in the fragrant steam. With their dying breath they open their shells and release their ocean juices, making a pot elixir that is equal parts vineyard and seashore. And since their basic flavors are iodine and sweetness, they pair well with other flavors.

And yet . . .

I fish for a pen and a piece of paper. "We *have* to write this down for Greg." We backtrack a few restaurants. Erin reads and I record:

Moules au basilic
Moules au l'estragon
Moules à curry
Moules au cidre fermier
Moules au Calvados
Moules crème, ciboulette
Moules aux poireaux
Moules Roquefort
Moules marinières
Moules Provençales
Moules crème à l'ail
Moules à la moutarde

And then, finally, since Normandy *is* the home of the granddaddy of all French cheeses:

Moules Camembert

"That's it. I've seen enough."

It's nearing lunchtime and the waterfront grows crowded with folks ready for their obligatory mussels. Erin and I swim against the tide counterclockwise toward the merry-go-round, the crowd doing as we had done, stopping eagerly at each menu. *Why do they even bother? Isn't it painfully obvious what they're going to eat?*

"Honfleur seems like the kind of place where you'd bring the person you were having an affair with," Erin observes. "Like, have you ever read *Madame Bovary?*"

We're supposed to stay in Honfleur for three nights. But we check out the next morning.

CHAPTER
38

"**Y**OU'RE ABSOLUTELY, totally positive you don't want to come with us to Corsica?" I ask Erin three days later. She's catching a bus north in Dijon. Dressed in turquoise-and-green silky harem pants and a bright yellow T-shirt emblazoned with a picture of Bob Marley, she looks ready to do some damage.

"Amy . . . Amsterdam. But have a great time at the beach. I'll be careful, I promise."

"Don't do anything I wouldn't do!" She drags her backpack and duffel into the crowded bus station. "We'll see you when we get back! I love you!" She waves good-bye over her shoulder.

YOU KNOW HOW THE GRAND CANYON IS BEAUTIFUL? Majestic? Heavenly? *Grand?*

Well, now take the Grand Canyon and invert it. Turn it inside out and push it up and up and out and surround it with a sparkly turquoise sea: ridiculously tall mountains ragged and red, draped in the tallest trees you've ever seen, with gorges running every which way through them and roads like roller coasters with herds of cows and droves of pigs all blasé-like wandering in the middle of traffic, just daring you to hit them . . . and that's Corsica. It is the most sublime place I have ever seen, beholden to no one, wild as all get out. I was bewitched, standing on the deck of the Marseilles car ferry as we sailed into the Ajaccio harbor. Corsica is the kind of place people are still *dying* to protect. Not that I'm advocating this—*at all*—but do you know what the Corsicans did when a McDonald's tried to open on their island back in the 1990s? They blew it up. There's *still* no McDo on Corsica.

There are beaches. Red-rock calanques. Pirate coves. Hiking trails. Museums. Monuments. Pristine forests. Food. Greg has to keep reminding me: "Amy, this is our *vacation*."

AND THEN, wouldn't you know it? It starts raining.

And raining.

And raining.

Once he gets the Internet to work—it requires a cell phone, a jerry-rigged antenna, Uncle DD's land line in Paris, and several fraught phone calls to our Ajaccio-based service provider—Greg checks the weather forecast. He mumbles something that sounds a lot like *several days*. I go up and down the slick tile stairs of our tiny mountain rental, looking unsuccessfully for things like extra sheets or extra towels. Everything in the house is damp. Which will be murder on the kids. They've come here already looking busted—rashes, intestinal issues. My plan to practice California medicine and heal them with sunshine looks screwed. It's *freezing*. I've wrapped them in one of my sundresses for extra warmth.

"What?" I call over the stair railing.

"It's going to rain for the next several days," Greg says distinctly.

"*No*. That couldn't happen to us."

Even the town's plumbing eventually surrenders to the Biblical-type rain. Headline-news-in-Paris-type rain. People back home hearing we're under water and sending sympathetic e-mails marveling that we "just can't catch a break" type rain. "Hurry home," writes Mom. "It's gorgeous in San Diego!"

The kids just want to watch cartoons, and Greg has to work, so I take refuge in Madame Ceccaldi's regional shop, which is the right kind of place to be on a wet, miserable afternoon. Itself it's a little dark and dreary but the foodstuffs are a good distraction: everything made somewhere and by someone nearby, liminal touchstones. Madame Ceccaldi's husband raises pigs in the village chestnut grove. What's that like? He makes all her chárcuterie: *lonzu,* smoked and dried pork loin; marbled *coppa;* whispy *prizutti,* like prosciutto. Corsican honey will taste like the same dense, fragrant *maquis* used as cover by bandits and nationalist militants. How interesting. And when you say you're "eating out of the drawer" in Corsica, it means you're economizing, subsisting on chestnuts, chestnuts being to a Corsican what rice is to the Japanese.

Every few minutes, there's the hiss and sizzle of wet wheels on the road outside and then another wave of slicker-clad visitors washes into the shop shaking their umbrellas, released from a tour bus to buy souvenirs. Evisa, where we're staying, gets a lot of traffic. There are only a handful of roads traversing Corsica, and they string the mountain towns together as if they're connecting the dots. To get anywhere in the mountains you have to go just about everywhere else first. Covertly, I watch my fellow tourists buy their honey and their boxes of chestnut biscuits and then waddle back out into the downpour, board their buses, and drive off. I stay behind and fondle the merchandise, aimless and irresolute.

I must look pretty morose, too, because Madame Ceccaldi breaks protocol. Over the past couple days she's noticed me, watched me show up at her shop reliably each afternoon once *The Pink Panther* comes on TV for the kids. She's wondered whether and what I'll finally buy, and day after day I've left empty-handed. This is a waste of her time. Like everyone else in town, she knows *who* I am: I'm the lady with the tall husband and the dog who barks at cows and the two small kids, staying in André Lecca's converted *séchoir,* the one his grandfather built to dry the family's chestnuts. The Ceccaldis and the Leccas are two of the oldest families in town. There's a Ceccaldi depicted in stone on the town fountain, the one where we had to go draw water when the village plumbing went south. It's her prerogative to speak. *"Ça va?"*

Since I've been using her shop as my afternoon sanctuary, I'd figured eventually we would. But I'm prepared for the customary *Qu'est-ce que vous cherchez?* (I had a polite answer scripted for the polite question. *Chestnut flour,* I intended to say. I even have a follow-up prepared—*Can it be cooked like polenta?*—even though I already know the answer: yes. They serve it at the pizzeria under a braised *stufatu* redolent of wild rosemary, made with tough cuts of beef from the free wheeling cows.) When it came, I assumed our exchange would be totally meaningless.

But I have plunked myself down in her shop with a brooding face several afternoons running now and she wants to know *why.* In fact, the way she's phrased it, she actually wants to know if I'm *okay.*

And the answer to that is, of course, that *no,* I'm *not* okay.

Am I feeling sorry for myself? Yes. For all of us? Abso-damn-lutely.

Here's how I see it.

Fact: The seasonal employees have been on Corsica since April, which is officially the start of the summer season here. Down the hill in Porto, where we went to the indoor aquarium, I saw a bunch of them standing on the empty restaurant terraces, hands out, feeling the big, fat drops that kept falling and falling and falling relentlessly, and they looked as woebegone as I felt. Their tips must be lousy.

Fact: Scarlett is afraid of crashing thunder, which means that for three nights in a row now, Greg and I have shared our minuscule futon in the two-room *séchoir* (not two bedrooms; two *rooms*) not just with Doobie, who's no fan of loud weather, either, but also with a quivering, crying, snoring, and sprawling toddler.

Fact: When we get home to San Diego in a month, our homecoming will be a shared celebration. And then real life, regular life, will resume, and about that I am pretty nervous. Corsica was my parting gift to us.

Fact: So sure was I that we'd be spending our celebratory vacation lounging on a beach, I didn't even bother to pack warm clothes. And if that isn't tempting fate—Me! Tempting fate!—then I don't know what is.

Conclusion: God hates us.

"It's raining," I moan.

Madame Ceccaldi just looks at me.

And *looks* at me.

And the longer she looks at me—silently, intently—the more ridiculous I feel.

She's *still* looking at me . . . Is she still looking at me?

Okay . . . She's still looking.

But she's probably *not* looking at me for as long as it seems . . .

Except that she is . . .

Oh my God! She's *still* looking at me!

And then I start to sort of freak out. Is she giving me some sort of Corsican evil eye or something? Because if you're Corsican and your family has been around long enough, then something bad has certainly happened to *your* family before, too. Except that in a Corsican family, something bad is, like, your uncle got knifed in a bloody family feud, or your brother was accused of being a nationalist militant and shipped off to prison in France for the rest of his life, or—if you go far enough back in time (and Corsicans have long memories)—somebody or maybe a whole bunch of somebodies in the family got massacred by one of the island's former occupying powers: the Pisans, the Genoese, or the French. It sort of puts things into perspective. I blush as pink as the *lonzo*.

Madame Ceccaldi comes out from behind the counter and crosses her shop in three bossy footsteps, to the table in the middle of the room where a rack's hung with dark, nearly black, slender sausages speckled with white nuggets of fat like shiny stars. She takes one down and hands it to me. I already know what it is. It smells like the lair of some wild thing and it is cool and dry to the touch.

"Figatellu." It isn't a suggestion. Her voice has the command of one of Indiana's Jedi masters, so I pay for it without word or fuss or a single question and walk out into the rain.

"Is it a blood sausage?" Greg inspects the *figatellu* suspiciously, smelling it and balking at its musty, fusty odor.

"Sort of."

"What's 'sort of' mean?"

"It means yes, it's made with blood . . . and with pork kidneys, hearts, and livers."

He looks nauseated. He turns it over and over in his hands. "Is it fresh?"

"This one's dried. You only make fresh *figatellu* in the winter when you've just slaughtered a pig. You eat those grilled." I cut two thin slices with my pocketknife. Inside, the *figatellu* has the moist texture of bread pudding, beaded with greasy perspiration. "Here. Taste it."

"Um, no thanks."

"Come on, just taste it."

"No! Sorry, disgusting. Indy, you try it."

Indy doesn't even avert his gaze from the screen. "Never."

"Greg!" I stamp my foot and startle Doobie from under the kitchen table. "Just eat it! Come *on*. This is what we came for!"

"Maybe it's what *you* came for," he laughs, nudging Indy and Scarlett over to make room for him on the futon. "I came for the beach. *You* eat it."

And then the cryptic message Madame Ceccaldi no doubt meant for me to discover in the *figatellu* hits me. Leave it to a Corsican to remind me that—*again,* how many times and in how many ways will I hear the same message?—there's only one thing to do when life hands you something ugly, something you would much, much rather not deal with: just eat it.

CHAPTER 39

T HE NEXT DAY DAWNS—literally dawns—clear and bright. Scarlett the rooster is on the stairs. *Pad pad pad.* My eyelids are crusted
with sleep but she's wide awake and beaming. "Good morning, Mama!"

"No . . . It's too early, baby."

Me, I had been up all night with the *figatellu,* stealing clandestine
nibbles from the refrigerator, then sneaking back under the covers, each
time swearing that bite had been the last. Its flavor had intoxicated me,
juiced me up, made me feel as if I was high on vitamins or something. (It
was probably all that iron.) I hadn't slept.

"Can I draw?" she asks.

"Um-hm."

For a long hour I sleepily shoo her away like she's the snooze button
when she tries to rouse me. At seven Greg heads upstairs for a shower
and I roll off the futon. Damn. My notebook's in her lap, a stack of its
neatly folded ripped pages in her hands. "This is you and this is me,"
she translates, pointing to two side-by-side oblongs, each with a pair of
truncated stick arms and stick legs. "And this," she fingers the scribbles
across the top of the paper, "says, 'I love my mom, I hope that she had a
good sleep, love Scarlett.'" Ever the coquette, she gifts me the treasure
and bats her eyelashes.

"Thank you, sweetheart. I love it."

"And this one . . ."

We go through page after page . . . She's been busy. Greg finishes his shower and comes downstairs with wet curls. "Do we have a plan for the day?"

"Go upstairs now and put on your clothes, baby," I tell Scarlett.

"Good morning, Daddy." She's had my undivided attention for breakfast and scurries up the stairs compliantly. Over the banister she shouts, "Show him my drawings!"

I gather them into a stack on the counter. "The plan: I need to get some more *figatellu*." Greg makes a retching sound. I ignore him. "And then since it's finally sunny we should go hiking. Can we be out the door in ten minutes?"

Twenty minutes later, we're still at the overlook in the center of town. Yes, the view is gorgeous. Greg takes pictures. He takes picture after picture after picture after picture.

"I'm taking Indy," I say, and, grabbing his hand, head uphill toward Madame Ceccaldi's. "Scarlett's with you," I shout behind me. If Greg said anything in response, I didn't hear it: I was thinking about *figatellu*.

When we come back out, Greg and Doobie are walking up the street. Greg's hands swing freely, he's whistling, and he has a relaxed I-am-not-on-duty look on his face. My heart stops. "Where's Scarlett?"

And then he says it.

I now know that the most terrifying words to pass between parents are not, "I want a divorce," they are, "I thought she was with you."

"Damn it, Greg!" I speed down the hill to the overlook, dragging Indy behind me, certain she's there. Unconsciously, I am counting: There are six storefronts between the shop and the overlook. Indy and I have taken seventy-four steps. It's as if my brain is parceling the distance between us, calculating how far she could possibly have wandered (not far), how much closer to her I am with each footstep (almost there). There are dozens of cars in the parking lot. Twenty or more people milling about. Two tour buses. But the bench where she and Greg had been sitting is vacant. "Isn't that where you were?" He's come down the hill behind me.

"I told you I was taking pictures," he says. Vaguely, I understand that he's explaining, or rationalizing, or whatever. I scan the row of benches, expecting she'll suddenly pop out of the crowd, like a fairy ring.

She's not on the benches.

She's not anywhere around the benches.

She's not on the stone wall behind the benches.

She's not in the parking lot in front of the benches.

So my heartless mind conjures a hologram Scarlett—red shirt, jeans, blonde ponytail—that flickers everywhere she *should* be. It plays with a stick, and hides behind a car, and chases a cat, but every time I draw close to it, it disappears. It's been five minutes now.

On the other side of the overlook wall is a sheer twenty-foot drop into somebody's garden. "Go look, Greg," I whisper. He goes and leans over the stone barrier, looking for her on the ground below. He travels all the way to the far, far right and then back again all the way to the far, far left, all along the wall, a hundred paces, scouring the garden rim intently. I mouth a silent mantra: *Please please please but no no no.* And she isn't there, either.

"Go with your dad, Indy."

But he clings to me. "I want to stay with you!"

I charge back up the street breathless with altitude, exertion, and panic. Had she followed me to the shop? Only Madame Ceccaldi is there. It's been seven minutes. And then it's been nine, and Indy's sobs are unhinging me right when I need to stay focused and positive. She must be okay. But when an eternity of fifteen minutes has passed, and the group of old men at the café have dispersed looking for *la fillette blonde* who's staying in André's *séchoir,* and Greg and I have reconvened at the lookout and he's acknowledged that she isn't at the house or in our garden or around the car, either, against my will I start to consider the worst: the cars pulling in and out of the parking lot, the buses pulling in and out of town, the strangers and the visitors, the split second it would take to grab our daughter and drive off, or yank her silently behind a closed door—that these gruesome things actually happen to people.

As I stalk the streets I call Scarlett's name, but this time, because only silence answers, I must call it over and over and over again. I realize that I will howl her name until I have no voice left. If we don't find her, I will have to stay here for the rest of my life, obsessively searching, certain she's just behind that tree over there, or around that wall, or right on the other side of that fence.

"I want my sister!"

A woman from the café approaches. "Let me take your son." Her soothing voice is disowned by a face tight with concern. "He can sit with me while you look, right over there." Gratefully, I nod and turn to go.

"I want to stay with you!"

"It's okay, Indy. I'm going to find Scarlett." I untangle and crouch on the still-wet pavement. "She's okay. Stay with the lady."

Then I begin to run.

I race around the village chased by regrets. Why was I buying *sausage*? Why am I *here*? So plain it seems: that I am meeting fate. The penance dealt to an inattentive, divided mother; the punishment for ever asking whether my children were *enough*.

Greg and I meet again at the village stairs, he running up, me running down, and though his face is drawn he still grabs my hand and promises, "She's okay," but I shake him loose. After yelling for twenty minutes, I'm hoarse, and have no encouraging words for him anyway. If this time our world is actually falling apart, I will not dissemble. I plunge the stairs two at a time, racing the same direction where Greg has just been, but looking nonetheless.

"Scarlett! Answer Mama, please! Scarlett?!"

A few more minutes later, far off, I hear a woman's faint voice. But it's indistinct: I can't tell what she's saying. Maybe she's just calling for Scarlett, too—her name rings out over the mountain. But still, I sprint toward her voice. "Scarlett?"

Closer, her words become plain: *"Elle est là! Elle est là!"* She is here!

I'm beckoned down an ally and around a corner and down another ally into a part of town I've never seen. And then there they are: a short older woman flanked by her own preteen daughters, sheltering sniffling Scarlett under a stairwell. And the relief is like morphine, such a flood, my knees buckle.

She doesn't speak English and I find I can't speak a single word of French; we babble our entwined stories unintelligibly. Kindly, because we are intimates now, she offers her hand. I grasp it and repeat endlessly, thank you, and thank you, and thank you: my heart feeling as if it's been defibrillated, pounding the rhythm of my gratitude and my resolve—*This is my life. This is my life. This is my life.*

<hr />

REMARKABLY, soon enough, though—especially for Scarlett, with the benefit of her goldfish memory—it's all over. We thank the villagers, take the kids to the café for a self-conscious *sirop,* and the day recovers a semblance of normalcy. And we still go hiking.

On the trail outside town, light filters through the broad leaves of gnarled chestnut trees. "Put me down, Mama," Scarlett scolds, so, reluctantly, I release her. But Greg and I trot close behind her as she and Indy dash down the trail with Doobie faithfully on their heels.

The trail goes up a hill and across several of the lazy creeks that flow toward the big river. It passes under the straight, tall towering boughs of laricio pines that were planted hundreds of years earlier by the Genoese, masts for their sailing ships. "That's how the Genoese ruled the world," I tell Indy, pointing into the canopy.

"Trees?"

"Power," says Greg. "Money. Soldiers."

The river's tumult grows abruptly louder where the trail descends into a crop of gargantuan boulders. "I don't think we can do it, Greg," I breathe anxiously. To follow it, we'll have to scramble over the moss-mottled rocks. Surely, this path wasn't meant for little kids! But Indy is already leaping from rock to rock as sure-footed as a mountain goat. The river hides behind these rocks.

"Don't you want to see the waterfall?"

"I do! I do, Dada!" Scarlett cries. "Come *on*, Mama!" I've scaled obstacles like these before, but I'm still shaky doing it one-handed helping Scarlett, jolting when my foot slips or when a hand grip comes loose in a shower of gravel. *Don't let her fall. Don't let her fall. This is* your *job. Don't let her fall.*

White water gushes over jumbled rocks strewn about as if we've interrupted a pair of mountain giants playing pétanque. The river, the rocks, the trees, the brush—it is all impressive and overgrown and overlarge, the way I remember creeks looking in my childhood, before I got big and my growth shrank them back down to their true proportions, before they disappeared for real under parking lots and subdivisions. I really do want Indy and Scarlett to see the waterfall, but a slender suspension bridge dangling across the river, twenty feet up in the air, probably thirty feet across, is the only route to the trail on the other side.

"No, that's way too dangerous, Greg."

The metal slats are spaced widely, six inches between them at least, nearly wide enough apart for Scarlett to slip right through. Between them you can see the raging torrent below: it'll be like walking on thin air. The only handrails are two thin wire cables slung between posts spaced at least six feet apart. The bridge is already swaying back and forth precariously, propelled just by the breeze generated from the crashing, roaring river, and only a fool would attempt such a feat with two kids. I grab Scarlett and hold on to her for dear life. "Indy, no!" My voice is so stern, he stops in his tracks, crushed.

"Come on, we have to!" Greg yells over the noise of the river. "On the other side we'll have lunch, and then we'll hike back. Okay? It'll be fine! "Really!"

Why isn't he ever fazed? "Really?" I shout back, petrified, and clutch Scarlett. "How can you? We almost *lost* her today!"

"I know. But we *didn't*!"

His words hang like a bridge over the water.

To move forward now or fall back? That's really it, isn't it. It's the same question that brought us to France: Having come so close to disaster, having almost lost everything that we loved, *now what do we do*?

And since Provence, when Mom reminded me that so much more still lay ahead, I've been realizing that I will never have the satisfaction of having this question asked, answered, and settled once and for all: it's a moving target and the central issue of marriage—for better or worse. When you take your vows they sort of clue you in right there that things are destined to eventually, and repeatedly, go south. As a new bride or a new mother, maybe I didn't want to admit that before. But the past eighteen months have made it abundantly clear: we will always face problems. So, now, how do we move on and make life better? Do we always play it safe? Avoid all the roaring rivers? Cling to the misplaced hope that things are fine as long as we don't talk about anything that isn't fine? Risk nothing? Change nothing? And what will we do when the worst just happens anyway, the lightning bolt out of the blue? When another crisis strikes or there's a real tragedy? What will Greg do? And what will I do? Wait for someone to save me? Save myself?

"Will you help me?" I call. "I can do it, but you'll be right behind me, right? I'm not just talking about the bridge, Greg. I don't ever want us to bail on each other again when bad things happen." Before I can place one foot on that bridge, which is our way forward, I need to hear him say it out loud, to make sure that we're really ready, because we promised each other a life of adventure, after all, but this question has burned us badly once before and he knows it.

"From now on, I will always be right behind you," he answers steadily, and I know that when he puts his hand over his heart, he's touching that flying bird. "Hold Scarlett, I'll carry Doobie. Indy, you're big. Ready?"

CHAPTER

~❦ 40 ❦~

I CAN'T DO IT. I tried, but I just can't leave Corsica without telling you one last thing.

We did make it to the beach eventually. We found a marvelous white sand one within sight of the mooring yachts in Calvi where we ate local lobsters, and a pebbled one speckled with beach glass on a headland near home. Just as I'd hoped, the kids threw off their clothes and played happily by the water's edge, looking healthier than they had in months.

But the best part of the beach trips, I hadn't anticipated. On the long drives home, the kids conked out, fanned by warm wind blowing through the windows, lulled by the Rolling Stones and Bob Marley on the iPod. And in that moving cocoon, Greg and I talked as if, having openly laid the past to rest, we were getting reacquainted.

Some of our talks were about Corsica. Can it last? Outside Calvi we picked up a new straight road of fresh asphalt cutting through vineyards and slicing into the mountains. Like everything does in Corsica, it reminded me of when I was little. There used to be a wonderful steep, twisting road that scaled the mountain behind our house, called Steele Canyon Drive. At the top of it were a few houses and a liquor store where Mom would buy Casey and me Coca-Cola after school. One summer, we three sat by our pool watching the mountain burn, and I wasn't afraid, because my mother was there. Instead, it was exciting. Soon after, Mom married Jerry, and not long after that, we moved away. And soon after *that*, all of the wild places around the old house disappeared: the horse meadows and open fields, rocky hillsides where rattlesnakes lurked. The worst was when they straightened Steele Canyon Drive to accommodate SUVs and new rows of identical peach stucco houses. Their inhabitants are, I guess, spared the dizzying descent, but they'll also never know the thrill.

The glory of Coriscan food is its charcuterie, because it tastes inimitably of wild Corsica. And in this, it tastes as much of a wild people as it does of the island's wild nature—chestnuts and the myrtle, lavender, rosemary, and thyme of the *maquis*. But here are some sad statistics: About twenty-five percent fewer pigs are raised on Corsica now than were raised there a short decade ago. And according to an official with the Association for the Defense and Promotion of Corsican Charcuterie quoted in the *New York Times*, it is possible that only ten percent of the charcuterie now sold on Corsica is actually made from pigs born and bred on the island. The association made a study of imported pork and found that some of it was coming from as far away as China. On the streets of Paris you can buy a counterfeit Louis Vuitton purse. On the streets of Ajaccio you can buy counterfeit *figatellu*. And that just makes me sad.

CHAPTER
~ 41 ~

S OPHIE AND MARC ARE BOTH WONDERFUL COOKS, though they'll
each humbly claim otherwise. Marc professes to have only a handful
of recipes up his sleeve, including a duck breast with green peppercorns
in hommage to Sophie's favorite meal at the Auberge Ensoleillée. Now
it's his go-to dish whenever they're having, as he puts it, fancy company
(like for one of the orgies). Sophie insists she's just a master of quick
dishes: couscous with dried fruit, vegetables, and chicken, or savory
crêpes for dinner. But I've seen them each do truly inspiring things in
the kitchen. And they both cook. A lot.

Take the night Marc made us that second fondue. I know I said that
nothing could make it truly pleasurable, but I lied: Marc made it remarkable. Before he let us eat, he schooled us, passing an old pepper mill
around the table so we could sprinkle our plates with freshly cracked
pepper. "You dip, then you dip," he explained. "First into the cheese,
then into the pepper. *Voilà*. It's the only way to get the proper balance of flavor and texture." When the last traces of fondue—his special
blend of Savoie white wine, Beaufort, Emmenthal, and Gruyère—were
left in his ancient enameled pot, he hovered over it like a nurse over a
newborn, eyes glazed with pleasure and concentration. "We call this the
religieuse," he said mischeviously, never looking away from the sizzling
cheese slick. "Because it's the best part, and you keep it for yourself like
a greedy priest."

"Marky, it's ready." Sophie stuck a fork in the pot.

He swatted her hand playfully. "Wife! No, a little more. It must be quite crisp and exquisitely golden. And . . . *voilà!*" He attacked the pot with two forks, violently grating and scraping the crust. "Your plates," he commanded, and we obediently held up our dishes. On each he deposited a small mound of crumbly golden gratings. "With the wine," he ordered. We finished our glasses, and the third bottle of wine for the night, with the cracklings; the texture of sand, buttery and salty. Magnificent.

Today is Lulu's birthday, and when Sophie arrives at my kitchen door she finds me in a flop sweat, frantically whisking a bowl of oil and egg yolks, muttering curses and prayers under my breath. "Would Scarlett like to help me make Lulu's cake?" I nod but keep whisking wildly, so Sophie shepherds Scarlett out the door, casting a bemused backward glance at my mayhem. The kitchen is a wreck, eggshells strewn all over the counter as if an unfortunate chicken had exploded, and pools of sticky egg whites congealing in nasty blobs on the sideboard. On the table are three other discarded bowls holding the disastrous, broken evidence of my previous attempts to make mayonnaise.

I hate mayonnaise.

My abiding terror of mayonnaise began in culinary school, creeping up on me along with a deep sense of inadequacy over my intractable inability to *make* it. *Everyone* else could make mayonnaise. In the *garde-manger,* people whipped up mayonnaise as if they were throwing back happy-hour cocktails, all easy, breezy, and nonchalant. I made curdled egg soup. So I kept my dirty little secret from Chef and wheedled Sandra into making mine for me.

And I've kept my dirty little secret to this day. But over the years, the farther I drifted from cooking, the more mayonnaise bothered me, *symbolically.* Mayonnaise is the fluffy white incarnation of my shortcomings. So I've hid my ineptitude and gutlessness behind spurious justifications; claims that the jarred product was possibly superior to homemade, and *at least* sufficient.

And is it? Let's just say this: the difference between homemade and jarred mayonnaise—even your very favorite jarred one, the one that makes your BLT a moment of celebration, your potato salad a work of art—is like the difference between black-and-white and Technicolor: one is sophisticated and atmospheric, the other obvious and bright. Made without corn syrup, homemade mayonnaise isn't cloying; just rich and full, a little tart, with a customizable edge of saltiness. It's more delicate, and because it's delicate, it enhances, instead of hides, the flavor of everything it touches: fish, cold meat, dipped, boiled vegetables. Because I've had homemade, my claim that jarred mayonnaise was a perfectly fine substitute always rang hollow in my ears. But making mayonnaise makes my heart palpitate like a hummingbird and my fingernails go numb. The degree of physical distress it causes me is downright embarrassing.

So here I am, struggling—but struggling valiantly.

But you know what? It makes not a lick of difference to my mixture. The eggs and oil in the bowl stubbornly stay liquid. They won't emulsify. Just flat-out *won't* do it. The mixture is basically laughing at me. So I whisk, and whisk . . . *and whisk* . . . and then, "Damn you to hell!" I finally cry in frustration, and launch the bowl and whisk right into the sink, sloshing a yellow wave of eggs and oil all over the countertop right as Erin walks into the kitchen. She's been packing. She leaves tomorrow, and for her farewell dinner tonight, she wants some violet artichokes that we bought together in Saulieu: *with mayonnaise.* I could hit her. Or cry. She looks anguished. "Aim, we could just buy mayonnaise."

But I reach for another couple of eggs. "Oh no, Erin. We can't. The only way to be a good cook is to cook. If you let fear win, you start taking shortcuts. And all those shortcuts eventually accumulate on you. Get that vinegar, would you?" I crack an egg, toggle the yolk back and forth between the shells to separate it, and dump it into a clean bowl. I beat it with the whisk. "Now, add a teaspoon full."

"Why vinegar?" she asks.

"Acid," I explain, blending yolk and vinegar and adding a careful teaspoon of mustard and a sprinkling of salt to the bowl. "Mayonnaise is just fat droplets suspended in acid. The mustard helps stabilize it and keep it from breaking."

"And by breaking you mean . . ."

With a sweeping hand I indicate all my discarded bowls. "My suck-ass mayonnaise." I take a deep breath and hand Erin a precisely measured cupful of oil. We lock eyes. She looks frightened. "Are you ready?" My grip on the whisk is growing sweaty but I try to be calm. "Now, slowly . . . slowly . . . drop by drop you add the oil while I whisk. And . . . go . . . *slowly.*"

Painstakingly, she drips a single drop of oil into the bowl and I start whisking like crazy, brow furrowed in concentration. "Okay. Another," I say, and another tiny droplet falls. We go on, me stirring frantically between dribbles, nervously examining the mixture. There should be a color change and a discernible difference in texture as it emulsifies. It should lighten and thicken and look like whipped butter. But ours remains liquid and bright yellow. Maybe it'll still come together. "Okay, now, I think you can pour it more steadily, but still slowly." I whisk faster. The oil descends in a slow, steady stream and I whisk and whisk and whisk and . . . then . . . aaaaagggggghhhhhh! Damn!

"Is that right?" Erin asks.

"Does it look right?!" Dribbles of yellow soup fall from the whisk back into the bowl. There's not an ounce of fluffiness. "I don't get it! Do you know, Erin, how many recipes and instructions for mayonnaise I've read? Hundreds! Seriously. By now, hundreds! Blogs! Magazines! Cookbooks! Technically, I get it, but I can't do it! Good God I suck."

"Want to go to Lulu's party instead?"

Stupid mayonnaise.

My frustrated scowl and the dried egg yolk on my shirt elicits Sophie's concern. "What's wrong?" A single-layered chocolate cake sprinkled with slivered almonds bakes in the oven. Sophie will dust it with cocoa when it's cooled.

"Can you make mayonnaise, Sophie?" I love this big, bright kitchen, especially the fireplace in one corner and the giant dining table made by Marc from an off-cut of quarried limestone.

"Of course." Of course she said of course. Why did she have to say of course?

"Can you teach me?" I reach for a pen and a scrap of paper.

"Of course." She cracks an egg, puts the yolk in a glass bowl, then sloshes in a bit of red wine vinegar and reaches for the mustard.

"Wait, Sophie! How much vinegar was that?" I demand, scribbling instructions.

"I don't know. Not too much." Then she adds a spoonful of mustard.

"And how much mustard?"

"A spoon? Not too much." She taps my paper with her whisk. "Stop writing: watch."

I am terribly confused. Every mayonnaise recipe I've ever read emphasizes precision, but Sophie just dumps things haphazardly, *recklessly* into the bowl. I'm no slave to measurements, but this is mayonnaise after all. Most unkind of sauces! I'm almost embarrassed for her, assuming we're headed for yet another broken mess. Maybe I shouldn't look . . .

The oil is *glubbed* into the bowl. No dribbling, no dripping. Her whisking has no urgency to it. I lend her mine: my wrist moves of its own accord, beating the air as if I'm trying to beat the mayonnaise for her.

But right before my eyes, a miracle occurs: the yolk lightens, the mixture thickens, and there's a light, fluffy cloud of perfect mayonnaise. If I hadn't seen it, I wouldn't have believed it.

Sophie scoots the bowl across the counter for me to taste. "I think you make it too hard on yourself. Too complicated. You must relax, Eh-mee. But *alors,* now you try, okay?"

She hands me a bowl and, feigning her confidence, I add an egg yolk, a slosh of vinegar—not too much—a sprinkle of salt, and a spoon of mustard. She smiles in solidarity as I grip the oil bottle in one hand and the whisk in the other. And then . . . I do it. With no warp-speed whisking, no precious dribbles and drops, I let the oil stream slowly into the bowl while I whisk patiently and evenly, as if I *believe* . . . and . . . holy mackerel . . . I make mayonnaise! "I did it!"

"See? It is not so difficult."

"Sophie, it's a miracle! Eight years I've been trying to make mayonnaise!" I fly across the counter to kiss both her cheeks. "I have to go home right now and do it again!"

And I do! Back to back I make three more bowls of cookbook-gorgeous mayonnaise, one right after the other, enough mayonnaise for twenty artichokes, all the while cackling in glee to myself, mesmerized by my new ability. Buoyant, jubilant! Reborn as a cook! I feel like roaring: *I can make mayonnaise!* It is almost unfathomable to me what has changed.

But I do have a theory.

It's possible, I think, that the lightness of one's mayonnaise may be directly proportional to the lightness of one's attitude. And one's attitude in the kitchen is, as in life, a function of the extent of one's courage. Simply put, the more you cook, the bolder you get.

Being uptight is anathema to good cooking: the let-go instinct is obligatory. Think about it. Already the kitchen is a pretty lawless place, full of chaos and mess, and blood and flame and sharp objects, and the cook stands willfully in the middle of it all, creating harmony from discord. Which, for me, ranks cooks among the bravest people I've ever known.

And none are braver than those who cook at home, because they're the ones who've always been asked to do the most with the least: with salt and pepper, butter, olive oil, and herbs, with eggs and wine, with trash fish and scary mushrooms, with nearly burnt cheese and the unlovely bits of carcass and bone that others would just throw away. And seriously, what's scarier than facing down your hungry, needful loved ones, never wanting to disappoint, always wanting to delight? And how many people stay out of the kitchen essentially because they're afraid? Afraid they can't do it, afraid they'll mess up, afraid they'll make a mess, afraid they don't have the time, or the energy, or the right pans, or *whatever*. Home cooks are warriors.

And home is where French food began. For all the fine and famous chefs that have perfected it, and the restaurants that have profited from it, and the magazines and television shows that have promoted it, French food was born quietly and unceremoniously at home: the accumulated, shared genius of generations of bossy, opinionated, discerning, brassy, inventive home cooks. Which is why to me it's all the more sad and significant that that's where its practice in France is fading fastest, done in as elsewhere by the pace and pressure of modern life and the seduction of easier, more convenient, but wholly insufficient substitutes. Ironic, too, because cooking is actually the best antidote I know to modern life: it creates a pocket of timelessness through ritual and recipe.

A true cook is seldom overwhelmed by life's monoliths, and that's my aim. Instead, three times a day, a cook practices and cultivates the values that have always served us all well, and the values that I want for myself and my family in and out of the kitchen, the ones I think we need the most, now more than ever: courage, resourcefulness, and humility.

So . . . cook! And if you already cook . . . cook more!

And have no fear of mayonnaise.

I FEEL LIKE WE SHOULD HAVE SPECIAL T-SHIRTS," I tell Greg. "Mine would say, *I Ate My Way Around France and All I Got Was This Dumb T-Shirt and a Muffin Top.*"

He puts down the shirt he's folding, comes around behind me, and encircles me with his arms. "Thank you."

"Don't. You'll make me cry." I drop the dress of Scarlett's I'm folding and it joins ranks with the rest of our worn-down and worn-out clothing, items laundered nearly beyond recognition, each article a little more precious to me this morning as we enact the ritual of packing for the very last time.

It's our very last trip.

Over the next ten days we'll make another giant loop: put the final miles on the faithful Kid. We will travel north, up through the lush Loire Valley to Tours, then down along the western coast to Bordeaux just in time for the first day of summer, and then on and over France's mountainous southern border into Spain, seeing and tasting the world of the Basques from both sides of a border that many of them don't actually recognize. Then we'll circle up through Périgord's chalky cliffs and drive over the hills to Burgundy. When we get back, there will be just enough time left for good-byes and to sell the Kid, to pack our lives back into our luggage, to bid farewell to fields and creeks, to days of quiet and nights of starlight, to the tattered castle on the hill, to cows and sheep, to teachers and treasured new friends, to close a chapter and to board a plane.

"It seems impossible," I say.

"That's why it feels so good."

～ ⁓ ～

THE EEL IS SELDOM INCLUDED AMONG THE CREATURES of the animal kingdom noted for its inspirational qualities. In fact, poor guy, instead it's usually pretty well demonized, lumped in amid the creepy and the flesh-crawling. Greg, for example, is utterly repulsed by them, and wouldn't even consider a bite of the dish I ordered in Tours. "Taste it," I urged, extending a forkful. The eel was the most delicious fish I'd ever eaten: nuggets of firm white flesh pocketed with flavorful fat, simply sautéed in butter and garlic and some of the Loire Valley's white wine and sprinkled liberally with parsley.

But Greg cringed. "No way. No thanks."

"It's delicious . . ."

"It sounds slimy."

And there you go. Working against them, eels have bulgy, beady, lidless eyes with wide, round, humanlike pupils, and slender, sinuous bodies like snakes. ("Is it a snake?" Indy asked when my plate arrived. The chef had quartered my eel in cylindrical segments. If you placed them end to end, its tubular form was obvious. "Might as well be," Greg answered.) In fact, freshwater eels do slither rather more than swim, undulating through the shallows of lakes and ponds and rivers, including the Loire. (Which as rivers go is quite a slow-moving one, in places so sluggish that water lilies mass on its surface, tendrils curling around the reflected images of the valley's stately old châteaux.) Male eels ready to spawn have been found squirming their way across fields en route to water.

They live a mysterious and surprisingly long life. In the Basque country, where we visited Bayonne and Saint-Jean-de-Luz on the French side, and then San Sebastián over the Spanish border, teeny tiny baby eels called *txitxardin* were once plentiful—until overfishing and contaminated waterways took their toll. (Now that, like *rascasse,* they're rarer

and more expensive, some make do with a paltry substitute made of fish
purée.) But these "babies," thread-slender and wormlike, were actually
three or so years old by the time they were caught and consumed. It turns
out that eels are tireless migrators, and that both European and American eels have a common birthplace in the depths of the Sargasso Sea all
the way near Bermuda. Instinctually, the larvae travel for years to return
to their ancestral estuaries.

Eating the baby eels is a wintertime ritual in Basqueland, as is the
txarriboda, the traditional slaughter of a family pig. A similar ritual exists, or did, in Bordeaux, called simply the *tue cochon*—the killing of the
pig. In both places, a carnival-like atmosphere attends the communal
preparation of loads of *cochonnaille*—hams and loins and *saucisson* and
boudin and head cheese and the like—and then a feast of fresh, ephem-
eral dishes, usually bits of offal grilled over fragrant wood until they're
charred and smoky and hot when eaten with the fingertips. I stay in
touch with a girl from Paris named Alice. Her family is from Bordeaux
and still has a summer shack on the Bassin d'Arcachon. Before our trip
there she offered me three bits of eating advice: one, to have mussels and
oysters fresh from the Bassin at Chez Hortense on the tip of Cap Ferrat.
Which we did, joining tanned bourgeois-bohemian families fresh from
their summer retreats—men with long hair and open-necked shirts and
sunglasses, women breastfeeding at the table, children well-mannered—
digging into bivalves roasted in their shells and topped with coins of
grilled sausage (the oysters), or steamed in wine and tossed with the sausage ground to garlicky bits (the mussels). Two, Alice said, to feel the
soul of old Bordeaux we must *faire chabrot*: find somewhere rustic where
we could finish a bowl of soup by pouring in the dregs of a glass of red
wine (Bordeaux of course) and slurp it all down together. So we did. And
finally, she said we had to eat *tricandilles*: pork intestines marinated in
local Armagnac, slathered with garlic and mustard, and grilled—a *tue
cochon* specialty that is such a favorite, they serve it at restaurants all year
round. And we—or I, anyway—did that, too—no guts, no glory—at a

café near Bordeaux's captivating Marché des Capucins, still bustling after nearly three centuries. This last—chewing on the pig's rubbery innards on the first day of summer, drinking a really good bottle of Bordeaux, a little sandy from a day playing on the *dune de Pyla*—made me wish for such a ritual in my own life. One that regularly brought together death and life, food and community, the truly exquisite and the sincerely humble.

I've never killed a pig. Eventually—and probably soon, actually—it will be true that most Bordelais and most Basques will have never killed, or been anywhere near the killing of, a pig, either: EU health legislation now makes it technically illegal to slaughter animals on a small scale. (For *tue cochon,* some families now throw pork chops on the grill.) But I do know that a pig's death is loud and violent. And in the Périgord, home of foie gras, we visited a farm where hundreds of ducks and geese—after spending most of their life free-ranging under chestnut trees—are gavaged just before death to fatten their liver, force-fed rations of corn noodles by means of a rubber tube. Admittedly, their last days are not pretty.

But the point is this: with blood on your hands, it's hard to pretend that you don't know what you know. Like that cod fished far, far away and then whirled into a slurry and squeezed through a spaghetti maker is no substitute for an actual baby eel. Or that the presence of baby eels in the first place relies on mindful stewardship of their environments. Here's something I've learned over these months: being intimately involved in the procurement of food—through slaughter or harvest, gathering or tending—gives one great respect for the act of eating. It's not the only way, of course, to become a respectful eater, but it helps. I've also learned that acceptance of death can, or should, give one great respect for the act of living.

Which brings me back to the eels.

No creature clings to life more dearly than an eel. If you've ever seen a chef swing an eel like a wild lasso and then bash its head into a countertop, that act—unlike the bunny, dispatched with a single solid thunk—doesn't actually kill the eel: it just stuns it. What comes next—usually nailing its head to a board—doesn't actually kill it, either. That just keeps one end of the still-writhing creature somewhat stationary, enabling all the butchering that is yet to come. Slitting its belly and emptying its innards also doesn't seem to kill the eel: it still moves. Nor does ripping the skin from the eel's body. Decapitation, even, will not cause an eel to surrender. Maybe it's all just leftover electrical activity, but during its last moments, a headless eel will continue to jolt and wiggle as if, regardless, it's grateful to have that time.

Our very last stop on our very last trip was at the town of Rocamadour, etched right into the side of a cliff overlooking the Dordogne river. In ancient history, it was another pilgrimage town: Louis IX—who became Saint Louis, who went on a Crusade, and who built the lovely Sainte-Chapelle in Paris to house the relics of the Crown of Thorns—came here in the thirteenth century to worship.

In tribute, pilgrims at Rocamadour scale a flight of a hundred or so stone stairs ascending from the lower town up to the church complex midway up the cliff, and they're supposed to imagine that they're climbing up an eternal staircase. At the top of the stairs and around a few corners, a tunnel passes directly through the rock, and its length and orientation is such that somewhere right around the middle, each pilgrim encounters a split second of complete and total darkness before the proverbial light at the end of the tunnel appears. The church complex itself is a series of small candlelit chapels.

It had been a long day, a long trip. The climb up the stairs is supposed to be slow and meditative, but I hustled. I'd intended to get up the stairs to the chapels earlier, but first Scarlett wanted me to help her in the bathtub . . . of course . . . and then Indy couldn't find his pajamas . . . of course . . . and then Doobie threw up all over the bed from the celebratory foie gras that we brought him back from dinner . . . of course . . . and then Greg wanted to take a few pictures of the cliffs before the light failed . . . and so here I was, panting and hurrying and already exhausted. I flashed through the chapels just before sunset, never more than a scant minute ahead of the chapel minder, an old woman on my heels closing down the complex for the evening. There was no time for me to light my own candle. *Damn it. No!* I thought each time she appeared, rattling her keys. *We're leaving tomorrow!* And then I'd sprint toward the next darkened room.

But soon, I found myself sitting all alone in the chapel courtyard under a pale pink sky. "This is it," I grumbled. "And this isn't how it was supposed to end." I'd had a fairy-tale ending in mind, of course: I intended to light a candle in memory of Root and get on my knees and say thank you for France and for my family and for all the people who'd contributed to all of the meals that we'd eaten. I'd also put in a good word for the future of French food: that people would be respectful of traditions and return to the land and blah blah blah blah blah. As if one little word from me to the Almighty would fix everything. "I didn't even get to say thank you," I mourned.

Overhead, a little brown bird winged around the courtyard, keeping me company. It would stop and perch and twitter and sing for a moment to the setting sun and then fly off again. For a while, I watched it dive and twirl in a pretty impressive show of aerial acrobatics, and then, suddenly, *splat!* Whether a miscalculation, or a sign, or an act of avian anguish, I will never know, but the pretty little bird crashed headlong into one of the stone walls and dropped to the ground, dead as a doornail.

I went over and poked at its lifeless body with the tip of my shoe but it didn't move. And then I turned and walked slowly back out of the courtyard.

And as I walked through the tunnel, during that instant of darkness, I offered up this unusual vow: I will *be* thankful. No matter what may happen, I will make my gratitude as tenacious and as hard to quash as an eel.

⟡ EPILOGUE ⟡

S CARLETT GRIPS THE BASKET TIGHTLY WITH BOTH HANDS, face contorted with the effort of holding a basket nearly as big as she is. Barely able to see, she trips over her load again and again but doesn't complain. Occasionally, she stops to prod one of her charges back into the leaf litter scattered over the basket's bottom. Indy races ahead of us, searching. The cool morning air still feels wet from the night's storm, but it carries the promise of a hot afternoon. The lambs make a ruckus bleating as we pass, and a chicken cackles loudly: someone must have just laid an egg.

The snails we seek are extremely well hidden below the damp, high-growing grass in the roadside culverts. Every few feet or so, we stop to hunt.

"There's one!" Scarlett squeals. A snail the size of a golf ball glides along on its plump, ruffled foot, leaving behind an iridescent trail. I add it to our basket, where it disappears into its shell momentarily, hiding, before a timid eye stalk reemerges. Soon it's indistinguishable from the rest slowly but purposefully scaling our basket walls.

"That's three dozen," I inform the kids. "That's enough. Let's head back."

On the road we meet Monsieur Frigand on his tractor. "What's in the basket?" he shouts over the motor's roar.

"Snails!" Indy and Scarlett chime.

He scowls, then brightens. *"Alors!"* he cries. "It's July third, I forgot. It's the season now. Did you have good luck?" Scarlett holds up her basket so he can see and he hoots in appreciation. "*Magnifique!* Big ones! It's been a long time since I've gathered the *escargots. Bon appétit!*"

Back at the farmhouse, Indy and Scarlett pose for photos with their favorite snails—Scarlett has named hers Lulu—and then disappear next door for a last playdate before we fly home in the morning. Greg packs and repacks our bags upstairs, trying to condense the clothing and the souvenirs and books and toys we've accumulated back into no more than the five pieces of luggage we originally arrived with.

Which leaves me alone in the kitchen.

The first step in the preparation of *escargots bourguignonne* is the dispatching of the snails. They get cooked three times—actually four, if you count when you finish them under the broiler. The first dip into boiling water kills them, so that their bodies can be plucked from their shells. When you do, it's a surprise: their whole anatomy becomes apparent, the organs secreted away in a spiraling mass that's been curled within the shell. There's a single large lung and a heart and a stomach and a kidney, and a few glands for secreting the snail's lubricating mucus. You cut all that away and discard it and then the feet, only, get boiled a second time with white wine and aromatics: carrot, onion, leek, parsley sprigs, bay leaves, thyme, and a few cloves of garlic. When they are tender, an hour or so later, the feet are seasoned and stewed again in butter and chopped garlic, then stuffed back into clean shells. (You can use their own shells, provided they are first well boiled and sterilized in clean water and vinegar. Or you can buy them.) You make snail butter: softened, unsalted butter, whipped until it is glossy and smooth, mixed with many, many, *many* cloves of minced garlic and plenty of—but not too much, I now know—finely chopped parsley and salt and pepper. You seal the shell with a big knob of the butter, compacting it deep into the shell, and set the escargots, butter side up, onto special dishes with divots to hold them in place and keep them from wobbling. You place them under the broiler until the butter snaps and bubbles. When you eat them, they should be so hot that they nearly singe the roof of your mouth.

I put a big pot of water to boil on the stove and contemplate the snails. In just that short time, an enterprising few have nearly escaped. One is atop the basket handle, looking confused. Another is sliding surprisingly quickly across the countertop in the general direction of the kitchen door. I put them both back into the basket. The water boils. I consider the snails again. Is that one Lulu? "Greg! Will you come help me?"

He makes the ceiling shudder, lifting and tossing bags in the kids' room over my head, grunting. "Can't!"

For a moment, I consider taking all of the snails out to the yard and releasing them back into the fields. But instead, I pick up one by its shell and dangle it over the pot. "Thank you," I say to it. Out loud.

And then, "Courage," I whisper to myself.

And begin.

❧ ACKNOWLEDGMENTS ❧

I WOULD LIKE TO SAY THAT MY THANKFULNESS HAS PERSISTED—transformative, robust, and uninterrupted—throughout these many, many months since coming home from France, but that would be a lie. I'm human. Gratitude is a life's work. But I work at it, every day, and every day I do find something to be thankful for—including all of the souls who encouraged and nurtured this project through to its completion.

There's my husband, Greg. A funny story: Imagine me, wild-eyed with unwieldy words and lack of sleep, swearing at everything that moved. "Wow! You know what I just realized?" he declares from the comfort of our bed. (Bed! Sweet bed!) "Apparently, I was an idiot to think television would be bad. Because *this* has got to be worse." I glare at the computer screen. "Well, I guess you're finally getting what you deserve," I mutter. Greg went through hell and high water with me during the writing of this book, he took *two* for the team, and we've come out on the other side as tasty and delicious as vichyssoise.

Indiana and Scarlett are ever inspiring, and oh so happy to have their mama back now that her "stupid book" is finished.

My mother may seem to take a beating in these pages, but it's delivered by the wings of a fledgling learning to leave the nest. Her support has been unparalleled. Her belief in me, usually stronger than my belief in myself. Jerry deserves praise, too, because in the game of emotional dominoes, I fall on Mom, and Mom falls on him, and he finds a way to stay standing. My sister Casey gave birth to two human babies in the time it took me to birth this literary one, and still found time, and the patience, for stop-complaining-and-get-on-with-it phone calls. My sister

Diane knew precisely when to drag me to a Jazzercise (yes, Jazzercise, baby!) class, and mothered my children when I was indisposed. I am nothing without the solar system of my siblings: Bob, Erin, Michael, Yvette, and Tom. Thank you to my father, the first Greg in my life, who doesn't complain about being pushed to the clan's periphery, but who, I hope, knows how central he is to me. Thank you to Rosemary Brogan for tirelessly taking care of us all in times of struggle. Enjoy the frequent-flier miles! Finally, without Greg's parents, Jim and Ghislaine Schaefer, the kids may have starved and gone to school naked.

I'm still astonished that we'd never actually met Marc Verlez before the night he came to fetch us in Montbard and Greg nearly knocked him over hurling suitcases out the train door. It was destiny that we befriended Marc and Sophie and Julien, Joseph, and Lulu. Thank you to Colombe Jacobsen-Derstine for helping the stars align.

And speaking of serendipity, thank you to Rory Schepisi, JAG Garcia, Paul McCullough, Adrien Sharp, Michael Salmon, Tommy Grella Jr., Nikki Shaw, Patrick Rolfe, and Vivien Cunha. Also to Bob Tuschman, Susie Fogelson, Bobby Flay, Mark Dissin, Bruce Seidel, and the multitudes of Food Network producers, culinary whizzes, and handholders. Thank you to the viewers of Season 3 who gave me your votes and the fans of *The Gourmet Next Door* who gave me your eyeballs. Between Food Network and Inkwell Management were Michael Ruhlman and Anthony Bourdain, providing pivotal introductions. At Inkwell, Kim Witherspoon is both a kind ear and a keen agent. Thank you, too, to Alexis Hurley, Julie Schilder, and to early readers Rose Marie Morse and Ethan Bassoff for their insightful critiques. (Also, to Julie Noble, who read every word, twice.) Mark Lawless and Richard Hofstetter gave helpful practical advice, the kind I usually forget to ask for. I hope it goes without saying that this book is a work of nonfiction, but that in the interest of narrative, minor liberties have been taken.

Rica Allannic at Clarkson Potter understood exactly what I was trying

to say back when I was still in the babbling stage, and waited patiently—
and nudged gently—until I found my way there, too. Thank you.

Above all, thank you to the alchemist home cooks of France, who
turned meagerness into art, a trick we can all use.

And so, dear reader, cook!